UNDERSTANDING C

UNDERSTANDING C

BRUCE H. HUNTER

Berkeley • Paris • Düsseldorf

Cover art by Patrice Larue
Book design by Michael Snodgrass
Illustrations by Larry Baumgardner

This book is dedicated to

Dr. William P. Hogan

at whose suggestion this book was written, and who has been my friend,
consultant, confidant and inspiration over the years

and to

Karen Bradford Hunter

my life partner and primary editor, for without her help and dedication
and unselfish love, this book would not have been possible

also special thanks to

Leor Zolman

who brought C to most of us

Table of Contents

Preface

Understanding C was written to provide an introduction to the C programming language. It is intended both for the beginning C programmer and for the intermediate-level C programmer who wants to know more about C, under UNIX, CP/M, or MS-DOS. A great deal of care has been taken to make the C language, and techniques of programming in C, clear to anyone. But C is seldom a programmer's first language, and it is assumed that the reader is generally familiar with a programming language and with concepts of structured programming. Ample references to BASIC and a few other languages have been made, and some programs have been repeated in BASIC as an aid in the comprehension of C.

Understanding C uses a spiral approach to teaching C. Many books take a textbook approach, having the reader learn all of one set of programming concepts (e.g., strings) before starting another set (e.g., variables). This is not one of those books. The most basic elements of each set of concepts are dealt with first. Through a series of small, descriptive programs, the reader's understanding of C is continually expanded. Instead of referring to various "theories of programming," or saving the writing of programs until later in the book, the reader can start programming in the first chapter. You can't learn how to fix a car by merely reading a book, and you can't learn a programming language unless you get in there and use it! By the end of the first chapter, many of the fundamentals of C have been covered, and illustrated with numerous program examples. Each program is carefully dissected and explained in detail to demonstrate the programming principles involved, as well as the fundamentals of C.

Part One deals with the necessary C theory, providing a reference point for the rest of the book. Everything from files and redirected I/O to arrays and pointers is covered in the later chapters, continually using real-world programming examples chosen expressly to illustrate the concepts being presented. Each program is examined carefully and discussed as clearly as possible.

Besides the fundamentals and theory, which one would expect in a book of this nature, the reader will find that C is dealt with not as a theoretical language under a theoretical operating system, but as the real and ever-expanding language it is, running under CP/M, UNIX, and a multitude of other operating systems. After the reader has acquired a little knowledge of C in the first few chapters, an overview of the C language is given in the middle of the book. The amenities of the language, the writing style typical to C programming, and a definition of the commands are presented in a clear, easy-to-understand way. Several chapters deal with the functions from libraries of both UNIX 7 C and a representative sample of 8- and 16-bit compilers available today. That C can be used not only as a systems language, but also as an applications language, is shown in the chapter on number crunching. No other language has the flexibility to cover the range of applications that C does, and this chapter indicates how to use that flexibility. UNIX is both father and son of C, so an entire chapter is devoted to UNIX and UNIX-like operating systems and utilities. C, when run under UNIX, takes on an entirely different flavor, which is demonstrated by a small sampling of true UNIX C programming.

To close the book, the features of a large and representative group of C compilers are compared in table form. By the end of the book, the reader should have a reasonably full understanding of the C language, the C environment, and C systems. The reader will have had the opportunity to understand the majority of C as it exists today.

Acknowledgements

A very special thanks to Dr. Jonathan Kamin whose editorial improvements substantially contributed to the quality of this book.

Also thanks to Mike McGrath who took a chance. And to those on the production staff at SYBEX who worked so hard, among them: Valerie Robbins, Laura Meany, and Ellen Campbell, who word-processed the text through many drafts; Michael Snodgrass, who designed the book; Brian Akers, who typeset the manuscript; Laura Bennett and Lorraine Aochi, who carefully proofread it; and Larry Baumgardner of van Genderen Studio, who completed the illustrations.

Finally my gratitude to the people in the industry whose contributions benefit us all. I especially want to thank George Eberhard, Walt Bilofsky, Richard Roth, Tom Gibson, Jim Colvin, Leor Zolman, and Carmine Governale for their suggestions and support.

Part One

The C Language

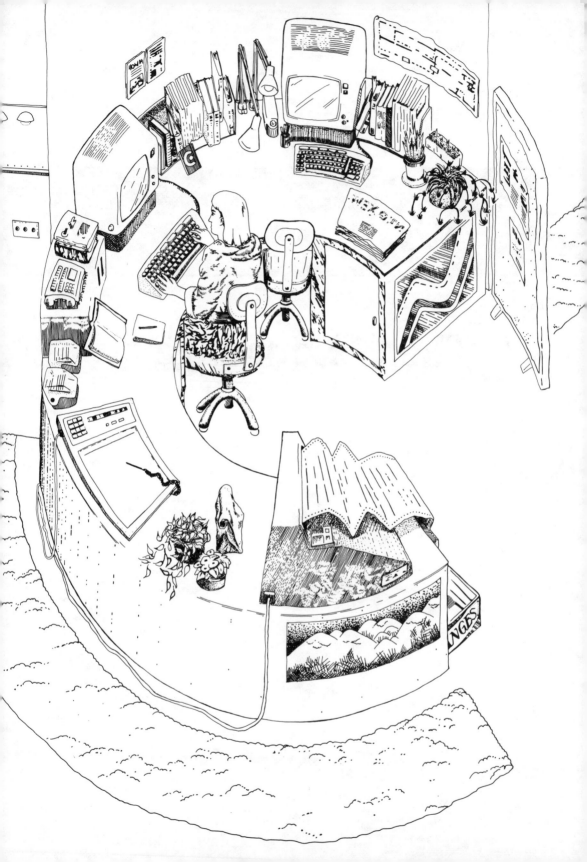

Introduction:

What is C?

This book will present C as it truly exists today, in many various versions running under numerous operating systems. There are three major families of operating systems available on microcomputers today, including the CP/M and MP/M family of operating systems; MS-DOS and PC-DOS; and UNIX and its emulators. Both the text and programs in this book are directed to all three families of systems.

C and UNIX were created side by side. The C language as it exists on UNIX Version 7 is defined by Kernighan and Ritchie's book, *The C Programming Language*. Programs written in UNIX 7 C are largely devoid of input and output capabilities, because UNIX 7 C depends on UNIX's ability to redirect its input and output. Other operating systems, such as CP/M or MS-DOS, do not provide redirection, and versions of C running under these operating systems must handle file I/O like any other language.

Understanding C deals with both environments. One chapter is devoted entirely to C as it exists in the UNIX environment. All other chapters deal with C on other operating systems. The majority of programs in the book were written on CP/M and MS-DOS compilers, and will run on either family of operating systems.

The importance of C as a serious and major programming language increases daily. Because of C's unique ability to operate well at systems level and still do applications programming, the creators of languages, operating systems, and utilities have created their own versions of C for sale. Even more significant, they are using C as their in-house systems language to develop their own products (a task traditionally done in assembly language).

Operating systems are a natural product of C. UNIX was written in C. MicroShell, a UNIX-like overlay to CP/M, is written in C. C's ability to replace assembly programming is making it the major language of this decade.

But C can also be an excellent applications language. The extremely large function libraries that have been developed for C have given it ample power in all sorts of applications. Business systems and scientific applications are easily programmed in C. In the chapter on number crunching you will find a program to calculate the construction of helical compression springs. A program of this nature would normally be programmed in FORTRAN or PL/I, but in C it takes less code than in either of these languages.

A BRIEF HISTORY OF C AND UNIX

It is difficult to separate C and UNIX, particularly in their early history, because they were developed side by side. Legend has it that UNIX was developed in an attic at Bell Labs in Murray Hill, New Jersey. Way back in 1969, Ken Thompson of Bell had managed to get his hands on an abandoned DEC PDP-7 that had no software. Ken was doing some programming research, and he set about to write a series of programs to help him develop software. In the period from 1969 to 1972, with the aid of Dennis Ritchie, he developed these programs into an operating system. In 1972, the system was recoded to run on the newer PDP-11, in a new language also developed by Bell, called C.

C, whose principal author was Dennis M. Ritchie, was an offspring of Martin Richard's BCPL, by way of a language called B (believe it or not) written by none other than Ken Thompson on the original PDP-7 under the original UNIX in 1970. Thompson's early development work on both UNIX and C has marked him as the pioneer of both. Ritchie's contribution was the expansion of B (a language without data types, not entirely dissimilar to PL/M) into the typed, extensible language that is now C.

By 1973, the joint contributions of Thompson, Ritchie, and many others at Bell had been refined into the system that Western Electric finally distributed to colleges and universities, thus extending the fame of both the operating system and the language. By 1975, Version 6 of UNIX was released. In early 1979, UNIX Version 7, which is today's standard, was released. It was coded almost entirely in C.

Most notable in the early development of UNIX and C is that they are largely the work of two individuals, Thompson and Ritchie. Obviously extraordinarily brilliant system programmers, they developed a language and an operating system *by* programmers *for* programmers. Most languages in common use today were developed by committees. Whether by a university committee (BASIC and Pascal) or an industry commitee (PL/I, FORTRAN), they are still designed by committee. Remembering that the camel is reputed to be a horse that was designed by committee, this practice can sometimes be counterproductive. C, on the other hand, was spared this process. It was, and is, a relatively "pure" language, unrestricted by compromise. Not that this is entirely good. C seldom checks itself, and as a consequence, this "free" language is at liberty to create impossible data structures, and to throw pointers to places where pointers should never be, such as the heart of the operating system. UNIX is equally "unfettered" with user-friendly messages. A single command from UNIX will destroy every file in the system without so much as a single "Are you sure?" The other side of the coin is this: C and UNIX are a language and a system that are capable of doing almost everything you might want a computer to do.

The definition of the C language was released to the public in 1979 in the now-classic book, *The C Programming Language*, by Brian Kernighan and Dennis Ritchie. The computing public was swift to recognize a good language. C compilers intended out of necessity to operate *outside* the UNIX operating system proliferated quickly. In fact, the majority of these C compilers were designed for the 8-bit environment, which is totally foreign to UNIX. Once the cord was cut, C was on its own. Unfortunately, the "cord" was the "pipe," UNIX's means of directing, or more precisely redirecting, the I/O from outside the program. The programmers of C compilers and libraries, however, were quick to overcome this deficiency with a large library of C functions, most of which were for I/O. Today there are over a dozen C compilers for 8-bit computers alone, and most will never see a UNIX environment.

On the other hand, C was not about to steal the limelight. An operating system as ingenious as UNIX was hard to ignore. Just as C developed a life of its own, UNIX would be emulated and would develop a life of its own as well. Because of UNIX's unique features, especially redirected I/O and pipes, numerous UNIX-like utilities have come into existence, and there are the UNIX-like Shell overlays to other operating systems, which combine the best of CP/M and UNIX. Unquestionably, most operating systems will in time incorporate some of the UNIX flavor. The *PWB/UNIX Overview*, by Dolotta and Haight, described UNIX as being able to run on hardware costing "as little as $60,000" and on "typical" systems costing about $120,000. Today, systems under $2000 can support a reasonably good facsimile of the UNIX Shell running with the CP/M operating system, the software cost of the Shell emulator being around $150.

C ON THE MICROCOMPUTER

C's history under CP/M and MS-DOS is relatively brief. When UNIX found its way into universities and limited commercial environments in the mid-'seventies, its potential quickly became apparent to all who used it. Languages have a way of transcending the operating systems on which they were created, and a few adventurous souls were quick to write new C compilers for other systems. Until 1982 CP/M was the dominant operating system for microcomputers. It was natural that CP/M was to be the target system for the first microcomputer versions of C. The first C versions to make their appearance were tiny-c, BD Systems C, and Small-C, all running under CP/M.

Early Versions of C for Micros

tiny-c is a small C-like language that has both an interpreter and a compiler. The interpreter was written by Tom Gibson in 1978. Like many of the earlier versions of C, tiny-c was not originally written for the commercial market. Tom Gibson was working for none other than Bell Labs, and he created tiny-c in order to teach C to his son Paul. Tom realized the commercial value of his effort and marketed his product. A neighbor of Tom Gibson's, George Eberhart, author of CI-C86, wrote the tiny-c compiler. tiny-c went on to become the father of Small-C, which spawned C-80, QC, CW/C, and many others.

Many people who have used C for awhile probably cut their teeth on BD Systems C. The BDS C compiler is the product of the genius of Leor Zolman. Leor got into C in the 'seventies, while working at MIT's computer science lab. Leor has a penchant for programming games. He discovered the game Othello on UNIX, and wanted to run it on his own micro. First he attempted to program Othello in assembly, but finding it a pain, he wrote a subset of C to do the job. Having a running C compiler, he realized that he had something that just might be marketable! Since it is the oldest C in its class, it is not surprising that there is a BDS C User's group. Their software is in the public domain, and probably more people have been introduced to C through BDS than any other single version. A great deal of software has been written in BDS C as well, including MicroShell, a UNIX emulator.

The advent of the 8088 and 8086 16-bit processors brought about 16-bit versions of C under CP/M-86. In addition, IBM's decision to use the version of MS-DOS called PC DOS on the IBM PC firmly established the MS-DOS family in the field of 16-bit systems as well. C thrives in large-memory environments, and a number of C versions quickly appeared for MS-DOS and CP/M-86.

TYPES OF PROGRAMMING LANGUAGES

Before your introduction to C begins, let's talk about programming languages in general, and define a few terms. Programming languages come in all sizes and varieties, each filling a specific need. Some, such as assembly language, are very close to primitive machine instructions. Each of the computer's internal mechanisms for handling data must be accounted for when writing assembly-language code. For example, if a character is to be sent to the screen, the low-level language program must provide the instructions to put the character into a register in the central processor, and then issue a command to direct the character to be output to the screen. Low-level language code is difficult to read, because it is geared more toward computers than toward people. Consequently, it is also rather difficult to learn to write! It is tedious as well, because so much code is needed to accomplish even simple tasks.

High-level languages more closely resemble the English language. This makes them easier to read and write, and they are therefore easier to learn. Fewer lines of code accomplish the same tasks, and the programmer need not be concerned with most of the internal mechanisms that perform the program instructions—they are handled automatically.

To illustrate this point, let's say you want to write a program to print "hello" on the screen. A low-level language requires many lines of code to do the job, but a high-level language requires considerably less, and in some cases only one line is required. For example, a BASIC interpreter handles the job with only two words:

```
PRINT "HELLO"
```

High-level languages are not necessarily powerful, however. A powerful language is one that accomplishes a great deal with a minimum of code and programmer effort. COBOL is a high-level language that I would definitely *not* classify as powerful, because it is excessively verbose, taking many more lines of code to complete a program than any other high-level language.

Some languages are intended to teach programming. Pascal and BASIC are prime examples, and they are often called teaching languages. Others are designed for writing programs for specific applications, such as payrolls, statistical analysis, and so forth, and they are called *applications languages*. PL/I, FORTRAN, COBOL, and enhanced versions of BASIC and Pascal are applications languages. Still other languages, such as PL/M, work at more primitive levels, to create code for operating systems and utilities, and they are called *systems languages*.

Where does C fit into all this? The C programming language is unique among languages, because it is a mid-level language. It is not a high-level language like BASIC, PL/I, or Pascal; nor is it a low-level language like assembly language. Mid-level languages are meant to replace assembly language and still perform the tasks of high-level languages. C fits this description "to a T" because it can function as both a systems language and an applications language.

C is a language of uncommon power. Power in a language or utility, at least in my definition, is the ability to do a great deal with very little code. In one of the later chapters of this book, you will see a utility coded in C called a *filter,* which filters out everything from a piece of text except the words themselves. The entire filter is written in less than a page of code. In fact, the executable portion is less than half a page. It is joined to a Shell command program only three lines long. So what does it do? It will produce a dictionary from any piece of text. That is power!

C has the ability to work at the system level, and it gives the programmer the leeway to write almost anything he needs. Yet, as I mentioned, C is sufficiently versatile to do applications programming, too. Writing a general ledger in C, for example, is not a difficult task. However, the most powerful feature of C is its ability to extend itself. C libraries are easily expanded in size, and C library functions are very easy to write once you get the hang of it. Typical C functions call other C functions. The result is that C need never be a static language like COBOL or FORTRAN, or even my beloved PL/I. C grows with the programmer's skill and exposure until eventually a C programmer's library becomes unique to his own programming requirements.

Because C programs consist solely of a series of functions, C can justifiably be called a function-oriented language. In most languages, a function serves as a vehicle to accept values (called arguments or parameters), to process them, and ultimately to return a single value to the main program. In C, functions take on an elevated significance because they also serve as *procedures* (collections of instructions to perform a specific task). Even the main program block is a function in C, from which the rest of the program is directed.

Structured Programming

For those of you coming into C from BASIC or other nonstructured languages, the term *structured language* might be new, so let's take a closer look at this concept. Nonstructured languages like BASIC and FORTRAN start at the top of a program and work their way in a straight line down to the bottom, executing each instruction one at a time, unless a GOTO or a branch directs the program flow elsewhere. This is often an adequate way of handling program logic. However, because most program logic is too complex to be handled in a straight up-and-down series of instructions, branching soon gets out of hand. Code with a lot of GOTOs is difficult to read. You've all heard of "spaghetti-string" programs with so many branches and GOTOs that the main line of the program logic is obscured. A number of years ago, a language called ALGOL (from the term ALGOrithmic Language) was created to handle program tasks separately by putting them in blocks. This type of program has a main block that directs the flow from block to block. ALGOL spawned a number of structured languages that became very popular in the United States, including Pascal, PL/I, and C.

COMPILERS AND INTERPRETERS

As we proceed through the text, there will be many references to compilers and interpreters. A note or two of explanation is in order.

Interpreter languages read and execute one line of code at a time. They don't know what's going to happen in the code after the line they are executing, and they don't even care. There are some pleasant features of interpreters that make them suitable for beginning programmers. When you are finished writing a program in an interpreter language, all you do is save it and then type RUN or some similar command, and the program executes immediately, one line at a time. It's easy to fix errors in interpreter code. You correct the code, save it, type RUN or CONTINUE or some similar command again, and away you go. Interpreter languages are limited in scope because of their line-by-line execution, but the most significant disadvantages of interpreter programs are that they execute very slowly, and their variables are all global, known to every part of the program.

Compilers are quite different from interpreters. Compilers know everything about what will happen in the program and when, because compilers "parse" (read each line of the code from the beginning of the program all the way to the end) several times in the compilation process. To people used to interpreters, the compilation process can be a confusing experience. Let's look at what happens when code is compiled in a typical C compiler. (Compilers are relatively standard in the way they compile code, but there are small individual differences from one to another.)

Let's say you have just finished writing your source code. The first step in the compilation process is accomplished by the *preprocessor*, which follows the instructions of the header file in your source code to "include" any header-defined files or redefined functions, or constants. It also prints

The Creation of Source Code

out any apparent syntactic errors. The next step is performed by the compiler proper, which translates the code parsed by the preprocessor into *intermediate code*, usually assembly code. Then the *optimizer* optimizes the intermediate assembly code, making it more efficient. At this stage, most compilers make what is called a *relocatable module*, which is intermediate code that will be relocated to its final address at link time.

Finally, the *linker* links the program proper to the functions called by the program, and to any other modules specified at linkage time, to produce the final *object code*, which is in machine language. Only then is the program ready to run.

The biggest advantage of compiled code is that it runs very rapidly and is very compact. Sophisticated programming features can be built into compiler languages, and that is a distinct advantage as well. The only disadvantage of compilers is that it can be tedious to correct the code, because you have to recompile the code each time.

You are about to embark upon a joyous journey into C, and to a small extent into UNIX. I hope that I will be the one to lead you there.

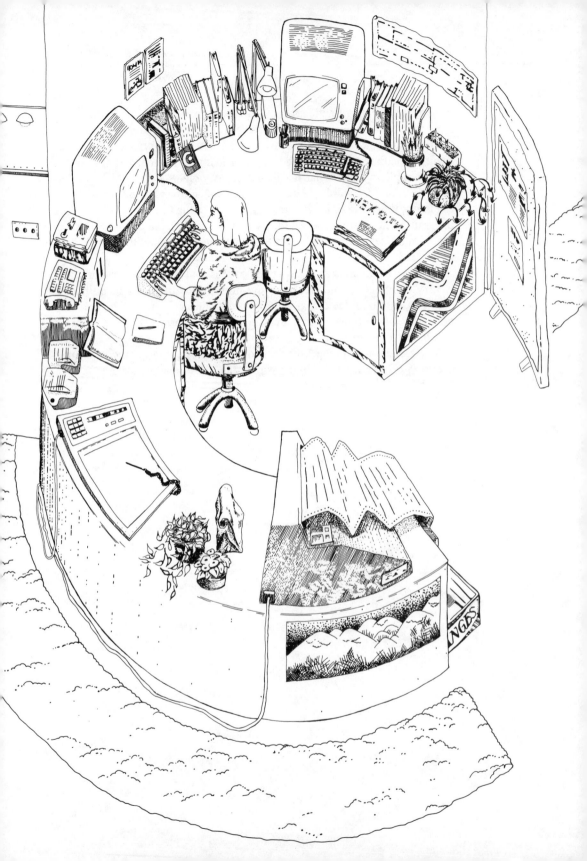

1:

Getting C Programs Up and Running

Chapter 1 will give you a general idea of what to expect from the C programming language. This book takes a spiral approach to learning C, and that involves being exposed to concepts in stages, with each stage providing more thorough coverage than the last. In this, the first stage, I will lightly skim over the C language to give you a "feel" for it. If you don't understand some of the concepts or terms presented in the first chapter, don't worry about it. They will be covered again several times throughout the book, and the presentation of these concepts and terms will be expanded continually. By the end of the book you will have a comprehensive introduction to the C language.

THE STRUCTURE OF C PROGRAMS

Let's begin by looking at the construction of a C program:

```
/ * First Program * /
#define CLEAR 12

main ( )
{
    putchar (CLEAR);
    puts ("\n\n\n\t\t This is C.");
}
```

For comparison, here is the BASIC equivalent of this program:

```
10 REM FIRST PROGRAM
20 PRINT CHR$(12)
30 PRINT: PRINT: PRINT
40 PRINT "THIS IS BASIC"
```

C's block structure is evident at first glance. Each block is delimited by a pair of curly braces, and everything within that block is executed sequentially unless a statement within the block redirects the program flow. In the case of our simple program, the only block is the main block. The first command of the program is to put a character to the screen. The putchar ( ) function outputs the single ASCII character 12, a nonprintable character that clears the screen on many terminals. Routines to clear the screen depend on the hardware, rather than the language. The constant CLEAR is defined by the line

    #define CLEAR 12

which replaces every occurrence of CLEAR with the ASCII character 12 (base 10) when the program is compiled. This is an example of a *preprocessor command*. Preprocessor commands are acted upon by the first pass of the C compiler before any code is compiled. The keyword main instructs the compiler that this is a main program block, and the empty parentheses indicate that there are no arguments—values with special meaning to the block—being passed to the program.

The last instruction, puts, is a printing function that prints the series of characters enclosed within the parentheses to the screen. Everything within the double quotes is a *string* (or *literal*) and is output to the terminal. Characters following a backslash \ are control characters. The command for a newline is \n, and the command for a tab is \t. The terminal outputs three newlines and two tabs before printing the string

    This is C.

Comments—words that you don't want the program to act on, but that you may want for program clarity—are surrounded by slash/star pairs:

    / ∗ comment ∗ /

Another thing you notice right away is the unique appearance of C programs. White space is used liberally in C. Program lines are indented, and blank lines and spaces are inserted freely. Because C is a "free-form" language, you can insert white space anywhere in the program, and this has one great advantage: program clarity. Writing clear code is important in any language, but it is especially important in a language as cryptic as C.

Here's an example of how using white space makes the program clearer. The C compiler will read and act upon the following statement with no problem:

    if (ch == '/n') break;

However, the same statement is clearer to people reading and maintaining the code if it looks like this:

```
if (ch == '/n')
    break;
```

The if statement and the logical expression it evaluates are on one line, and the action that may result from this evaluation is on the next line. C recognizes that this is one statement because the compiler continues to read until it sees a *statement terminator* (a semicolon).

Spaces can also be used in a program line to add clarity. An expression such as

```
quad = a*x*x+a*b*x*y+b*y*y;
```

is much clearer as

```
quad = (a*x*x) + (a*b*x*y) + (b*y*y);
```

thanks to spaces and parentheses.

There are no rules for using white space other than plain old common sense and the desirability of clear programs.

C does its work by way of functions. Even the main (or controlling) block is a function. The basic C language has no input/output functions. The C libraries, on the other hand, are rich with every sort of function. It is easy to define and implement functions in C.

The next program illustrates the incorporation of a user-defined function called clear.

```
main ( )
{
    clear ( );
    puts ("\n\n\t second program");
}

clear ( )
{
    putchar (12);
}
```

Following is the BASIC equivalent of this program, here written in CBASIC.

```
DEFFN CLEAR = CHR$(12)
CLEAR
PRINT: PRINT
PRINT TAB(8); "SECOND PROGRAM"
```

Now there are two blocks: the main function and a function to clear the screen. Within the main function, the first command calls the function clear. The function is then executed by outputting an ASCII 12 or 0C hex, which clears the screen. Then the program returns to the line below the function call and executes the puts( ) statement by outputting the string. The *return* is implicit in all C functions. When the end of a function has been reached, the program returns control to the line after the line that called the function. Note that the function is not nested within the main program block, as in Pascal or PL/I, but is separate from, and outside of, the main block. It seems to want to tell you that C does not know what is happening within the function, as indeed it does not. The scope (area of operation) of the main block and the function block are self-contained. Everything within is local, which means that variables are known only within the blocks in which they are declared. Scope will be mentioned frequently throughout the book.

You have seen output. Now how about a little input?

```
/ * Third Program * /
main ( )
{
    char name [64];

    putchar (12);
    puts ("\n\nThe third C program\n\n\n");
    puts ("Enter your name: ");
    gets (name);
    puts ("\n\nHello ");
    puts (name);
    puts ("\n\t*");
}
```

Now the plot thickens. A variable, name, has been declared as a character array with a length of 64 characters. C, like other computer languages, declares its variables at the top of a program. This shows the system what the variables are and allocates storage for them. C cannot handle strings in the sense that BASIC or PL/I does; instead it puts them into an array of characters, as Pascal does. All C string functions (and there are a lot of them) are equipped to handle the array. The first line of executable code, putchar (12), clears the screen on many terminals. The second line prints two line spaces, then the program title, and then skips three more lines. C takes nothing for granted; if you want to skip a line, you must tell it so. The next line instructs the user to enter his name. Aha, something new! The function gets asks for a string, or literal, from the console.

```
    gets (name);
```

The BASIC equivalent of gets is INPUT, and the equivalent BASIC line would read INPUT NAME.

Getting C Up and Running

The program now reads the input string one character at a time, inputting it into the array with the first character in the first position in the array, which starts with position zero. The last character input from the console is a carriage-return/line-feed pair, which causes the system to input a binary zero to the array. In the C vernacular, the last character input is a \0 (a string terminator). If the name that is input is Chad, it is stored as

C	h	a	d	\0

The first character, stored in name [0], is C. The second, stored in name [1], is h, and so on. A reference to the array without the subscripts produces the entire array, starting at position 0. The program prints the name when it encounters the next line, puts (name). To demonstrate that the line feed is not automatic (as it is in BASIC), the last line outputs the string \n\t* to print a star as the last line of the output. The last three lines would output

```
Hello Chad
        *
```

If you have access to a C compiler, now is a good time to try it out. As with any language, the more you create actual code and run it, the faster you will learn.

THE FOR LOOP

Now it's time to get into a few of the concepts used in C. First let's look at the *for loop*. A loop is a part of the program that comes back and repeats itself (loops) until everything in it is repeated as many times as necessary. Consider the following problem: during the Festival of Lights, two candles are burned on the first day. Each day thereafter one more candle is lit, and the holiday lasts for eight days. How many candles are used altogether? The program in Figure 1.1 can be used to calculate the answer, and it also nicely demonstrates the for loop.

Let's look at it more closely. Most of the programs in this book will be "dissected" a few lines at a time to show how the program and the language work.

```
main ( )
  {
     int n, i, total;
```

The variables n, i, and total are declared to be type integer; this statement causes C to allocate or assign storage for 3 two-byte integers, because all (short) integers take two bytes.

```
total = 0;
n = 1;
```

The program declares three integer variables and initializes (assigns initial values to) two of them: total to 0 and n to 1. Had they both been initialized to 0, the statement could have read

```
n = total = 0;
```

While it is making the assignments, C reads the line from right to left. In this case 0 is stored first, total second, and then n.

Now let's look at the loop statement:

```
for (i = 1 ; i < = 8 ; i++)
```

This for loop is typical C syntax. C is characteristically cryptic, compact, and curt. A statement with the form

```
for ( ; ; )
```

tells the program to loop. The first statement in the parentheses initializes the loop index i to 1. The next statement is a test to terminate the loop. As long as i is less than or equal to 8, the loop executes, because the statement is true. (The loop continues to execute as long as the expression that tests the loop is true.) The last statement increments the index. The statement i++ increments i by one *after* executing the loop. If it were ++i, it would

```
main ( )
{
    int n, i, total;
    total = 0;
    n = 1;
    for (i = 1 ; i <= 8 ; i++)
    {
        n += 1;
        total = total + n;
        puts ("\n day ");
        putdec (i);
        puts ("\n candles ");
        putdec (n);
        puts ("\n total ");
        putdec (total);
    }
}
```

Figure 1.1: The Candle Counter (Illustration of the for Loop)

increment i *before* executing the loop. The index can also be decremented by the operators i-- or --i. So what do you have? A loop starting at the index 1 and increasing by ones to 8.

The next program block calculates the number of candles and prints the results to the console.

```
{
    n += 1;
    total = total + n;
    puts ("\n day ");
    putdec (i);
    puts ("\n candles ");
    putdec (n);
    puts ("\n total ");
    putdec (total);
}
```

Now the execution proceeds a line at a time, grinding straight down. n, which started out as 1, is incremented by the statement

```
n += 1
```

which is the same as N = N + 1 in BASIC.

Do you remember how offended you were the first time you saw the statement a = a + 1? It went against everything you had ever learned in algebraic notation. In computer languages it is all right, of course, because it is an *assignment statement* saying that the contents of the variable a are now equal to itself plus one. a += 1 is a shorthand notation for just that. So now you know that the line

```
total = total + n;
```

can also read

```
total += n
```

Here is the code to accumulate the total candles used:

```
    puts ("\n day ");
    putdec (i);
    puts ("\n candles ");
    putdec (n);
    puts ("\n total ");
    putdec (total);
}
```

This block puts out the statement "day" and follows it with the integer i, the loop index. Notice that putdec (meaning "put decimal," which is not implemented in all versions) prints a character representation of the integer. C takes nothing for granted, nor does it do anything automatically. If you tell it to print 48 without enclosing 48 in quotes, it will print a 0, because 48 is the ASCII number for 0.

When the program executes, it produces this:

```
day 1
candles 2
total 2
day 2
candles 3
total 5
day 3
candles 4
total 9
   .
   .
   .
```

What if you want the total last, without a running total? The program in Figure 1.2 shows what you should do. Now here's a program of another color. The loop executes by printing days and candles, but it doesn't print the running total, because the block stops before the statement that prints the total. Once the block is exited on the eighth iteration, the last two lines execute.

```
main ( )
  {
    int n, i, total; /*declare n. i, total as integer*/
    total = 0;       /*initialize total to zero*/
    n = 1;           /*initialize n to one*/
    for (i = 1 ; i <= 8 ; i++)
    {
        n += 1;
        total += n;
        puts ("\n day ");
        putdec (i);
        puts ("\n candles ");
        putdec (n);
        puts ("\n");
    }
    puts ("\n total ");
    putdec (total);
  }
```

Figure 1.2: The Candle Counter with Accumulated Total

USING THE FOR LOOP
TO CREATE A CHARACTER ARRAY

By now the for loop should be familiar to you, so let's use it to create a character array, to get the feel of character input and strings. The for loop can be used to create an array one character at a time. Take a look at the program in Figure 1.3.

Tearing it apart, the executable part of the program starts with a loop to get up to 64 characters:

```
for (i = 0; i < = 64; i + + )
{
    puts ("\ninput character: ");
    ch = getchar ( );
    if (ch == '\n')
        break;
```

The console asks the operator to input a character, and the command getchar ( ) gets the characters one at a time. Note that ch is declared as a single character, not as a character string. The character ch is tested to see if it is a

```
/*str_ary.c    creates a character array*/

main ( )
{
    char ch, chstring [64];/*declare a 64 character string array*/
    int i;                 /*declare an integer variable i*/
    putchar (12);
    puts ("\n\n\n\n\n\t\tCharacter and String demo\n\n");
    for (i = 0; i <= 64; i++)
    {
        puts ("\ninput character : ");
        ch = getchar ( );
        if (ch == '\n')
            break;
        puts ("\ncharacter is ");
        putchar (ch);
        chstring [i] = ch;
        puts ("\nstring is ");
        puts (chstring);
    }
    chstring [i++] = '\0';
    puts ("\n\n final string ");
    puts (chstring);
}
```

Figure 1.3: A Character Array

newline \n (just a line feed, not a carriage-return/line-feed pair—see glossary). If it is a newline, the loop is exited with the break command. This command is one of the ways C can change program flow within a loop. The break forces the execution to move to the line after the end of the block, in this case to

```
chstring [i++] = '\0';
```

If you used the command exit ( ), it would cause the program to exit or quit and return to the system. If you used the command continue, it would stop forward execution and go back to the loop statement.

If ch is not a newline, the for block continues:

```
puts ("\ncharacter is ");
putchar (ch);
chstring [i] = ch;
```

After the character is echoed back to the screen, it is assigned to the end-most position in the character array.

The next step is to output the string:

```
        puts ("\nstring is ");
        puts (chstring);
    }
```

The accumulated string is displayed by the statement puts (chstring). The concept here is important. This statement is telling C to output the array chstring starting at position zero, where the first element in the array is stored.

The string array is completed by ending it with a string terminator \0. It is then output to the console:

```
        chstring [i++] = '\0';
        puts ("\n\n final string ");
        puts (chstring);
    }
```

THE WHILE LOOP

As long as we are doing loops, let's do it another way and look at the while loop. The while loop is shown in the program in Figure 1.4.

For the sake of having something to process, the string chstring is input from the terminal. Now the string needs to be torn apart a character at a time:

```
while (chstring [i] != '\0')
```

The while is similar to PL/I's and Pascal's WHILE and the WHILE. . . WEND found in some versions of BASIC. While the expression in parentheses is true, it executes. In this case, we are using a *not* condition for while-not-true because the operator != literally means "not equal to." So what we have is this: while the individual characters of the string chstring are not the string or null terminator, the contents of the while block outputs each character of the string by using the putchar ( ) function (not puts ( ), which outputs a string) to print the individual characters:

```
{
    putchar (chstring [i++]);
    puts ("\n");
}
```

The loop index i is incremented at each execution by [i++]. A line feed is added to keep the characters separated. The results of the program are the characters of the input string, output as a column.

THE DO-WHILE LOOP

There is another form of looping, the do-while (which is actually a "do-until" if you want to nit-pick, because the test is at the end of the iteration rather than at the beginning). The program in Figure 1.5 is Figure 1.4 redone as a do-while loop.

As you can see, there's nothing new here except that the test is at the end. In fact, that's the point! The while statement tests the loop condition at the beginning of the loop. The do-while statement tests at the end of the loop.

```
main ( )
{
char chstring [64];
int i;

    i = 0;
    puts ("input string: ");
    gets (chstring);
    while ( chstring [i] != '\0')          /*the while*/
    {
        putchar (chstring [i++] );
        puts ("\n");
    }
    puts ("\n\t");
    puts (chstring);
}
```

Figure 1.4: The while Loop

OK. I've looped until you are dizzy. Now let's stop going in circles and make a decision.

THE IF STATEMENT

No self-respecting language is without an if statement. C's if is one of the best. It executes not only like the IF statement in FORTRAN, but also like the IF-THEN-ELSE statement in BASIC, and the if-else-if statement in PL/I. C's if statement works like this:

```
if (condition)
    statement;
        else
            statement;
```

The expression (condition) inside the parentheses must be true for the statement that follows to be acted upon. If it is not true, the else statement will be acted upon.

As an example, let's use red and green as integer variables:

```
if (red)
    stop ( );
        else
            if (green)
                go ( );
                    else
                        reverse ( );
```

```
main ( )
{
char chstring [64];
int i;

    i = 0;
    puts ("input string: ");
    gets (chstring);
    do
    {
        putchar (chstring [i++] );
        puts ("\n");
    }
    while (chstring [i] != '\0');
    puts ("\n\t");
    puts (chstring);
}
```

Figure 1.5: The do-while Loop

When C examines a logical expression such as if (red), it evaluates the expression and internally assigns a 0 if it is false. The if statement considers a zero to be false and anything else to be true.

Notice that the code is markedly indented. The reason for the indentation is clarity. The above if-else-if-else sequence nests in levels. Each retest and alternate action is nested deeper than the last (given a subordinate level), and the code reflects this nesting. For example, the else is subordinate to the if. Clear code is a necessity.

It is important to be careful in placing the curly braces. If they are not balanced, one left brace to one right brace, the compiler will probably refuse to go any further. Even if it is a "friendly" compiler, the code still will not compile. To be sure that your braces are balanced, place each right brace directly in line under the left one. For example, the following brace placement is difficult to check:

```
if (red) {
    stop ( );
    exit ( );
}
```

Blocks like the one above can get confusing, and you'll find that it's easy to forget the right brace. Instead, construct the block this way:

```
if (red)
{
    stop ( );
    exit ( );
}
```

This makes reading and correcting the code substantially easier, and it's a snap to check whether you have the same number of left and right braces.

Now it's time to demonstrate the if statement (and sneak in a few other concepts). Take a look at Figure 1.6. Examine the first few lines:

```
main ( )
{
    char instring [64], ch;
    int i, nword, charval;
```

In the line char instring [64], ch; two character variables are declared, a single character variable (also called a *scalar*), ch, and an aggregate variable, the string array instring. The remaining variables are of integer type. Now let's look at the next three lines:

```
nword = 1;
puts ("input a sentence: ");
gets (instring);
```

The number of words (nword) is initialized to one. The puts prints the string "input a sentence" to the console. Then gets (instring) inputs the character string to be used as a sentence to the program.

Next we find our old friend, the for loop:

for (i = 0 ; instring [i] != '\0' ; i++)

The variable i is initialized to 0, the loop is repeated until the end-of-string character \0 is encountered, and the loop is incremented by one on each iteration. Now each character of the array is assigned to the variable ch one at a time:

```
{
    ch = instring [i];
    putchar (ch);
```

The value of the string-array member is stored in the scalar variable ch. A *scalar* is a variable that represents a single value. Now it is a character and therefore can be output with the function putchar ( ).

Next a newline (\n) is output. (CP/M automatically adds a carriage return on output.):

```
    puts ("\n");
    charval = atoi (ch);
```

Here's a new concept, a *built-in function*. Built-in functions are those supplied with the language, as opposed to those that the programmer

```
main ( )
{
    char instring [64], ch;
    int i, nword, charval;

    nword = 1;
    puts ("input a sentence: ");
    gets (instring);
    for (i = 0 ; instring [i] != '\0' ; i++)
    {
        ch = instring [i];
        putchar (ch);
        puts ("\n");
        charval = atoi (ch);
        printf ("character value %2d \n", charval);
        if (ch == 0X20)
            nword += 1;
    }
    printf ("\n\nthe sentence has %2d words %2d characters", nword, i);
}
```

Figure 1.6: The if Statement

creates. Alpha to integer (atoi) converts the character into its ASCII number equivalent and returns it as a decimal (base 10) integer. It is stored in the integer variable charval.

Remember, characters are integer variables and integers are character variables, in the sense that ASCII characters are the integers from 0 to 127. C deals in system primitives, and it recognizes that the distinction between an ASCII character and its numeric equivalent is a fine one. The statements (ch == 0X20) or (ch == 32) could just as well be (ch == ' '). They all compute the same. Hex 20 is decimal 32, and the 32nd character in the ASCII sequence is a blank.

Another point to dwell on is the logical equal (==). The single equal sign (=) is for assignment, like Pascal's := . The logical equal (==) is for comparison, like FORTRAN's .EQ. If you use the assignment (=), C does not give you an error message. It simply considers everything as true because the expression does not generate a zero value or false. Remember, all logical statements will internally generate a 0 if they are false.

The next statement is a new concept, followed by the now-familiar if statement:

```
printf ("character value %2d \n", charval);
    if (ch == 0X20)
        nword += 1;
}
```

Some programming languages are able to format the output of variables to print a specific number of characters or digits. The printf ( ) statement is a formatted print. Note the %2d. That is a *mnemonic*, or C's way of saying that the variable to be printed there is a decimal integer two bytes long. The program now looks for a variable at the end of the literal enclosed in quotes. The decimal integer stored in the variable charval is then printed after the words character value. If the character is a blank, nword is incremented.

Then the program tells us how many words and how many characters are in the string that has been input:

```
printf ("\n\nthe sentence has %2d words %2d characters", nword, i);
```

The integers stored in the variables nword and i appear in the output to replace %2d.

C is not very big on checking for errors. It assumes you have already done so. Unlike PL/I, which searches the line for any remaining format, C gives unpredictable results if the formats and variables don't match. If the format is too narrow for the value of the variable intended, the result will be a truncation. For example, if the string "Thomas" is formatted with a %4s, the output will be "Thom". C is very literal!

The result of this program is that the string input, a sentence, has each character converted to its ASCII value and output in a column. At the end of the loop, the length of the string and the number of words are output. Although this is a nonsensical program, it demonstrates the way text processors and compilers check characters. Does it seem that it could be programmed more easily? Figure 1.7 shows another version of the same program. The major simplification is the line

> if (instring [i] == ' ');

which avoids the need for conversion to a decimal integer.

Although strings can be compared one character at a time, C does not allow one string to be *assigned* to another with a simple assignment such as

> string1 = string2

String assignment will be examined in more detail as we go along, but it is a good idea at this point to be aware that C cannot handle strings as BASIC does.

SUMMARY

Before going on to the next chapter, let's stop for a minute and briefly review some of the concepts that have been covered so far.

Functions

In this chapter we saw that each programming module or program block is a function, including the main program block. There are several types of

```
main ( )
{
    char instring [64];
    int i, nword;

    nword = 1;
    puts ("input a sentence:  ");
    gets (instring);
    for (i = 0 ; instring [i] != '\0' ; i++)
    {
        if (instring [i] == ' ')
            nword += 1;
    }
    printf ("\n\nthe sentence has %2d words %2d characters", nword, i);
}
```

Figure 1.7: Word Count

functions, and one of them is the built-in function (we looked at puts ( )). Built-in functions are provided by the writer of the C compiler; the more sophisticated the compiler, the more built-in functions you will find. The way they "tick" is not visible to the programmer. You simply use them and they work. We also looked at functions that the programmer needs to create, like clear. There is a lot more to learn about functions, and because functions are so important in C, they will be mentioned throughout the book. Four chapters are devoted just to the C function library and the care and modification of that library.

Strings

Strings are groups of characters, similar to words in the English language. Many languages deal with strings as a separate type of variable, but in C they are dealt with as an array of single characters called character arrays. A five-letter word is stored in an array of six elements, 0 through 5, with the last element being a binary zero to demarcate the end of the string. C, like most programming languages, starts counting at 0.

Loops

The process of iterating or repeating a statement or block of statements is called looping. There are several kinds of loops. We looked at the for loop, the while loop, and the do-while loop. Each kind of loop repeats until some kind of condition is satisfied. The for loop and the while loop test for this condition at the beginning of the loop, and the do-while loop tests for this condition at the end of the loop. The for loop has the distinction of having a loop counter incorporated into its basic structure (for i = 1 to 10); sometimes it is called an incrementing loop.

The if Statement

We also touched lightly on the if statement in this chapter. It is only one of many program constructs that will be discussed in this book.

Now here is a concept to take with you into Chapter 2—the concept of the Boolean or logical test. Boolean or logical operators are those that compare their operands and yield one of two possible answers: true or false. The symbols for these Boolean operators are $<$, $>$, $<=$, $>=$, $==$, and $\div$. The symbols &&, ||, and !, the logical operators for and, or, and not, are also used in conjunction with symbols. Boolean or logical expressions are those incorporating Boolean operators.

Boolean expressions are used to test or satisfy a condition in certain program constructs. The for loop we examined is one of these constructs. The index i <= 8 actually can be only true or false. How? If the current value of i is 5, then the statement is true, because 5 is undeniably <= 8. If the current value of i is 9, then the statement is evaluated as false, because 9 is clearly not <= 8. If the expression is evaluated as false, it is internally assigned the value of 0. If the expression is evaluated as true, it is internally assigned the value of anything else, or a "nonzero" value. The while loop and the if statement are other program constructs that require a logical or Boolean expression. In the next chapter a great deal of attention is given to the many operators used in conjunction with logical expressions.

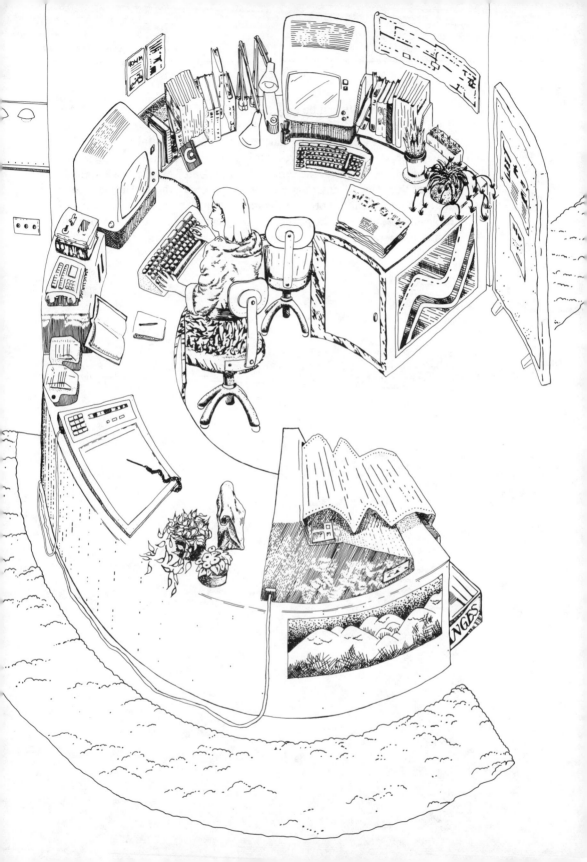

2:

Operators, Hierarchy, and Associativity

A lot of ground is covered in this chapter. All of these definitions are meant to be used primarily as a reference, and most of them will be covered later in more detail. Don't get bogged down trying to learn them all at once. Just know that they are here when you need them. (And you will need them!)

OPERATORS

C's rich set of operators approaches PL/I's in number and variety. Operators are what make things happen. By definition, an operator is a symbol that specifies an operation to be performed. The simple assignment operator = , as in

```
x = 0
```

tells the computer to assign the value zero to the variable x. The symbols

```
+ - / *
```

are all familiar operators.

The order in which operations are performed is called the *order of precedence*. It is also called *hierarchy.* The expression

```
a = b + c
```

obviously wouldn't work if the assignment were done before the addition operation were completed.

The *direction* in which operations are done also becomes important. The addition of b and c is done from left to right, but what about the assignment? The assignment must be done from right to left, or how else would the results of the expression b + c get into a? The direction in which operations are done is called *associativity*. So when you deal with operators, you must also deal with order of precedence and associativity.

Operators fall into three classes:

1. *Unary:* those that operate on a single value: − n
2. *Binary:* those that operate on more than one value: 2 − n
3. *Ternary:* This one is unique. It operates on three values:
   a = (b > c) ? d : e

C has a wealth of operators. With the exceptions of the @ and `symbols, there are no printable nonalphanumeric characters that are not used alone or in combination with another as C operators. The operations are as varied as the symbols that represent them. At this point we must clarify a couple of concepts before we get into the definitions of the operators themselves.

LVALUES

An *lvalue* is a variable or constant with a permanent address in memory. Typically, an lvalue is on the left side of an expression such as an assignment:

    a = x∗x + x∗y + y∗y;

In this example, a is an lvalue. The concept of lvalues is critical in C, and is covered in depth in Chapter 4.

SCALARS AND AGGREGATES

Variables are either scalars or aggregates, depending on whether they have one value or many. A scalar has a single value:

    a = 1

An aggregate, on the other hand, is a variable that has multiple values, as in an array or structure. (Structures are covered in Chapters 3 and 8.) This is an initialization of an aggregate:

    for (i = 1; i <= 10; i++)
        a [i] = n++;

DEFINITIONS

Operators

+   *The traditional addition operator*

With arithmetic operators, both operands must be arithmetic (integer or float), except for pointer arithmetic, in which case one is pointer and the other integer. Examples:

```
c = a + b;
new_ptr = ptr + 4;
```

++   *The increment operator*

The increment operator increments the value with which it is associated. The value must be a scalar, and the result of the operation is to increment the value by one. Examples:

++i   increment i first, then operate

i++   operate, then increment

−   *The traditional subtraction operator*

Both operands must be integer or float unless one is a pointer, in which case the other must be an integer. Examples:

```
c = a − b;
old_ptr = ptr − 4;
```

−   *The unary operator for negation*

The result of − a is an *rvalue* that has the opposite sign of the lvalue a. The object of the unary operator, in this case a, must have assigned storage (lvalue). The result of the operation is a simple expression that does not have an assigned memory location (rvalue). To keep the value, it must be reassigned to a variable with a permanent address (lvalue). The variable a must be integer or float. Example:

```
c = − a;
```

−−   *The decrement operator*

The value decremented must be scalar. The result of the operation is the value minus one. Examples:

−−i   decrement first, then operate

i−−   operate, then decrement

⋆   *The traditional multiplication operator*
Example:

```
c = a ⋆ b;
```

⋆   *The indirect operator*

⋆ptr refers to the contents of the address to which the pointer ptr points. ptr must belong to the data type *pointer* (see Chapter 4 on pointers).

/   *The traditional division operator*

Both operands must be arithmetic. Precedence (hierarchy) is the same as for multiplication. In the following example, the result is the quotient of b divided by c. Example:

    a = b / c;

=   *The assignment operator*

This operator is the same as Pascal's ': ='. a is an lvalue (by its very definition); both values must either be scalar or an element of an array, structure, or union. In the following example, b is forced into the data type of a. If a is a pointer, b may be a pointer; otherwise both must be arithmetic, or both must be single character. Strings *cannot* be assigned to strings, because they are aggregates. Example:

    a = b;

+=   *Add new value of a variable to its old value*
Example:

    a += 2 is the same as a = a + 2

−=   *Subtract new value of a variable from its old value*
Example:

    a −= 2 is the same as a = a − 2

⋆=   *Multiply new value of a variable by its old value*
Example:

    a ⋆= 2 is the same as a = a ⋆ 2

==   *The logical equal*

Don't confuse this with the assignment operator. This is used for comparison and will return only a Boolean true or false. Example:

    if (a == b)

!=   *The not-equal operator*

The values on either side of it are *not* equal. Example:

    if (a != b)

<   *The less-than operator*

The value on the left is less than the value on the right. Example:

    if (a < b)

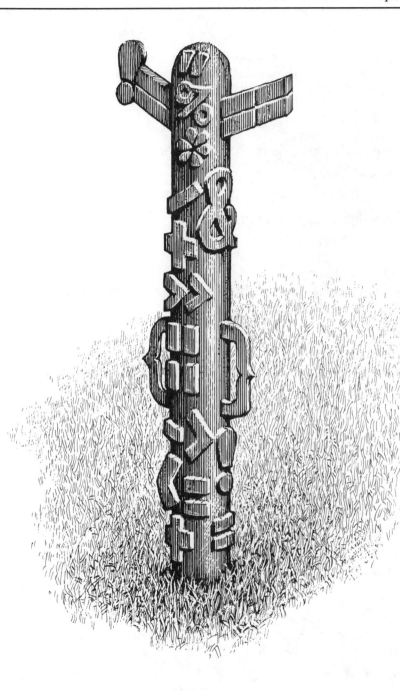

C Operators

<=   *The less-than-or-equal-to operator*
The left value is less than or equal to the expression on the right.
Example:

>   if (a <= b)

>   *The greater-than operator*
The value on the left is greater than the value on the right. Example:

>   if (a > b)

>=   *The greater-than-or-equal-to operator*
The value on the left is greater than or equal to the value on the right.
Example:

>   if (a >= b)

&   *The address operator*
This causes the variable to which it is attached to return its pointer or
address. The variable must be an lvalue. Example:

>   &x   the address of x

&&   *The logical-and operator*
This performs a *logical* or *Boolean and* on the expressions on either side
of it. Example:

>   if (a == b && c > d)

|| *The logical-or operator*
This performs a *logical* or *Boolean or* on the expressions on either side.
Example:

>   if (a = b || a = c)

!   *The logical-negation operator (also called the "not" operator)*
This reverses the condition of the expression it precedes. The expression
evaluates to a scalar. The result of the operation is true if the expression is
0; it is 0 (false) if the expression is true. Remember, logicals are Boolean
operators. Example:

>   while (! EOF)

~   *One's complement operator*
This returns the one's complement of its operand, represented in the following example by j. j must be an integer. Example:

>   b = a & ~j;

->   *Structure-pointer operator*
In the following example, p must be coerceable to a pointer to a struct or

union having a field named struct_memb (see Chapter 4 for a discussion of structs and unions, and Chapters 9 and 14 for a discussion of coercion). Example:

>   p -> struct_memb;

%   *Modulus operator*
This returns the remainder of a division. Both operands must be integer. Precedence is the same as for traditional multiplication. Example:

>   remainder = a % b;

Note that there is no exponentiation operator. Exponentiation is handled by a function.

The following operators are all used for various types of *bit manipulation,* and are included for the sake of completeness. Bit manipulation is an advanced concept that will be of little use to beginning and intermediate programmers, and is not supported by many C compilers.

<<   *The left-shift operator*
This is used for bit manipulation. Example:

>   a << 2   shift a 2 positions to the left

>>   *The right-shift operator*
This is also used for bit rotation. Example:

>   a >> 2   shift a 2 positions to the right

&   *The bitwise-and operator*
This performs a *bitwise* or a *binary and* on the values on either side of it. Example:

>   a = a & mask

| *The bitwise-or operator*
This performs a *bit or* on the values on either side of it. Example:

>   a = a | mask

^   *The bitwise-exclusive-or operator*
This returns an *exclusive or* of the integer on which it operates. Example:

>   b = c ^a;

Escape Characters

Some nongraphic or unprintable characters are represented in C by an escape sequence starting with a backslash \. The backslash is an escape character that modifies the meaning of the character that follows it. To avoid any chance of confusion, the ASCII value of the character is listed as well (in hex) with its corresponding control character. 0x, or 0X, is standard C notation for hexadecimal.

\	An escape character to represent character constants		
\n	Newline (line feed)	0X0A	^J
\r	Return (carriage return)	0X0D	^M
\0	Null terminator (for strings)	0X0	^@
\t	Tab	0X9	^I
\\	Backslash	0X5C	\
\oo	Escape for octal constants, for example, '\032' (32 octal or 1A hex, 0X1A)		
\f	Form feed	0X0C	^L
\'	Single quote	0X27	
\"	Double quote	0X22	

Formatted Print and Scan Conversion Characters

%_	Format conversion operator for formatted print and scan functions such as printf ( ) and scanf ( )
%d	Decimal integer, for example, printf ("%5d", i); prints the decimal integer i right justified 5 places
%o	Octal integer
%x	Hexadecimal integer
%h	A short integer (system dependent, may not be implemented in some subsets of UNIX 7 C)
%u	Unsigned decimal
%s	Character string
%e	Exponential notation
%f	Floating point number
%g	Uses a %e or %f, whichever is shorter

Miscellaneous Symbols

? :   *Ternary operator*
It works like this:

```
a = (b > c) ? d : e ;
```

which is the same as

```
if (b > c)
    a = d;
        else
            a = e;
```

*Precompiler character*
This is not an operator at all (see Chapters 5 and 9). Examples:

```
#include
#define
```

_   *The separator*
Also not an operator, the underscore is a legal C separator. Example:

```
separ_ate
```

A separator serves to provide a visual space between items to make them easier to read, but won't confuse the compiler into thinking the items are separate variables, as a blank space would.

Punctuation

As long as symbols are being looked at, let's look at some C punctuation:

{   The *left brace,* used for starting a block

}   The *right brace,* used for ending a block

(The *left parenthesis,* used to enclose an expression and/or give an expression precedence over hierarchy

)   The *right parenthesis,* used to complete the enclosure

[The *left bracket,* used to enclose an array subscript

]   The *right bracket,* used to complete the subscript enclosure

'   The *single quote,* used for enclosing any ASCII-representable character to yield its ASCII numeric value. Example:

```
asciinbr = digit + '0';
```

"   The *double quote,* used to surround literals (string constants). Example:

```
printf ("%s\n", "string");
```

,   The *comma,* used to separate variables and operations. Example:

```
printf ("name = %s index = %d", n, i)
```

.   The structure-member operator, a period, used to connect the structure and member name (see Chapter 5). strct must be an lvalue in this example:

    strct.member

:   The *label terminator,* for example:

    label:

;   The *statement terminator,* for example:

    if (a == b) c = a = b;

ORDER OF PRECEDENCE (HIERARCHY) AND ASSOCIATIVITY

A *hierarchy* is a group of persons or things arranged in order of rank. In this context it means the order of precedence on arithmetic and logical operators. Without the aid of parentheses to force precedence, operations will be performed in the order dictated by hierarchy.

Associativity refers to the direction in which the operators associate with the operands, whether from left to right or right to left.

Figure 2.1 illustrates how the concepts of hierarchy and associativity

Operator	Direction of Associativity	Description
( ) [ ] → .	→	primary
! ++ -- - * &	←	unary
* / %	→	multiplicative
+ --	→	additive
<< >>	→	shift
< <= => >	→	relational
== !=	→	equality
&	→	bitwise
^	→	bitwise
|	→	bitwise
&&	→	logical
||	→	logical
?:	←	conditional
= += -=	←	assignment
,	→	comma

Figure 2.1: Table of Hierarchy and Associativity

work together. The table is arranged in order of hierarchy. Primary operators ([ ], ( ), ->) are those that are performed first. They are acted upon before unary (single) operators, the second category on the list. Unary operators, in turn, take precedence over multiplicative operators (those that multiply, divide, and yield the modulus), and so forth. The associativity of each descriptive group of operators is shown with an arrow indicating the direction in which the operation will be performed.

Our little table clearly shows that association is an important concept. The assignment, for example, being right to left, allows

$$a = b = c = d = e = f = 0;$$

C starts out at the right and associates (in this case assigns) 0 to f, then f to e, then e to d, and so on, ending with a.

The table illustrates that hierarchy is of equal importance. The expression

$$a = x * x + x * y + y * y;$$

is performed as follows:

$$a = (x*x) + (x*y) + (y*y);$$

The multiplication operator has precedence over the addition operator. Hierarchy can be changed with the use of parentheses; expressions enclosed in parentheses are completed first:

$$a = x * (x + x) * (y + y * y);$$

3:

Data Types, Storage Classes, and Storage Management

I realize that the last chapter was drier than the throat of a Mojave green rattler in August. Let's just say that C's richness of operators, data types, and storage classes keeps the fundamentals of C from being copied onto the inside of matchbook covers for use as crib sheets! In other words, there is a lot to learn before mastering this language.

Unfortunately, you are not through the "heaviest" part yet! If you thought for one minute that the BASIC interpreter can get mean over a syntax error, or that PL/I is nasty about expressing its ire over a run-time error, you've got a surprise in store for you. C will silently watch while you make mistakes. It will allow you to truncate a hundred billion dollars off the national debt without even telling you that your file field isn't wide enough to hold the answer. C will allow you to put a pointer out into the depths of "never-never land," or worse yet, right into the operating system, and it won't so much as beep at you when the entire memory goes whizzing before your very eyes.

What I'm trying to say is that rules are rules, and if you want to keep C up and running, sooner or later you're going to have to learn them. The good news is that C is an extremely powerful and versatile language that will allow you to program anything from systems to applications. Once the basic concepts are mastered, you can mentally soar like an eagle, so C is worth all the work of learning it. And, as with the last chapter, you don't have to memorize this chapter. It is meant to be a reference. Although sooner or later you must come to grips with each concept, the chapter can be skimmed over for now and returned to again (and again).

DATA TYPES

There is a great deal of confusion about character data versus integer data in C. To help clear up the confusion, here are a few points to remember.

All data coming from and going to the system are handled as 8-bit integer data. The basic building block in data transmission for high-speed digital computers is the 8-bit byte. A byte can represent a single character or two numerals (usually hex). The eight bits that make up the byte are numbered 0 through 7. Pure ASCII character data has the last (seventh) bit "turned off" (set to 0). Having the high-order bit set to 0 gives the now 7-bit integer the opportunity to represent 128 different characters. By no coincidence, the ASCII character set consists of 128 characters. The first 33 of these characters (0–32 decimal) are unprintable. They are blanks, tabs, carriage returns, line feeds, form feeds, the bell character, and so forth. (A blank can be referred to as ' ', 020 hex, or 32 decimal.) The characters 33–126 decimal are printable characters, just like the ones you're reading right now. (Capital A in ASCII is 41 hex and 65 decimal.) The last character (127 decimal) is a delete character.

Now that is exactly half of the story. When the seventh bit is "turned on" (set to 1), the byte can have an additional value. These last 128 characters are normally negative numbers (the concept of one's complement). As characters they have meaning in EBCDIC (which is never used in microcomputers) but not in ASCII. No character data in C using ASCII will ever have a negative ASCII value. The CP/M physical end-of-file mark (EOF) is not an ASCII character, and it has a value of -1.

When C receives or puts out a character, it outputs a byte. If the byte is to be intelligible to the console, which is the C's standard input/output device, it must be a character (the seventh bit must be set to 0). The confusion comes in here: because all characters are 7-bit integers, a single character can be represented as an integer (data type *integer*) as well as a single or scalar character (data type *character*). Therefore, all scalar characters can be integer. This comes in very handy in detecting the end-of-file marker, as you will see. If you are still confused about this, keep reading.

Data is differentiated into various types in C. Whether integer, float, character, struct, or whatever, you must specify the data type. If you don't, C won't know how to handle the program's data, nor will it know how to store it. The trick is knowing *which* data type to specify! Let's take a closer look at each data type.

Character

When using character arrays, C's method of handling strings, the data type *char* is the one you want to use. When using character data, you may want to use the data type char; however, character data can also be handled with the data type integer. A look at the following program will clarify this point. The purpose of the program is to take character input and copy it to the program's output. Here's what it looks like.

```
main ( )
{
   int c;

   c = getchar ( );
   while ( c ! = EOF)
   {
      putchar (c);
      c = getchar ( )
   }
}
```

Notice that the character c is declared integer. Initially, one would assume that because character input is being handled, the data type naturally would be character—but not in this program. Why? Because the character c must be type integer to read the end-of-file mark (EOF), −1. If c were declared as type char, the program could not read the numeric EOF mark.

Another point: in C the data type character is not a string (as it is in BASIC and PL/I). A character in C is a single, scalar character. A string in C is an array of characters terminated by \0. When any character is put between single quotes such as '0', C returns the integer value of that character. '0' will return 030 hex. If you doubt it for even a second, try this:

```
main ( )
{
   if ('0' == 0X30)
      puts ("true");
      else
         puts ("what?");
}
```

It will display "true" because the character 0 is ASCII 030 hex. You should have trusted me!

As you may know, in an 8-bit system a *word* is two bytes (16 bits), and an *integer* is the value yielded by two bytes. It naturally follows that integers are *machine words*, but words are not always integers. Bearing in mind that there are *signed integers* (such as − 32, + 12, and so forth) and *unsigned integers* (such as 843, 9, and so forth), it behooves you to know that they are represented differently internally. Unsigned 16-bit integers give the numeric values 0 to 65,535. To allow for signed 16-bit integers, the concept of *one's complement* is usually applied. This effectively cuts the available number of positive integers in half, giving a range of $-32,768$ to $+32,767$ for signed short integers. An integer can be *short* (two bytes) or *long* (four bytes), depending on the machine. Normally it is the length of the machine's word; an 8-bit processor has a 16-bit word, and 16-bit processors have 32-bit words. In the smaller 8-bit versions of C, signed short integer is normally the only arithmetic class available.

float

The data type *float* is a floating-point number of standard precision, as opposed to double precision. System-dependent, it is usually four bytes. The actual precision of float varies from one implementation to another. It is both hardware- and software-dependent. For example, Digital Research's C has a mantissa precise to seven digits and a range of $1.18 \times 10^{\pm 38}$. This is the maximum number that this version of C can output with full precision. Anything larger forces the output into scientific notation or causes zeros to be added to the end of the number. Examples of float data are 3.14159, .314159e1, and so forth.

Double Precision

A double-precision number (type *double*) is a floating-point number of very long precision, usually eight bytes. For example, DRC's type double-precision floating-point numbers range from 9.46×10^{-308} to 1.80×10^{308}.

struct

struct (meaning structure) is an aggregate data type consisting of one or more data types, either scalar or aggregate (see glossary). By analogy, raisins and cherries and cake are all separate things, but fruitcake is one thing. The C struct is a "fruitcake" of data types, or an *aggregate data type*. The struct forms a memory template to define the data types. Unlike PL/I's *structure,* struct may not be freely passed back and forth to files as a single entity. For further reference, structs and unions have a chapter of their own, Chapter 8.

Array of

Arrays are repetitions of a single data type. Unlike the fruitcake analogy, an array is like a carton of extra large grade AA eggs. Arrays can be of type integer, float, character, pointer, or structure, or can be arrays of arrays of these data types. They free the programmer from all limits but those of his or her own creativity. The possibilities can get pretty wild, such as arrays of arrays, arrays of structures of arrays, arrays of pointers to arrays, and so on. Arrays are dealt with in detail in Chapter 4.

union

The data type *union* is a real garbage can. A union is a programmer-defined area large enough to hold any data type that the programmer anticipates will pass through it. Refer to Chapter 8 on structs and unions.

bitfield

The data type *bitfield* is an integer subfield. It is always declared as a member of a struct. Since a bitfield is less than a byte, it has no address—therefore you may not use the address operator & in reference to the bitfield.

Pointer

A *pointer* is an unsigned integer that is used to hold the memory address of a variable or constant. Refer to Chapter 4 for more information on pointers.

typedef

If you find that C doesn't give you enough data types for your programming needs, C allows other data types to be defined (as Pascal does) by using the *typedef* facility. This is C's way of never having to say it's sorry.

typedef creates new data type names. typedef means that the name so modified shall now be recognized as a specified data type. typedef is not associated with any particular object until it is used with the object in a declaration. Here is the way typedef is used:

    typedef [type specifier] [list];

Where you see [type specifier], you can insert integer, char, float, struct, or union. Where you see [list], you insert the new variable name. A classic use of typedef would be

    typedef char *string;

making string synonymous with character, no doubt an aid to dyed-in-the-wool BASIC programmers.

STORAGE CLASSES

One of the great advantages of a structured language like C, Pascal, or
PL/I is that it allows storage to be allocated and freed as required. If you
need to sort something in a program, for example, the storage required for
the sorting array is permanent to the program unless the storage is allowed
to be deallocated or freed. By sorting in a subroutine (or in a function in
C), the array can be local to that block of the program. Note, however,
that when the block is exited, it is possible to free its storage requirements.

Data Types and Storage Classes

This is done by using *local variables*. A local variable is one that has meaning only in the block in which it appears. Those that are known to all blocks are *global* to the program.

extern

A variable declared as *extern* (external) is known outside of the area in which it is declared. If it appears outside of the main program block, it retains its meaning for common use by any file that uses the program and the same variable name. When used internally to a program block, the variable name is known to any other block that also declares the name. External variables have their storage allocated for as long as the program is running.

The character length of variables external to the main program block is system-dependent. It is reasonable to assume that a length of six characters is safe. Fewer than six characters is an even safer variable length. When in doubt, read the manual.

The program fragment in Figure 3.1 demonstrates the use of extern. In this skeletal example, the variable buffer is declared explicitly external to the main program block. It is declared explicitly external to read ( ) and write ( ) within their blocks. The variable buffer is therefore known to the read ( ), write ( ), and main program blocks, as well as to any file that may call it.

Because it is easier to create external variables implicitly than explicitly, some C compilers do not support the use of the variable extern. The program in Figure 3.2 makes use of an implicitly declared external variable (buffer [ ]). It is almost identical to the program called B.C. in Chapter 4, which is used to demonstrate pointer passing from function to main and main to function. Compare the program in Figure 3.2 with B.C. on page 66. Notice that in the following program, buffer [ ] is known to the entire program.

The header line

```
#include "bdscio.h"
```

or

```
#include <bdscio.h>
```

causes the compiler preprocessor to open and read the header file bdscio.h. It becomes a part of the program. I/O header files like bdscio.h and the classic stdio.h define I/O constants like EOF, stdin, stdout, stderr (standard input, output, and error), and other standard program constants like TRUE, FALSE and ERROR. Header files will be discussed more fully in Chapter 5.

```
            #include "std.h"
            extern char buffer [BUFSIZ];

            main ( )
            {
                char reply [1];
                int rn;

                clear ( );
                puts ("\n\n\n\n\tMenu\n\"");
                .
                .
                .
                if (rn == 1)
                        read ( );
                        else if (rn == 2)
                                write ( );
                .
                .
            }

            read ( )
                    extern char buffer [ ];
                {
                    .
                    .
                }

            write ( )
                {
                    extern char buffer [ ];
                    .
                    .
                    .
                }

            clear ( )
                {
                    putchar (12);
                }
```

Figure 3.1: Program Fragment Illustrating Use of extern

```
    /*
            b1.c

            a program to write to and read from a buffer
            by external declaration

    */

    #include "bdscio.h"

    char buffer [129];          /*NOTICE THAT BUFFER IS EXTERNAL
                                TO THE BODY OF THE CODE*/
```

Figure 3.2: A Program to Write to and Read from a Buffer by External Declaration
        (continues)

```
main ( )
{
    char reply [1];
    int rn;

    puts ("\n\n\n\n\tpointer buffer program");
    for ( ; ; )
    {
        puts ("\n\n               menu");
        puts ("\n\n 1              read string  ");
        puts ("\n\n 2              write string ");
        puts ("\n\n\n\t enter selection  : ");
        gets (reply);
        rn = atoi (reply);
        if (rn == 1)
            read ( );
        if (rn == 2)
            write ( );
    }
}

read ( )
{
    char dummy [1];
    char buf1 [129];

    clear ( );
    puts ("\n\n\nenter string : ");
    gets (buf1);
    strcpy (buffer, buf1);
    puts ("\n  buffer = ");
    puts (buffer);
    puts ("\nenter to continue");
    gets (dummy);
}

write ( )
{
    char dummy [1];
    char buf2 [129];

    clear ( );
    puts ("\n\n\t\tstring output\n");
    strcpy (buf2, buffer);
    puts (buf2);
    puts ("\n enter to continue");
    gets (dummy);
}

clear ( )
{
    putchar (12);
}
```

Figure 3.2: A Program to Write to and Read from a Buffer by External Declaration

static

Like the static class in PL/I, *static* ensures that the storage allocated for the variable with the static class will remain in existence for the executable life of the program. The difference between extern and static is that although the permanence is retained, a variable declared as static outside the main program block is not known to the calling files. The program fragment in Figure 3.3 leaves the character array buffer external and global to the entire program, but it will not be accessible to any other files (programs).

auto

Automatic storage is declared with the class *auto*, very much like PL/I's automatic storage class. It can be declared only within the block that uses it, and it guarantees that the block that uses it will free it when execution exits the block. Most variables are implicitly auto. In the Figure 3.2, the buffers buf1 and buf2 are implicitly auto. Be sure that automatic storage is what you want when you use it. If you leave a function block and return to it later, you will find that the previously stored values of the variables for that block are gone.

register

register is a storage class that gives the variable "register preference" in execution. The registers of the processor are the ultimate in high speed storage, so register is used to promote rapid data transfer. Like auto, register must be declared within the block, and it is in existence only while the block is executing. Care must be exercised not to overuse register, because there is only so much register space available.

```
#include "stdio.h"

static char buffer [BUFSIZ];

main ( )
{
        char reply [1];
        int rn;

        clear ( );
        .
        .
        .
```

Figure 3.3: Program Fragment Demonstrating static Declaration

DECLARATIONS

The very first portions of nearly all C programs, and certainly all non-trivial ones, are the precompiler commands and the declarations. The declarations assign and associate the scope of the variables declared, the storage class, and the data type of the identifier.

Declarations take the form

storage_class type <list> initializers

as in

static int i = 0;

meaning that i is an integer that is static and has an initial value of zero (initializers assign the initial values). The storage class is optional, as is the initializer. In fact, initialization of variables in the declaration is not supported by all compilers. The declaration must end with a semicolon.

A list of multiple declarations on a single line is permissible and encouraged. Identifiers are separated by commas:

auto int i, j, k, len, nflag;

In this statement i, j, k, len, and nflag are integers and are allocated automatic storage.

Pointers are declared as the type of the identifier to which they point:

char string [MAXLINE];
char *strptr;

or

char string [MAXLINE], *strptr;

Parentheses can be used within declarations legally. As usual, they change the precedence of the declaration:

float *funx ( );

is a function *returning* a pointer *to* float, while

float (*funx)( );

is a pointer *to* a function *returning* float.

There are a lot of rules on declarations, especially as they relate to structures and unions, but I want to cover them a little later. For now this is enough to cover the basics.

STACK ALLOCATION

There is a certain breed of programmer who revels in the esoteric delights of programming in assembly. I know of a few isolated individuals who not only love assembly language programming, but won't even program in anything else. There are many more people who view the prospect of programming in assembly language with emotions ranging from skeptical reticence, determined defiance, anxious dismay, and sheer panic all the way to martyred resignation. Whatever category you fit into, if you program for long, especially in a language as sophisticated as C, you will inevitably get into some assembly language, or something very close to it.

Most of the written material about assembly language programming covers the assignment of memory and the register activity. Little has been written about the stack. Stack storage is highly volatile, changing addressable and nonaddressable areas of storage that take up the slack between register and addressable memory. Languages such as Pascal, PL/I, and C use a form of stack memory called *heap* (*based storage* in PL/I). Heap or based storage is not the stack proper, but an area of memory usually found above the addressable allocated storage area. Similar to another stack, it is allocated and freed from the program by the programmer.

As you may have noticed by now, C doesn't do a heck of a lot on its own. A mid-level language, it makes few assumptions. It expects that the programmer is indeed able to invoke all the routines required to make the program run. Allocating the heap is no exception. You don't get it if you don't ask for it. C functions call other C functions, and although it may appear that heap allocation is not required, more than likely, it is needed. Buffered file I/O is a good example of functions needing heap allocation. The function for heap allocation is alloc.[1] For more information on heap allocation, refer to *The C Programming Language* by Brian W. Kernighan and Dennis M. Ritchie.

STORAGE MANAGEMENT

The primary goal of this chapter is to show you how C uses the declaration of variables by data type and storage class to allocate storage. What exactly does this knowledge mean to you? Before a program written on a C compiler can run, the compiler must know where to find the variables and constants it is going to use in the course of executing the program. In more specific terms, this means that it must know the addresses or pointers to the lvalues used in the program. The data types tell C how many bytes to use. The storage classes tell C whether they will be used outside or inside of the program. If they will be used inside of the program, the storage classes tell where they will be used.

When the C compiler reads the source code for the first time, it takes its first parsing pass. (*Parsing* the code for the first time is like settling down to read the Sunday paper. Before beginning, the reader glances through the paper and decides which section to read first, which section to read second, and so forth.) The first parsing pass gives the compiler enough information to allow the compiler's next pass to create intermediate code with either absolute or relative addresses. In simpler terms, parsing the code several times gives the compiler the information it needs to always be aware of what will happen throughout the program. This gives the program much more power than one written in an interpreter, which only reads the program line by line, not knowing what will happen beyond the line it is reading. Declarations are what make compiled code possible.

Before continuing, let's review what you have learned so far. In Chapter 1, you saw some of the mechanics of how C works: how C programs make decisions, how they perform loops, and most important of all, how they deal with standard input and output involving the keyboard and console. You studied some of the basic theory of C in Chapters 2 and 3, a necessary but not necessarily exciting pastime. It's time to go up to a higher level in our exploration of the C language.

To give you a taste of what is to come, consider that what you have learned so far gives C about as much power as a programmable calculator. Where computers leave the lowly calculator behind in the dust is in the ability to use mass storage. One vehicle for mass storage is high-speed computer memory—not the disk drives, which are another vehicle for mass storage, but the memory I'm talking about is the memory built into the computer itself. To create a list of variables large enough to take advantage of this mass storage area above the program might seem a nearly impossible task—you not only run out of meaningful names, but you can easily lose track of the names you have used. To avoid this, masses of variables with the same name but with different subidentifiers (numeric subscripts) are assigned, called *arrays*. To locate the data in the various addresses in memory, you need a way to keep track of it all, and you do this with handy little devices called *pointers*. To utilize arrays, pointers, and other programmer's tools, you rely on a single source—the *function*. Get ready to learn about all of these concepts and more in the next chapter, called "Functions, Pointers, and Related Concepts."

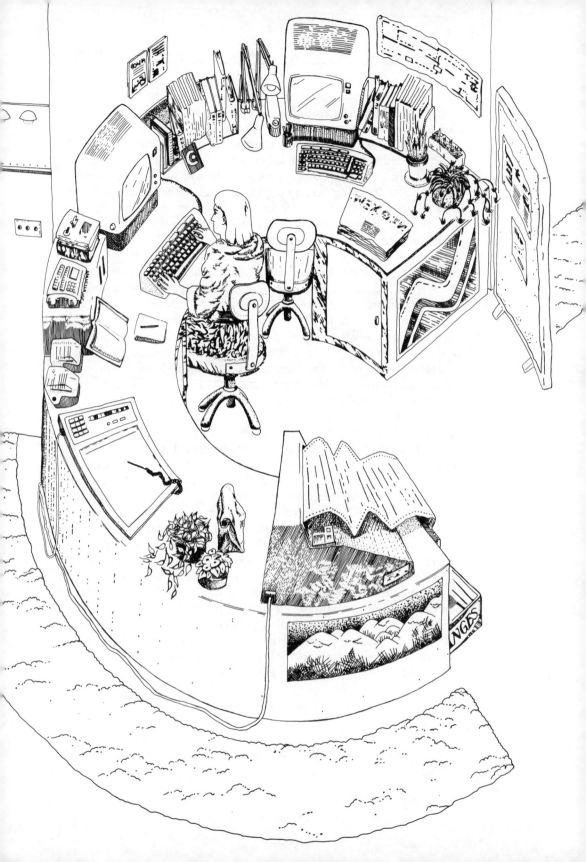

4:

Functions, Pointers, and Related Concepts

Among the many topics discussed in this chapter, there will be a long look at pointers. To do any real programming in C, you must understand pointers, and there are many things to learn. You will learn what a pointer is. You will learn the C syntax for using pointers with unary operators. You will learn how pointers allow functions to deal with multiple values such as aggregates (unions, arrays, structs) and have those values known outside the function. You will learn debugging tips to help you get your pointer programs up and bug-free quickly, specifically as an aid to learning pointers. You will even learn how pointers point to arrays, arrays of arrays, and even more exotic structures. But that is not enough. The most important concepts to learn about pointers are not merely how they are used, but *why* they are used and how they actually *work*.

Most authors won't touch pointers with a ten-foot pole, and those that do tend to cover them superficially. I'm not going to do that. I intend this book to be a *complete* introduction to C. In this chapter we will go into pointers in depth, because one of C's great strengths is the ability it offers the programmer to manipulate pointers with virtuosity. The only way to give yourself the power of pointers as an effective programming tool is to understand them inside and out. In this chapter I will try to get you well on your way towards this goal.

This chapter also deals with functions. C is one of the most powerful languages in common use today, and one source of its power is the unique way that it uses functions as its basic building tool. Every program block in C is in fact a function block, including the main block. Because C, unlike Pascal, Ada, and PL/I, does not have procedures, the lowly function takes on vital importance, for C programmers need to learn to use the functions to do everything. A function usually returns a single value, but it can also be made to act as a procedure by having it alter data values. It does this by reaching out to the stored data locations and by changing the values stored there.

Functions and pointers work together in C. For example, a function can alter stored values only by addressing a pointer. This concept is not easily learned, and it has been the downfall of many a would-be C programmer. To prevent you, the reader, from brushing over the critical concepts of pointer handling, lvalues, rvalues, the indirect operator and its relationship in functions and arrays, a great deal of this chapter will be devoted to defining, explaining, and reiterating these concepts.

Each programming language has its forte. C's fortes are its power, speed, and versatility, and its ability to build upon itself. In a philosophical sense, it is a recursive language, calling upon itself to gain greater power. The language's exclusive use of the function as its program building block is neither an oversight nor an omission. Functions, once created, are permanent tools. They are stored in the programmer's libraries. The most frequently used functions are stored within the *language's* function library.

Such power is not without a price, however. The price is that the programmer must learn to handle the housekeeping tasks that less powerful languages do automatically. Pascal and PL/I permit a value to be given to a procedure by "reference." These languages deal with the stored values by making pointer handling transparent or invisible to both the program and the programmer. On the other hand, the C language will not risk the integrity of the program's data by allowing the data to be altered accidentally by the unwitting programmer. Instead, it passes only an *image* of the stored data to functions. This is called *passing by value*. The rest is up to the C programmer. A programmer who wants to change stored data values must do so by reaching the data "where it lives." The data can only be reached by knowing its address, and that is what pointers are for. All of this is interrelated and takes a bit of effort to sort out. Let's start by looking at how data are stored.

STORING AND MANAGING DATA

Storing and managing data are what computing is all about. Data management is memory management. Sometimes data are stored in variables that can hold only a single (scalar) value. For example, IQ = 125 (125 is the value assigned to the variable IQ).[1] However, if you stored data *only* in this way, you would soon run out of meaningful variable names. In addition, keeping track of the variable names would become more of a problem than storing the variables. Because large groupings of data usually have something in common, particularly if they are of the same data type, it is convenient to store that data in a matrix or array. An array is a data aggregate. A data aggregate consists of more than one data element (as opposed to a scalar, which contains a single data element).

All data stored in high-speed memory are stored at addresses. The address is the exact location of a particular piece of data, which is indicated by an unsigned integer (a number with no + or − designation) that is a machine word. For example, in an 8-bit, 64K machine, the available addresses would be 0 to 65535 (64 × 1024). Memory is analogous to storing letters at the post office in boxes, giving each box a number. The box number is the address. Similarly, the pointer is the address of the data. Using pointers is another way to manage memory. A variable does not have to have a name as long as it has an accessible pointer.

Languages that support arrays (most do) access the arrays internally by way of pointers. Even BASIC has arrays, but BASIC does not have a data type pointer; it has pointers, but you can't see them—the pointers are transparent to the user. BASIC is a teaching language, and pointers are not only dangerous for beginning programmers, they are also relatively difficult to understand. That's why it was thought best to leave pointers out of the definition of the BASIC language. C, on the other hand, was created for programmers. It places nearly every available tool at the disposal of the programmer. Pointers are among these tools. Consequently, any element of any array can be accessed in C, either by using the array name or by using a pointer to the element.

FUNCTIONS AND THEIR RELATIONSHIP TO POINTERS

By general definition (not C's), a function is a block of code of one or more lines that returns a value to the expression that uses it. C functions (unlike PL/I's, Pascal's, BASIC's, etc.) do not have to return a value. In C the job of a function is to perform a specific task or tasks. Most often, functions are given specific data to work with. Naturally, there has to be a special name for that data, and that name is *parameter* or *argument*. In programming terms, parameters are "passed" to the functions. In C it frequently is necessary to pass a pointer (to the data) to the function. You will see how this works later in the chapter. For now, just be aware that pointers are used with functions.

C is a block-structured language. It looks a little like PL/I, some of the ALGOLs, and Pascal, except that it has no "call" and there are no "procedures." In fact, outside of the main program block, the only thing C has in the way of any form of subroutine is the function. Consequently, while functions in BASIC are handy "tools" for the programmer to use, in C the use and creation of functions are skills you *must* master.

There are two forms of functions, user-defined functions (those that the programmer creates) and built-in or library functions. The library functions supplied with most versions of C are versatile and varied. You can use them to do almost anything. But one of the most important aspects of C is that it allows you to create and enlarge functions with ease by using other functions. Brian Kernighan, one of the developers of C, is well known for his books on software tools, which deal specifically with creating functions by using previously existing functions. The ability to expand itself in this manner is what makes C such a powerful language.

In order to broaden our understanding of functions and how they operate, let's take a closer look at parameters and related concepts.

Parameters

The data that are "passed" (given to) a function are called *arguments* or *actual parameters*. When they are "received" (acted on) by the function, they are called *formal parameters*. More commonly, they are simply referred to as *parameters*. The following program fragment illustrates the difference between actual and formal parameters.

```
power (x,n); / * actual parameter list * /
.
.
.
}
power (nbr, pwr) / * formal parameter list * /
int nbr, pwr;
{
```

(Note that there is no semicolon after the parentheses when the function receives the formal parameters, because it is the beginning of the function block.)

Scope of Variables

The scope of variables refers to *where* variables are known by the program. Variables declared inside the main program block are known to the main program block only. It is said that they are *local* to the main block. Variables declared within a function are local to that function. Variables declared outside of the main block are known—they are *global*—to the entire program.

In the skeletal program in Figure 4.1, the character array datbuf is global to the entire program. The variables i, j, and x are local to the main block. The variables nbr, pwr, and i are local to the function power ( ). Thus, i represents two different variables, having one value in the main block and something different in the function power( ). Thus the scope of j is the main, the scope of nbr is power ( ), and the scope of datbuf is the entire program.

In Figure 4.1, when the variables x and j are passed to the function power, they are *received* as nbr and pwr. nbr and pwr are passed *by value*. If they are altered by the function power, the values of x and j are not affected. To affect these values, the *address* of the variables would have to be passed to the function. This is called passing a pointer.

The majority of functions receive variables as parameters from the calling block to the function. In computer languages, we talk of passing parameters *by value* and *by reference*. A parameter passed by reference

```
        char datbuf [MAXLINE];

        main ( )
              int i, j, x;
              {
              .
              .
              .
              power (x, j);      /*The call to the function power*/
              .
              .
              }

        power (nbr, pwr)    /*The first line of power*/
        int nbr, pwr;
              {
              int i;
              .
              .
              }
```

Figure 4.1: Skeletal Program Demonstrating Parameter Passing

passes (points to) the address of the variable. Therefore, any changes to the variable are permanent. PL/I can pass parameters by reference. On the other hand, when parameters are passed by value, the function receives an "image" of the variable by having it placed on the stack when it is passed. Changes to the image do not affect the variable itself. C can pass variables (as parameters) *only* by value.

For most people, this could be considered merely academic, but it has a large impact on programming in C. Why? Let's look at two program fragments in which parameters are passed to functions and find out.

Let's say that you want to use the function max to get the largest of two variables:

.

.

.

```
x = y * max(a,b);          /*This is where the max function is
                             needed to get larger of a or b in
                             order to perform the multiplication
                             of this equation. This is like a
                             "call" to the function. */
```

.

.

.

```
int max(n1,n2)             /*Here we see the function itself.
                             This is where the parameters a
                             and b are received as n1 and n2.
                             The function now compares the
                             values of n1 and n2 and returns
                             an "image" of the largest back to
                             the expression that called the
                             function. */
```

.

.

.

Now to calculate x, only *images* of the variables a and b have to be passed to the function max. max will return the larger of the two values to the expression, and x is then calculated. What is important to the understanding of passing by value is that the values of the variables y, a, and b are not changed by any of the code we see here. Only x is changed. Therefore, passing the arguments a and b to the function max *by value* is perfectly acceptable. In this example, passing a parameter by value doesn't present a problem.

Now let's look at a program of a different color. In the following program fragment, the value of one string variable is assigned to another.

```
        .
        .
        .
strcpy (a,b);              / *The call from the main to the
        .                    function. * /
        .

        .
}
strcpy (s1,s2)             / *The function body. * /
char *s1, *s2;
{
        .
        .
        .
```

Note that we want to copy the character array b into the character array a (in BASIC, the equivalent is A$ = B$). To do this, the *value* of a must be changed. If only an *image* of the string a is passed to the function strcpy, its value cannot be changed, and the program does not accomplish the desired results. To change the value permanently, a pointer to a must be the parameter that is passed. As a pointer to the address of a, it allows a new value to be put into the variable address at the location in storage pointed to by s1. The change is permanent; a will have the value of b as its contents.

Remember, the only way to affect the *value* of a variable is to affect its stored value. Variables (or constants, for that matter) have an assigned storage location that is permanent for the portion of the program in which they have scope. Global variables are permanent for the life of the program, as are those variables that are local to the main program block. If their value is changed at their permanent address, the change is permanent for the life of the program. If it is changed while it is on the stack, it is a temporary change that will not affect the stored value.

To help understand this, we need a convenient terminology. Variables with permanent addresses are called *lvalues*. The name comes from the fact that the value on the left of an assignment always has a permanent address. It is not a register or stack variable with no address. I'm going to harp on this point a lot because it is a very important concept.

Let's go through a short exercise in pointers and related et ceteras:

```
x = 1;
```

Here's the simple but important assignment. The variable x contains the value 1. Remember, all assignments in the main have permanent storage allocated.

But what if we do this:

       ptr_x = &x;

ptr_x is a pointer. It is set to the *address* of x by the operator &. The unary operator & can be used *only* with lvalues. This is a major concept in C. Spend some time on it:

       z = *ptr_x;

The unary operator * (the indirect operator) tells you that you are dealing with the contents of the address pointed to by ptr_x. The indirect, when used with a pointer, will yield the *contents* of the pointer.

       z == *ptr_x

This logical comparison now will be evaluated as true, because both variables have the same value.

The program in Figure 4.2 demonstrates reading and writing from buffers by pointer addressing. This program doesn't have a lot of practical value, but when we get into disk files (buffered files), the concepts demonstrated here will be invaluable.

Breaking it down is the best way to examine the concepts:

       #include "bdscio.h"
       char buffer [129];

```
       /*
                 b.c

                 a program to write to and read from a buffer
                 by pointer addressing

       */

       #include "bdscio.h"

       char buffer [129];

       main ( )
       {

             char *bufptr;
             char reply [2];
             int rn;
```

Figure 4.2: A Program to Write to and Read from a Buffer by Pointer Addressing (continues)

```
        bufptr = &buffer;   /*Assign the pointer to the buffer*/
        putchar (12);
        puts ("\n\n\n\n\tpointer buffer program");
        for ( ; ; )
        {
            putchar (12);
            puts ("\n\n                menu");
            puts ("\n\n 1    read string ");
            puts ("\n\n 2    write string ");
            puts ("\n\n\n\t enter selection: ");
            getchar (reply);
            rn = atoi (reply);
            if (rn == 1)
            {
                read (bufptr);
            }
            if (rn == 2)
            {
                write (bufptr);
            }
        } /*end for*/
}


read (p)

        char *p;    /*declare p as a pointer*/
{
        char dummy [2];
        char buf1 [129];

        putchar (12);
        puts ("\n\n\nenter string : ");
        gets (buf1);
        strcpy (p, buf1);   /*copy the buffer to the address
                            pointed to by the pointer*/
        puts ("\n  *p = ");
        puts (p);       /*print the contents of the address
                        pointed to by the pointer*/
        puts ("\nenter to continue");
        gets (dummy);
}

write (p)
        char *p;    /*declare p as a pointer*/

{
        char dummy [2];
        char buf2 [129];

        putchar (12);
        puts ("\n\n\t\tstring output\n");
        strcpy (buf2, p);
        puts (buf2);
        puts ("\nenter to continue");
        gets (dummy);
}
```

Figure 4.2: A Program to Write to and Read from a Buffer by Pointer Addressing

Pointers

Most C programs will have a "standard header" file, included at compilation time, to define the C program constants. Here the BDS C compiler's standard header is included, and a character array buffer of 128 characters maximum is established (128max + '\0'). This array is global to the entire program, because it is declared outside of the main.

Then bufptr is declared a pointer by the declaration ∗bufptr. Note the assignment technique. A two-character variable reply and an integer rn are declared as well:

```
main ( )
{

    char *bufptr;
    char reply [2];
    int rn;
```

The pointer bufptr is then assigned to the variable buffer. Now its address is known to the program.

```
bufptr = &buffer;
```

Next we find an old-fashioned menu trapped within a do-forever, an endless loop. The opportunity is presented to read or write a string. No big deal, except the reading and writing will be done from functions:

```
putchar (12);
puts ("\n\n\n\n\tpointer buffer program");
for ( ; ; )
{
    putchar (12);
    puts ("\n\n          menu");
    puts ("\n\n 1   read string ");
    puts ("\n\n 2   write string ");
    puts ("\n\n\n\t enter selection: ");
```

The next step is to convert reply from a character to an integer so that it can be tested. The function atoi (alpha to integer) does the trick. Two ifs perform a case (a multiple branch) and branch to the functions read ( ) or write ( ):

```
getchar (reply);
rn = atoi (reply);
if (rn == 1)
{
    read (bufptr);
}
if (rn == 2)
```

```
{
    write (bufptr);
}
```

The variable bufptr, the buffer pointer, is the argument passed to the function, and it is received as the parameter p:

```
read (p)

char *p;
```

Note that it is declared *outside the block*. Parameters are always declared outside the function block. More has been accomplished than passing the pointer to the function. Now the contents can be dealt with directly.

Next, internal to the function block, a single character array and a local buffer are declared:

```
char dummy [1];
char buf1 [129];
```

Then the screen is cleared, and the string is entered to the storage location assigned to the variable buf1, the buffer local to the function read:

```
putchar (12);
puts ("\n\n\nenter string : ");
gets (buf1);
```

C is not particularly casual about assigning one array to another—not many languages are. The assignment p = buf1 is therefore illegal. To overcome this handicap, the string copy function strcpy ( ) is provided to copy the newly received contents of buf1 into the address of buffer, and the pointer p:

```
strcpy (p, buf1);
```

To assure you that the address pointed to by p does in fact have the string in it, you just print it out by the statement puts (p);:

```
puts ("\n *p = ");
puts (p);
```

Now we come across an old trick to stop program execution temporarily. The gets (dummy) statement is satisfied by a carriage return:

```
puts ("\nenter to continue");
gets (dummy);
```

The next section should look pretty familiar by now. The pointer p is passed and declared as a pointer *outside* the function block. Then another dummy and another local buffer are declared:

```
write (p)
   char *p;

{
   char dummy [1];
   char buf2 [129];
```

The screen is cleared again, and the reemergence of the string is announced by the next puts ( ). The strcpy( ) function copies the string pointed to by p (buffer) to buf2. buf2 is the output buffer used by puts(buf2).

```
putchar (12); /* clear screen */
puts ("\n\n\t\tstring output\n");
strcpy (buf2, p);
puts (buf2);
puts ("\nenter to continue");
gets (dummy);
```

Compile this program and walk it through its paces to get the feel of variable assignments. If you don't feel that you understand the concepts, review this section again. If you think that you probably understand the main idea, review this section again before you write your first variable assignments in your first original program. lvalues are just too important in C to be passed over without a thorough understanding.

ARRAYS

Arrays are used so often in C that it is easy to take them for granted. Because all character strings are in reality arrays, even if they contain only one character, you may find yourself using arrays before you gain a complete understanding of them. C arrays, like Pascal arrays, are always single-dimensional.

However, C cleverly provides for arrays of arrays! Because of this, it can create, in effect, multi-dimensional arrays. (A point to remember: C array subscripts start at 0.) The following program segment creates three 3 by 4 matrices. The for statements prepare to step through the matrix in row major order (rows fastest, then columns).

```
main ( )
{
   int i, j;
   int a [3] [4], b [3] [4], c [3] [4];
```

```
for (i = 0 ; i < = 2 ; i++)
   for (j = 0 ; j < = 3 ; j++)
      .
      .
      .
```

You will find, however, that most arrays in C will be single-dimensional arrays, which are also called *vectors*.

Before moving too far ahead, here are a few rules:

- References to an array when it is unsubscripted are always to the element in the 0 position:

   x = *y

   This means "store the contents of y," but in this case, because y is an array, the expression defaults to the 0 element of y. This is the same as

   x = y [0]

   By the same rule,

   py = &y [0]

   is

   py = y

   It all makes sense when you remember that any reference to a string, which is in reality a character array, must be made to the first element. Strings and arrays are just about inseparable. Later in this chapter we will deal with both simultaneously.

- More C pointer/array idiosyncrasies:

   y [i]

   is also

   *(y + i)

   What they are both saying is that they reference i elements beyond y [0]. By the same token,

   py [i]

   is the same as

   *(py + i)

   because it is incrementing the pointer py i number of places beyond 0.

Array Passing

When an array is passed to a function, what is passed in reality is a pointer to the first element of the array, the element at position 0. Now you can't take a pointer to the bank, so you will have to perform a small but powerful bit of wizardry to get the array.

```
funct (array)
char *array;
    {
```

The pointer, here called array, is received by the function. Before entering the function block, it is declared with the indirect operator *. This tells C that you are dealing with the contents of the address, that is, the entire array. From here on, the variable can be referenced without the indirect operator:

```
strcpy (bigstr, array)
```

Working through the array from the element at position 0 in values is *pointer arithmetic*—the incrementing or decrementing of the pointer and/or array subscript. The next programming example keeps the pointer arithmetic as simple as possible, to avoid confusion.

Programs that alter the input before outputting it are called *filters*. The program in Figure 4.3 is a filter for names. It takes as input a name in the

```
/*

        NA.C

        a filter for names

*/

#include "bdscio.h"
char name [MAXLINE];

main ( )
{
    putchar (12);
    puts ("\n\n\n\tname filter\n\n");
    puts ("input name, first middle last : ");
    gets (name);
    lc (name);
    printf ("\n\n\nLowercase Name => %s\n\n", name);
    cap (name);
    printf ("Capitalized Name => %s\n\n", name);
    turn (name);
    printf ("Bureaucrat order => %s\n",name);
}
```

Figure 4.3: A Filter for Names (continues)

```
lc (nstr)
char *nstr;
{
    int i;

    for (i = 0; nstr [i] != '\0' ; i++)
        nstr [i] = tolower (nstr [i]);
}

cap (nstr)
char *nstr;
{
    int i;
    nstr [0] = toupper (nstr [0]);
    for (i = 1 ;nstr [i] != '\0' ; i++)
    {
        if ((nstr [i]!= ' ') && (nstr [i-1] == ' '))
            nstr [i + 1] = toupper (nstr [i + 1]);
    }
}

turn (nstr)
char *nstr;
{
    int i, j, k, idx;
    char first [62], mid [62], last [62];
    for (i = 0; nstr [i] != ' ' ; i++)
        first [i] = nstr [i];
    first [i++] = ' ';
    first [i++] = '\0';

    idx = 0;
    for (j = i - 1 ;    ; j++)
        {
        if (nstr [j] == ' ')
            break;
        if (nstr [j] == '\n')
            break;
        mid [idx++] = nstr [j];
        }
        mid [idx++] = '\0';
        j++;

    idx = 0;
    for (k = j ; nstr [k] != '\0' ; k++)
        last [idx++] = nstr [k];
        last [idx++] = ' ';
        last [idx++] = '\0';
        puts ("\n");

    strcat (last, first);
    strcat (last, mid);
    strcpy (name, last);

}
```

Figure 4.3: A Filter for Names

normal order: first, middle, last. The program reduces all the letters to lowercase. This allows the input to be either uppercase or mistyped:

aLFreD e NeUmaN

The next portion of the filter changes the first letter of each "subname" to a capital letter. So now the first, middle, and last names all start with a capital letter, with the rest of the name in lowercase. The last function changes the order of the name to last, first, middle, to allow for sorting and retrieval keyed on the last name. This is referred to in the program as "bureaucrat order."

Again, let's look at this program a few lines at a time. The main block lays out the plan of attack. It announces itself and proceeds to ask for the name input in normal order:

```
char name [MAXLINE];

main ( )
{
    putchar (12);
    puts ("\n\n\n\tname filter\n\n");
    puts ("input name, first middle last: ");
    gets (name);
    lc (name);
    printf ("\n\n\nLowercase Name => %s\n\n", name);
    cap (name);
    printf ("Capitalized Name => %s\n\n", name);
    turn (name);
    printf ("Bureaucrat order => %s\n",name);
}
```

main blocks should do as little work as possible; they should mainly (no pun intended!) direct the program flow.

Once received, the name is passed off to the function lc for lowercase conversion. C only allows for eight recognizable characters in variable or function names. When the variables are declared as externals, they may be restricted by your system to six characters. Consequently, the very descriptive names I've come to know and love in PL/I can't be used in C, so I had to settle for lc ( ) rather than the much clearer lower_case ( ). When the name is returned, it is printed by the print function printf ( ), which embeds or places a variable within its string constant argument, eg.:

printf ("Hi %s", name)

where Hi is a constant, %s is the escape indicating a string, and name is a variable. The name is then passed to cap ( ) for capitalization and again printed. Finally, it is passed to the function turn to have it turned around and redisplayed.

Notice that the name is declared outside of the main. It is therefore implicitly external.

The next section shows the lc function at work. The variable name was used as the argument in the function call lc (name). A pointer to name is passed to lc ( ) and received as a parameter (nstr). Before entering the function block, the pointer is declared with the indirection operator ∗. Now when the function block is entered, every reference to nstr will be an lvalue.

```
lc (nstr)
char ∗nstr;
{
    int i;

    for (i = 0; nstr [i] ! = '\0' ; i + +)
        nstr [i] = tolower (nstr [i]);
}
```

C has a wealth of string functions, but not the same kind that BASIC and PL/I have. Strings are arrays in C, and that allows for easy manipulation of the strings. The few string functions C has are unique and powerful. In most languages, a midstring or substring function would be used to step through the string. In C, each element is simply worked one at a time by the use of an indexed loop, the for loop.

The loop is initialized at 0, the beginning of all C arrays. It is tested to quit on the end of string, the termination character \0. Finally, it is incremented by one. The body of the for loop is an assignment statement reassigning each element of nstr (in reality the variable name) to its lowercase equivalent through the tolower ( ) function.

Now that the string name is entirely in lowercase, the next step is to capitalize the first characters in each "subname":

```
cap (nstr)
char ∗nstr;
{
    int i;
    nstr [0] = toupper (nstr [0]);
    for (i = 1 ;nstr [i] ! = '\0' ; i + +)
    {
        if ((nstr [i] ! = ' ') && (nstr [i-1] == ' '))
            nstr [i + 1] = toupper (nstr [i + 1]);
    }
}
```

The first character is capitalized by the function toupper ( ) before entering the loop. The loop is set to exit upon seeing the last character of the array, the null terminator \0. Within the body of the function, each character is examined to see if it is a blank. When blanks are found, the next character, the beginning character of the next substring, is capitalized by the function toupper ( ).

So far so good. Getting the names in reverse order is going to be quite another trick. The next function, turn ( ), declares three character arrays, first, mid, and last, to house the respective subnames. Note that they are declared *inside* the body of the function, not outside it like the variable nstr:

```
turn (nstr)
char *nstr;
{
    int i, j, k, idx;
    char first [62], mid [62], last [62];

    for (i = 0; nstr [i] != ' ' ; i++)
        first [i] = nstr [i];
```

The for loop steps from the first character, nstr [0], to the first blank by ones, copying the individual characters one at a time into the variable first.

Because first is a string in its own right, it must be terminated with \0. A blank is also needed on the end to keep it from running into the middle name. Note that the loop index is incremented at each operation by i++:

```
first [i++] = ' ';
first [i++] = '\0';
```

Extracting the middle name is a bit stickier. You can't start at the beginning of the string buffer, so the last index i is used as the beginning. However, you have to back up one character, because the index was left at the old null terminator.

```
idx = 0;
for (j = i - 1 ; ; j++)
    {
    if (nstr [j] == ' ')
        break;
    if (nstr [j] == '\n')
        break;
    mid [idx++] = nstr [j];
    }
```

Two conditions must be tested to exit the loop: end of string, in case there is no middle name, and the blank, to indicate the end of the middle name or initial. The expression

```
nstr [j] ! = ' ' || nstr [j] = '\0'
```

inserted in the for loop would do it, but then how could I show you the break statement?

Note that a separate index idx is created to start the string array mid at its beginning—mid [0]. The statement

```
mid [idx + +] = nstr [j]
```

increments mid as nstr is incremented by the for loop. Again, character for character, the portion of the name that corresponds to the middle name is copied to mid. mid is terminated with the string terminator, and the loop index is incremented to be positioned at the beginning of the next substring:

```
mid [idx + +] = '\0';
j + +;
```

The next section is nearly a carbon copy of the last subfunction—it differs in that it need test only for the end-of-string mark:

```
idx = 0;
for (k = j ; nstr [k] ! = '\0' ; k + +)
    last [idx + +] = nstr [k];
    last [idx + +] = ' ';
    last [idx + +] = '\0';
```

Notice the absence of braces after the for. This signifies that the next statement is the only statement that will be executed by the for. The following statements are executed *after* the exit (implicit break) from the for loop. The subnames (first, middle, last) are now separate entities.

The last task is to put them all back into the variable name. Remember, arrays can't be assigned as a whole, nor can one array be appended to another. Therefore, BASIC's

```
LAST$ = LAST$ + FIRST$ + MIDDLE$
```

is illegal in C.

The function strcat is the string concatenation function. It appends the last string to the first. The function strcpy ( ) is the only way C can assign a string to a string variable. So the first name is appended to the last, and the next strcat ( ) appends the middle name to last, first. The last line puts the resulting string into the array name, which is global to the entire program and is now printed by the main:

```
strcat (last, first);
strcat (last, mid);
strcpy (name, last);
```

If the last line were

```
strcpy (nstr, last)
```

the result would be the same, because nstr is a pointer to name.

DEBUGGING

An entire book could (and probably should) be written about debugging. A very large part of the time spent developing a program is expended on debugging it. When totally new algorithms are worked out, a substantial number of errors can occur. A "desk run" after outlining the main logical steps to the program should trap the logic errors, but compilers have one big problem: they do exactly what we *tell* them to do, which may not always be what we *want* them to do!

There are a number of ways to find out what is happening to the execution of a program. There are symbolic debuggers such as Digital's SID (Symbolic Instruction Debugger). They work with the assembly code produced by the compiler. The restriction is that the assembly code must be compatible with the debugger.

Another good debugging tool is the use of *stubs*. Stubs are pieces of code inserted into the raw code to help the programmer run or decipher the program results. You may want, for example, to find the contents of a variable at midexecution (in the middle of a program). The stub

```
printf(" x = %d, x)
```

prints to the console the contents of x at that particular point in the program's execution. In keeping with teaching by example, let's look at the stubs in the development version of the program in Figure 4.3. The stubs have been left in to show how they work.

The first stub appears within the turn function. The printf ( ) outputs the variable first and the index position of the array pointer:

```
}
turn (nstr)
char *nstr;
{
    int i, j, k, idx;
    char first [62], mid [62], last [62];
```

Run-Time Errors

```
for (i = 0; nstr [i] != ' ' ; i ++)
        first [i] = nstr [i];
        first [i ++] = ' ';
        first [i ++] = '\0';
        printf ("first = %s * index = %d \n",first, i); / * * /
```

Note the crowded construction:

```
"first = %s * "
```

This technique makes leading and trailing blanks immediately apparent. The stub is marked with a null (empty) comment, / * * /, so it is easy to find and delete the stub when you finish debugging.

There is nothing so frustrating as the dreaded "silent death," where the program appears to just go away. What is happening in reality is that the program is looping and producing no visible results. To find out how far the program execution has gotten, the simple message, "got here," will do beautifully:

```
idx = 0;

puts ("got here 1");                    / * * /
```

Note the second "got here":

```
for (j = i - 1 ; ; j ++)
        {
        if (nstr [j] == ' ')
            break;
        if (nstr [j] == '\n')
            break;
        mid [idx ++] = nstr [j];
        puts (mid);                      / * * /
        }
        printf ("%s\n", "got here 2"); / * * /
```

If the program goes away between these stubs, look for the problem inside the loop.

The next stub is inserted to display the variable mid and the current index position:

```
mid [idx ++] = '\0';
j ++;
printf ("mid = %s * index = %d\n", mid, j); / * * /
puts ("\n");
```

Setting the indices in a program such as this is not the simplest of tasks. If there is a mistake of 1 on an index, the loop tests at the blank preceding the subname, finds it to be a blank, and jumps out of the loop without as much as a hint of why the program bombed. Knowing the value of the index helps trace down the error.

Developing code is all logic, and so is debugging. We should all try to write error-free code. Expecting that you will write code with errors is a self-fulfilling prophecy, but errors do creep in, despite the best intentions. The point is to detect them as painlessly as possible. When learning a new language, it is easy to empty a box of printer paper just listing errors, so take all the debugging help you can get.

The last stub displays the variable last and the index position:

```
idx = 0;
for (k = j ; nstr [k] ! = '\0' ; k++)
    last [idx++] = nstr [k];
    last [idx++] = ' ';
    last [idx++] = '\0';
    printf ("last = %s * index = %d\n", last, k); / * */

strcat (last, first);
strcat (last, mid);
strcpy (name, last);
```

5:

The Standard I/O Header File

Including a header file in C code is taken for granted by experienced C programmers after a while. You get ready to type a file (program), deftly invoke the text editor, drive home the first / *, title the program, add a * /, and type the instruction to include the header.

> #include "stdio.h"

stdioh stands for *standard I/O header file*. Although only one of many header files that can be used in C, the standard I/O header file is the most necessary because it defines the I/O parameters, ports, and devices to be used. It also defines any function macros[1] that will be used in the program. It defines the common constants (TRUE, FALSE, EOF, ERR, CPMEOF, and FILE), creating buffers and buffer structures for file I/O. The precompiler includes the header file as part of the program by substituting all the values defined in the header file into the program by a process called macro substitution.

What has the header done? It has defined and declared all the pedestrian tasks that otherwise would have involved typing a page or two of instructions. Standard header files are included with all C packages. There are special header files as well, such as telecommunications headers, directed I/O headers, math headers, and others. You can also create your own headers, including standard headers. Figure 5.1 is a header file written for use with BDS C by Leor Zolman, which I modified for use on my Adds Viewpoint terminal.[2]

This "standard" header file is now customized to the system requirements and needs of a specific user. The inclusion of a CLEAR definition
now allows a program to clear the screen with the instruction

       puts (CLEAR);

```
/*
        stdio.h

        header file for bds.c for use on an Adds Viewpoint

*/

#define CLEAR '\f'        /*Adds clear and home*/
#define LST 5             /*CP/M printer call*/
#define MAXINT 32767      /*maximum signed integer*/
#define NULL 0
#define EOF -1            /*physical EOF*/
#define ERROR -1          /*general "on error" return value*/
#define JBUFSIZE 6        /*length of setjump/longjump buffer*/
#define CPMEOF 0x1a       /*CP/M End-of-text-file marker*/
#define SECSIZ 128        /*sector size for CP/M read/write calls*/
#define MAXLINE 150       /*longest line of input expected from
                            the console*/
#define TRUE 1            /*general purpose true truth value*/
#define FALSE 0           /*general purpose false truth valu*/
#define NSECTS 8          /*number of sectors to buffer up in ram*/
#define BUFSIZ (NSECTS * SECSIZ + 7)

struct _buf {
        int _fd;
        int _nleft;
        char * _nextp;
        char _buff[NSECTS * SECSIZ];
        char _flags;
};

#define FILE struct _buf
#define _READ 1
#define _WRITE 2

/*
storage allocation data, used by "alloc" and "free"
*/

struct _header {
        struct _header * _ptr;
        unsigned _size;
};

struct _header _base;           /*declare this external data to*/
struct _header * _allocp;       /*be used by alloc ( ) and free ( )*/
```

Figure 5.1: Header File for BDS C Using an Adds Viewpoint Terminal

Although putchar (CLEAR) would do the same thing, the puts function (put string) allows for the use of an escape sequence as well.

Every microcomputer programmer should acquaint himself with the ASCII table of codes. It is the table in which every alpha and numeric character is assigned numeric values in decimal (base 10), octal (base 8), and hexadecimal (base 16). For example, the capital letter A is ASCII 65 decimal, 41 hexadecimal, and 101 octal. Lowercase a is 97 decimal, 61 hexadecimal, and 141 octal. Various operations are assigned numeric values as well, such as the form feed, which is ASCII 12 decimal, 0C hexadecimal, and 14 octal. There is also a character called an *escape character* which is ASCII 27 decimal, 1B hexadecimal, and 33 octal. The escape character is used in conjunction with other ASCII characters to perform certain jobs.

Because the escape character is used with other ASCII characters, the entire set of characters is called an *escape sequence*. Escape sequences are usually used to get the hardware in your system to do something, such as clear the screen on your terminal, get the printer to change to another font, and so forth. In order for the hardware to get the message, escape sequences are pushed into the output stream by output statements such as printf, puts, and on. For example, to clear the screen on a Televideo 920 or 950 terminal, you use ASCII 58 (the :) in an escape sequence written in this way:

```
\33:
```

(The backslash indicates that the number following is in octal.)

Escape sequences are hardware-dependent—you can't clear every terminal's screen this way. Some terminals use control characters instead. Whichever your peripherals require, if they are unknown to the CPU (as they often are in computer systems), you've got to be able to control those peripherals, by embedding control characters and escape sequences in the output stream. Any programming language that does not do this easily does not meet the needs of a professional programmer. C shines in this area, because it allows the programmer to do this with ease.

It is conventional in C, and in just about all languages that include define and replace statements, to use uppercase letters for defined constants. This practice allows the reader or maintainer of the code to see quickly that the "variable" in a statement is not a variable at all but rather a constant. The statement

```
for (i = 0; i <= MAXINT; i++)
```

will loop, incrementing the loop index through the entire positive range of signed integers as defined in the header file. If MAXINT were in lowercase

C Headers

letters, someone reading the code might assume (incorrectly) that it was a variable.

The structs in the header file in Figure 5.1 define and declare the structures that will be used by the function alloc ( ) to allocate heap storage and free it:

```
struct _header {
    struct _header * _ptr;
    unsigned _size;
};

struct _header _base;
struct _header * _allocp;
```

Some C function libraries rely heavily upon alloc for functions requiring large buffers, such as the buffered file functions. SuperSoft C is one of them. It is therefore well worth adding these extra few lines of code to the header to be sure that storage has been defined.[3]

You may include as many header files in your program as you need. You can think up specialized headers for directed I/O, modems, and other hardware-dependent devices, ASCII character classification routines, non-local jump routines, macro defines for portability, and macro defines of any type, as necessary.

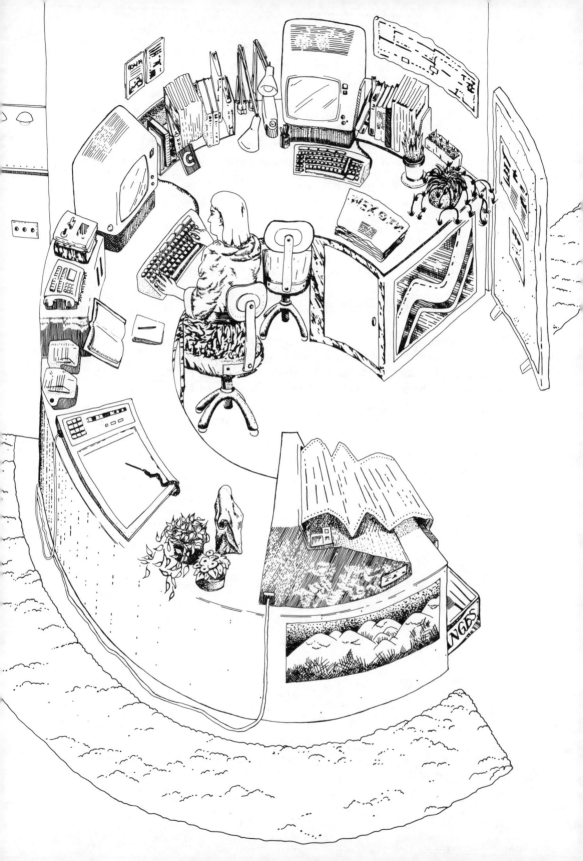

6:

Buffered Files

Disk files—something about that phrase says we're through playing around and are now ready to settle down to business. Disk files aren't easy to learn in any language or system. First of all, there is a whole new vocabulary, and that takes some getting used to. Then you start learning about the requirements of handling different file types.

Even in BASIC, disk files are not a piece of cake. BASIC's sequential files aren't all that difficult, but then all sequential files have to do is take all the character data given to them and copy it to disk. Random files, on the other hand, can be a nightmare in BASIC. Some BASICs are fussier than others, however. On one compiler, numeric data has to be converted to string data and reconverted when it is read. Another compiler might be a little easier to get along with in that respect, but you still have to deal with putting your variables into fields. Until you learn what you need to know, it almost seems easier to display the whole mess and copy it down with pencil and paper.

Pascal files are no easier. I know of a couple of expert senior programmers who just about gave up on some Pascal file versions, and who made no bones about it in a national magazine.

Where all of this is leading to is that disk files just aren't all that easy. But like everything else about learning to program in a new language, when you finally master the disk files, you've gained a significant amount of programming power in that language.

Before going into disk files, we need some definitions. Files are composed of individual records, and records are made up of fields. A file field is any separate piece of data in the data stream that can be logically separated from the record. A record is a collection of fields that have some logical connection. A file consists of a collection of records. Using the frequently cited phone-book example, if you put your phone book on disk, the phone book would be a file. Each listing (consisting of name, address, and phone number) would be a record. Each individual phone number would be a field, as would each name and each address.

Sequential files, sometimes called stream files, are files that are composed entirely of ASCII (character) data. The length of the records in sequential files is not regulated; therefore the records can be of any length. These files are opened only once for writing, and once they have been written and closed, they are closed forever. They cannot be appended or updated (unless you know some fancy programming tricks). Sequential files must be read from front to back (sequentially), and no single record can be accessed directly. Reading sequential files is kind of like eating strands of spaghetti. You start at one end and don't stop until you get to the other end.

Random files, sometimes called direct files, can be made up of either ASCII or binary (numeric) data. All records in random files must be the same length. Random files can be appended and updated, and any record can be accessed directly, as long as the number of the record is known. This is why they are sometimes called direct files.

The system keeps track of files by having a unique identifier for each open file. In BASIC the identifiers are frequently called stream numbers or file numbers. In C they are called the file ID, appropriately enough. The system keeps track of which record is in use with an internal file pointer, and does endless housekeeping to keep track of the file pointer.

Now that an elementary overview of disk files has been presented, I'll drop the other shoe. C files aren't like other files. C has two file types: raw and buffered. Raw files are handled in logical records (128 bytes long in the case of CP/M, 512 with UNIX), and raw-file functions move information directly, one block at a time. A typical use of raw files is to copy from file to file, without any intermediate processing such as a filter. Buffered files, on the other hand, move the disk data to and from *file buffers,* storage areas in high-speed memory. C does most of the housekeeping and fills or empties the buffers as required.

C handles all I/O by functions. Buffered file functions are described below. But before jumping right into them, here are a couple of the preliminaries: The parameters for each function are described below the function call. Parameters preceded by a star (*) require an lvalue, a variable, or constant that has allocated memory.

BUFFERED FILE FUNCTIONS

The fopen function

fopen (filename, iobuffer)

char *filename;
struct_buf *iobuffer;

The function fopen opens the file filename for input to the program and creates the buffer for the file I/O.[1] Once it is created, C fills the buffer from the disk as necessary. If any error is encountered, the function returns a −1.

The fcreat Function

fcreat (filename, iobuffer)

char *filename;
struct_buf *iobuffer;

The fcreat function creates the file named filename and opens the I/O buffer for output from the program.[2] Like fopen, it does all the housekeeping of filling and emptying the I/O buffer, except that it does not flush itself, that is, empty itself completely. The fflush function must be used to flush the buffer before closing the file.

The fflush Function

fflush (iobuffer)

struct-buf *iobuffer;

The fflush function flushes the I/O buffer. It is used before closing the buffer to get all the file information to the intended destination.

The fclose Function

fclose (iobuffer)

The fclose closes the I/O buffer and file, whether it was opened for reading (by fopen) or for writing (by fcreat) or fopen("fname","w"). If the file was opened for writing (fcreat), be sure to to use the fflush function before you close the file with fclose ( ), or some of your data will not make it onto the disk.

The getc Function

```
getc (iobuffer)

    struct *iobuffer;
```

The getc function returns the next byte (character) from the I/O buffer created by fopen ( ). It is equivalent to the getchar function for buffered files, except it reads from the console (stdin).

The unget Function

```
unget (character, iobuffer)

    char character;
    struct *iobuffer;
```

unget pushes the last character read back to the I/O buffer. unget is used, for example, if you want to read up to, but not including, the \n in a string. The \n could be pushed back into the buffer.

The getw Function

```
getw (iobuffer)

    struct *iobuffer;
```

The getw is similar to getc ( ), but it returns a *word* (two bytes—16 bits in an 8-bit system) instead of a character (byte).

The putc Function

```
putc (character, iobuffer)

    char character;
    struct-buf *iobuffer;
```

The putc function writes the character (byte) to the I/O buffer. As with most of these functions, it returns a − 1 when an error is encountered. It is equivalent to the putchar function for buffered files.

The putw Function

```
putw (word, iobuffer)

    int word;
    struct_buf *iobuffer;
```

The putw function writes a word (two bytes—16 bits for 8-bit machines) to the I/O buffer.

The fprintf Functon

    fprintf (iobuffer, format, arg1, arg2, . . . argn)

        struct-buf *iobuffer;
        char *format;

The fprintf function is similar to printf ( ), but the formatted output of the function is written to the I/O buffer instead of the console. This is unbelievably handy for formatting fields to simulate files of other languages or for outputting the data in the format you want to use.

scanf Functions

    fscanf (iobuffer, format, arg1, arg2, . . . argn)

scanf functions like scanf, sscanf, and fscanf format the input. The fscanf function in our program is similar to scanf ( ), but scanf scans data from the screen, while fscanf scans data from the I/O buffer. Again, this function is handy for reading formatted files from other languages.

The fgets Function

    fgets (string, iobuffer)

        char *string;
        struct_buf *iobuffer;

The fgets function reads a line of text, a string (in this case any block of characters terminated by a null terminator, the \0), from the I/O buffer and places it into the memory address specified by string. Again, note that string is an lvalue. It must have assigned storage.

The fputs Function

    fputs (string, iobuffer)

        char *string;
        struct_buf *iobuffer;

The puts function writes a conventional string (one terminated by \0) from the allocated memory variable string into the I/O buffered file.

COMMAND LINE ARGUMENTS

Before getting in any deeper, a few words about command-line argument passing are in order. You no doubt are familiar with passing another file name or two when invoking a program. A good example is loading or "bringing up" a text or screen editor and having it load or create a file. For example,

    a > ws newfile.txt

loads the WordStar word processing program, which loads or creates newfile.txt.

What has happened internally is that the operating system has stored the one or two additional file names along with the file name of the invocation for use by the called program. C makes provisions to use the names in the command line. The file names are argument vectors,[3] in C, argv. To keep track of how many there are, there is also an argument count—argc. If there is a second file name typed in at the console, it is argv [1] the first parameter, and the third file name is argv [2] the second parameter.

The argument count is straightforward. If two file names are present, argc (an integer) will be 2. If three names are present, argc is equal to 3. When passing argv to the program, you actually are referencing a pointer to a pointer. (Remember, C can put a pointer to any data type, including pointer.) The parameters and declaration look like this:

    main (argc, argv)
       char * *argv;

argc doesn't have to be declared, because it is built into the C language and it is a simple integer.

BUFFERED FILE INPUT

Now it's time to put argc to work. Most of the following programs were written in BDS C and uses its standard header, bdscio.h. To use them with any other compiler, either create your own header, or define any constants in uppercase, or change the constants to match the header you prefer. The header files define constants commonly used in C programs. If you're in doubt as to what to do, go back to Chapter 5 on header files.

Program 6.1 deals with buffered file input, inputting the files specified by the command line to a file buffer and then printing the files to the console.

Let's look at it in pieces:

```
main (argc, argv)
char * *argv;
{
    char iobuf [BUFSIZ];
    char outstr [MAXLINE];
```

The parameters argument count and argument vector are passed to the main block, and argv is defined as a pointer to a pointer. The I/O buffer iobuf is declared as a character array (in my system) of $8 \times 128 + 6$ characters by the header file. Obviously, the buffer size indicated by BUFSIZ is system-dependent, and is defined in the header file.[4] An output buffer is declared as well.

```
/*
    FI.C

    buffered file input

*/

#include "bdscio.h"

main (argc, argv)
char **argv;
{
    char iobuf  [BUFSIZ];
    char outstr [MAXLINE];

    clear ( );
    puts ("\n\n\n\n\tFile input program\n");
    if (argc != 2)
    {
        puts ("you must enter the input file name\n");
        puts ("along with the program invocation");
        exit ( );
    }
        if (fopen (argv [1], iobuf) == ERROR)
        {
            printf ("cannot open %s", argv [1]);
            exit ( );
        }
        while (fgets (outstr, iobuf))
            printf ("%s\n", outstr);
        fflush (iobuf);
        fclose (iobuf);
}
```

Figure 6.1: A Buffered File Input Program

```
clear ( );
puts ("\n\n\n\n\tFile input program\n");
if (argc ! = 2)
{
    puts ("you must enter the input file name\n");
    puts ("along with the program invocation");
    exit ( );
}
```

The test if (argc ! = 2) to see whether the argument count (argc) is 2 ensures that a file name is present to open, since the program will be argc [1]. If there is no file name, the program complains: you must enter the input file name along with the program invocation. Then it returns to the system so you can reenter the file name as part of the command line.

The next section is our first encounter with buffered file input:

```
if (fopen (argv [1], iobuf) == ERROR)
{
    printf ("cannot open %s", argv [1]);
    exit ( );
}
```

The fopen function opens the file having the name that was entered along with the file invocation, and it prepares the I/O buffer. C now opens the file and fills the buffer with data from the input file. It is refilled as often as necessary, with no further attention from the program or programmer. ERROR is defined by the header file as − 1.[5] If the file can't be opened for any reason, the program "complains" again and exits to the system. Remember, in comparisons like if, the operator must be a logical equal (==), not an assignment equal (=).

The next piece, believe it or not, is the program:

```
while (fgets (outstr, iobuf))
    printf ("%s\n", outstr);
```

The function fgets returns a 0 and exits the loop when it encounters the end-of-file mark (^Z in CP/M). fgets reads a line (a string terminated by a newline) and places it in the memory buffer outstr. The print function printf formats the string by adding a newline to its end; then it prints it on the screen.

Having done its thing, the execution leaves the loop, and the fflush function flushes the I/O buffer before fclose ( ) closes it:

```
fflush (iobuf);
fclose (iobuf);
}
```

Buffered Files

Most of the programs in this chapter "eat themselves." Once compiled, this program takes the invocation

    fi fi.c

indicating the program fi with the source file fi.c as the command line argument, and prints the source code to the screen exactly as it was typed.

The program in Figure 6.2, WC.C, is a word counter, counting words, lines, and characters. It is a variation of "Word Count" (written originally in RATFOR, a preprocessor language that generates FORTRAN), which first appeared in the ground-breaking book, *Software Tools* by Kernighan and Plauger. Unlike the last program, which deals with a line of data at a time, this one demonstrates the getc function, which deals with one character at a time.

The program differs from Figure 6.1 starting about here:

    inword = FALSE;
    nl = nw = nc = 0;

The flag inword tells the program whether it is *in* a *word* or not. The variables nl, nw, and nc (number of lines, number of words, and number of characters) are initialized to 0 by C's unique ability to initialize from right to left.

Then a conditional loop is set up, taking a character at a time from the I/O buffer and passing it to the character c, as long as it is not CP/M's logical end-of-file marker, ^Z. CP/M sets an ASCII 01A hex after the last character of a text file to indicate the end of text.

    while ((c = getc (ibuf)) ! = CPMEOF)

As each character is retrieved by getc ( ), nc (the number of characters) is incremented to acknowledge and count it:

    + + nc;

If the character is a newline, nl is incremented:

    if (c == '\n')
        + + nl;

Now, if the character is a newline (which is entered as a carriage-return/ line-feed pair in CP/M), a blank, or a tab, inword is set to FALSE to indicate that it is no longer within a word:

    if (c == '\n' || c == ' ' || c == '\t')
        inword = FALSE;

If the character was none of the above, and if inword is still set to

```
/*
        WC.C
        a fine C version of Word Count by W. P. Hogan
        counts lines, words, and characters
        from a text file
*/

#include "bdscio.h"

#define TRUE 1
#define FALSE 0

    int ifd, i, c, nl, nw, nc, inword;
    char ibuf [BUFSIZ];

main (argc, argv)
char **argv;
{
    clear ( );
    puts ("\n\n\n\t\t line, word, and character counter");
    if (argc != 2)
    {
        puts ("\nyou must enter the name of the file to be counted");
            puts ("\n as part of the command line");
            exit ( );
    }
    ifd = fopen (argv [1], ibuf);
    if (ifd == ERROR)
    {
        puts ("\ncannot open file");
        exit ( );
    }
    inword = FALSE;
    nl = nw = nc = 0;

    while ((c = getc (ibuf)) != CPMEOF)
    {
        ++nc;
        if (c == '\n')
            ++nl;
        if (c == '\n' || c == ' ' || c == '\t')
            inword = FALSE;
        else if (inword == FALSE)
        {
            inword = TRUE;
            ++nw;
        }
    }
    puts ("\n lines      words        characters\n\n\n");
    printf ("%5d %8d %11d\n", nl, nw, nc);
}
```

Figure 6.2: Word Count—Counts Lines, Words and Characters

indicate it is outside a word, it must be set to TRUE to show it is back in a word:

```
else if (inword  = =  FALSE)
{
   inword = TRUE;
   + + nw;
}
```

This technique is excellent for text programs and will be used again. Then the word-count variable nw is incremented.

Now all that needs to be done is to output the results of the computation:

```
puts ("\n lines      words        characters\n\n\n");
printf ("%5d %8d %11d\n", nl, nw, nc);
```

The puts function sets the header, and printf formats and prints the number of lines, words, and characters.

Compile the program and feed it itself:

```
wc wc.c
```

It will give you its own statistics.

BUFFERED FILE OUTPUT

By now you should have some sort of grip on the way C handles input from buffered files. So let's turn our attention to the other end of the process, and look at buffered file output.

The program in Figure 6.3 reads a file from disk and converts all the lowercase characters to uppercase. (Believe it or not, there are still uppercase-only computers out there.)

The program gets interesting about here:

```
if (fcreat (argv [2], obuf)  = =  ERROR)
   {
       printf ("cannot create %s\n",argv [2]);
       exit ( );
```

The fcreat function creates a new file with the name input appearing last in the command line. For example, in the following command, ucprog.c is the file created by fcreat ( ):

```
ucc lcprog.c ucprog.c
```

fcreat also opens an output buffer. The function returns a − 1 if the file fails to open.

The next section is the program proper:

```
while ((c = getc (ibuf)) ! = EOF || c ! = CPMEOF)
    if (putc (toupper (c), obuf) == ERROR)
    {
        puts ("disk error\n");
        exit ( );
```

```
/*
                    UCC.C
         file to file uppercase conversion
*/

#include "bdscio.h"

main (argc, argv)
char **argv;
{
    char ibuf [BUFSIZ], obuf [BUFSIZ];
    int c;

    clear ( );
    puts ("\n\n\n\t file to file uppercase conversion\n");
    if (argc != 3)
    {
        puts ("enter input and output file name\n");
        exit ( );
    }
    if (fopen (argv [1], ibuf) == ERROR)
    {
        printf ("cannot open %s\n",argv [1]);
        exit ( );
    }
    if (fcreat (argv [2], obuf) == ERROR)
    {
        printf ("cannot create %s\n",argv [2]);
        exit ( );
    }

    while ((c = getc (ibuf)) != EOF || c != CPMEOF)
        if (putc (toupper (c), obuf) == ERROR)
        {
            puts ("disk error\n");
            exit ( );
        }
    putc (CPMEOF, obuf);
    fflush (obuf);
    fclose (obuf);
    fclose (ibuf);
}

clear ( )
{
    putchar (12);
}
```

Figure 6.3: A Program to Read a File, Convert Its Lowercase Letters to Uppercase, and Write the Converted Records to Another File.

The character c is retrieved by getc ( ), as long as c is not equal to the end-of-file mark or CP/M's standard EOF marker, ^Z. At each iteration, c is converted to uppercase by the function toupper. If the character is not a lowercase character, it is left alone. If the putc function returns a − 1 (ERROR), the program will exit.

When the while loop is exited, the input file has been converted. To complete it, the CP/M end-of-file mark is written to the buffer to be the last character in the file.

```
putc (CPMEOF, obuf);
fflush (obuf);
fclose (obuf);
fclose (ibuf);
```

Of course, there are still the usual tasks of flushing the output buffer and closing both files. Compile the program, and let it process its own source code. The output will be all uppercase.

The program in Figure 6.4 is another program demonstrating buffered file output. It reads a file and outputs it a line at a time, numbering the lines during output. There's nothing really new here except for the last output line, which is a hard-working printf function. The variable lineno, the line counter, is incremented on each pass through the loop and put into the formatted output.

BUFFERED FILE OUTPUT
WITH PRINTER DRIVER

By now, this may be getting boring. How about putting the results to the line printer? Bad news, guys and girls! C has absolutely no provision for a printer.[6] What's that? If you knew that, you wouldn't have started in C? Don't give up—there is an answer. We'll create a printer driver.

The program in Figure 6.5 copies a disk file to the line printer by way of this new printer driver. Let's take a look.

It all starts here:

```
}
for ( ; ; )
{
```

The null for is a "do-forever" loop. It implies that the loop will be exited by a test within the for block. Here is the test:

```
if (! fgets (lbuf, ibuf))
    break;
```

The fgets function puts each line, as it is requested, into the memory variable lbuf (line printer buffer). When the system end-of-file mark or CP/M's end-of-file mark is encountered, the test is "if zero," and the break statement is acted upon.

Here is the program line that puts the output to the printer. The variable lbuf is passed to the function linepr (line printer).

```
if (linepr (lbuf)) continue;
```

PGLEN (page length) was defined as the integer constant 66 in the header. If there are more than two lines left to fill, the program goes through the loop once more without executing the line(s) beyond the continue, which will return the program to the beginning of the loop.

```
        if (lineslft > 2) continue;
        formfeed ( );
    }
    formfeed ( );
```

```
/*
                    NUMTXT.C

    a text line numbering program

*/

#include "bdscio.h"

main (argc, argv)
char **argv;
{
    char ibuf [BUFSIZ];                     /*1028 bytes*/
    char linebuf [MAXLINE];
    int lineno;

    puts ("\n\n\n\n\t\t Text Line Number\n");
    if (argc != 2)
    {
        puts ("the file to be read and numbered\n");
        puts ("must be included with the file invocation");
        exit ( );
    }
    if (fopen (argv [1], ibuf) == ERROR)
    {
        printf ("cannot open %s", argv [1]);
        exit ( );
    }
        lineno = 1;

    while (fgets (linebuf, ibuf))
        printf ("%3d: %s", lineno++, linebuf);   /*note printf*/

    fclose (ibuf);
}
```

Figure 6.4: A Text Line-Numbering Program

If there are fewer lines than two, the next line executes, invoking the function (you can't "call" in C) that performs a form feed.

Now for the heavy guns, Leor Zolman's printer driver:

```
linepr (string)
char *string;
```

```c
/*

                CP.C

        copy file to printer

        with an excellent driver written by Leor Zolman

*/
#include "bdscio.h"
#define FF 0X0c
#define PGLEN 66

int colno, lineslft;

main (argc, argv)
char **argv;
{
    char lbuf [MAXLINE], ibuf [BUFSIZ];
    int c;

    clear ( );
    puts ("\n\n\n\n\t Line Print File\n\n ");
    if (argc != 2)
    {
        puts ("enter input file name\n");
        puts ("with file invocation");
        exit ( );
    }
    if (fopen (argv [1], ibuf) == ERROR)
    {
        printf ("cannot open %s", argv [1]);
        exit ( );
    }
    for ( ; ; )
    {
        if (! fgets (lbuf, ibuf))
            break;
        if (linepr (lbuf)) continue;
        if (lineslft > 2) continue;
        formfeed ( );
    }
    formfeed ( );
}
```

Figure 6.5: Buffered File Output with Printer Driver (continues)

```
linepr (string)
char  *string;      /*note the lvalue asgnmt to string*/
{
    char c, ffflag;
    ffflag = 0;

    while (c = *string++)
          switch (c)
          {
          case FF:
                 ffflag = 1;
                 break;
          case '\n':
                 putlpr ('\r');
                 putlpr ('\n');
          colno = 0;
          lineslft--;
          break;
      case '\t':
          do
                 {
                 putlpr (' ');
                 colno++;
                 }
                 while (colno % 8);
          break;

          default:
          putlpr (c);
          colno++;
          }
          if (ffflag) formfeed ( );
          return ffflag;
}

putlpr (c)
char c;
{
          bios (5, c);
}

formfeed ( )
{
    if (FF)
        putlpr (FF);
        else
              while (lineslft--)
              putlpr ('\n');
    lineslft = PGLEN;
}

clear( )
{
    putchar (0X0c);
}
```

Figure 6.5: Buffered File Output with Printer Driver

lbuf, previously passed to the linepr function, is received as the variable string. Notice the next line, char∗string. You want string to be an object, a manipulatable area of storage, so you merely declare it an object by virtue of the indirect operator ∗. This tells C that string is the object of a pointer.

Two character variables are created now, the form-feed flag (ffflag), and a single-character variable c:

```
{
    char c, ffflag;
    ffflag = 0;
```

The ffflag is initialized to 0 to indicate a "no" condition, or FALSE.

C has a way of saying a lot more than immediately meets the eye. In fact, among C programmers, it can become a fetish to see just how much can be done in a single line or with a single command. It's best for beginning programmers to avoid this practice. The following line is relatively simple, although it packs a great deal of power:

```
while (c = ∗string + +)
```

c is the object of the assignment of ∗string. Because string is in reality string [BUFSIZE], it is an array. You can't assign an array, and C knows it. But what the statement is really saying is

```
c = string [index + +]
```

On the first iteration, ∗string was string [0], because any reference to a string array is to the first (0) element in that array. Each new iteration increments the implicit index of the array.

COMPOUND BRANCHING—THE CASE

Leor Zolman's printer driver has a very good example of a programming construct called a case. It is a major concept in programming, yet not all languages support it. The case is a multiple branch. It allows the code the choice of continuing in one of many different possible directions. A common example of a case is a multiple choice question where you need to choose one answer: A, B, C, or D. In its most primitive versions, the case is the arithmetic IF in FORTRAN and the ON-GOTO in BASIC. PL/I has no formal case, but uses its GOTO in conjunction with subscripted labels to make an exquisite case. Pascal also has an excellent case, but one of the best case structures to be found is in C.

The purpose of the case is to provide a multiple branch. C's goto, like any goto, provides a one-way unconditional branch to a label (for example, goto main). The if and if-else statements do a two-way branch (if one condition is met the program goes one way, otherwise it goes another way). With enough if-else-ifs, something similar to a case can be achieved (at a high cost—code clarity). The ideal vehicle for multiple branching of code is the case structure.

The case provides almost unlimited branching (255 branches in most versions of C). It functions by the switch statement, which houses the variable that is in essence the "argument" of the case structure. The case statement provides the vehicle to hold the constant that will act as a label for the switch. The function of the switch/case combination is that the switch compares the value of the variable assigned to itself with the labels, and then goes to or branches to the appropriate case label. The label itself must be an integer, character constant, or constant expression. Hand in hand with the switch/case combination is the break statement. The break provides an immediate exit from the case structure, preventing the program from automatically performing the other branches of the case. Lastly, a default is provided which acts as a last resort, because if none of the case labels are applicable, then the default will provide alternate action. A very good example of the full case construct is Leor Zolman's printer driver, which is part of the code in Figure 6.5, and which is the next section of code to be discussed in detail.

The following switch statement is a compound branch, which causes the control of the program to be transferred to one of the case statements following it. The expression that is the argument to switch is compared to the constant expressions following each case. Let's take a look at the first case:

```
switch (c)
{
case FF:
        ffflag = 1;
        break;
```

The way this case is written is very clever. The case switch is set to the character c. The first test within the case block is FF (form feed). (Notice the colon after case FF:, which is the case label. All labels are followed by a semicolon.) If the form-feed character 0X0c is received, it sets the form-feed flag to 1 or TRUE (a "yes" condition). Never forget to use the break statement, lest the execution fall through to the next line.

This segment of code is worthy of special attention for other reasons as well. Specifically, the FF: does not cause a form feed to happen, but rather sets a form-feed flag to be acted upon later.

Now let's look at the next case:

```
case '\n':
    putlpr ('\r');
    putlpr ('\n');
    colno = 0;
    lineslft -- ;
    break;
```

If a newline is received, a carriage-return/line-feed pair is executed. Except in a true high-level language such as Pascal or PL/I, you can't take anything for granted. You input a carriage return whenever you hit the return or enter key. This does not input a line feed. A line feed is therefore not stored. The only thing that keeps each successive line from overwriting the last line is that when it is output to the console, the console driver adds a line feed for you. In the printer driver, however, you, the programmer, must add the line-feed character.

Because a carriage return has been output, the print head has returned to column 0. So the column number colno must also be set to 0. In addition, to acknowledge that an additional line of text has appeared on the page, lineslft must be decremented.

Even the humble tab can't be taken for granted. The next seven lines are necessary to execute the tab:

```
case '\t':
    do
        {
        putlpr (' ');
        colno++ ;
        }
        while (colno % 8);
    break;
```

The case recognizes the tab character and puts the program into a loop where the tabs are expanded by outputting blanks. It prints the blank (020 hex) and increments the column number. The while statement tests the column number by doing an integer modulus division and testing the remainder of the division for a 0. As long as there is a remainder, indicating that the column is not an even multiple of 8, the loop continues to execute, printing blanks. When the result is 0, meaning there is no remainder, the test fails and the loop is exited. This is an excellent use of the do-while loop. Now it is apparent how all those columns are kept neat!

Many languages have a case structure. C's case is one of the best. It provides a default ("none-of-the-above") condition. If all the tests have failed, then the character must be a printable character. It is therefore passed to the function putlpr (put line printer):

```
default:
        putlpr (c);
        colno + + ;
    }
```

When that is done, the column number is incremented.

Now it's time to test the form-feed flag, and, if it's TRUE, invoke the form-feed function:

```
        if (ffflag) formfeed ( );
        return ffflag;
    }
```

After all that work you're still up a creek, because you don't know how to get the output to the printer! The answer unfortunately depends on your hardware, which is probably why it is not incorporated as part of the language. UNIX and C were created together to work side by side, and it is UNIX that frees C of I/O device dependency. Without UNIX, C has no choice but to rely heavily on file I/O functions. (UNIX expects the program's output to go to the "standard output," the terminal. If printed output is required, it is redirected to the printer.)

Working with CP/M, we must feed the characters to the operating system one at a time, by calling the operating system through the function bios. The function gets its name from CP/M's **B**asic **I**nput/**O**utput **S**ystem. The function bios has a number of "calls," corresponding to the various BIOS and BDOS functions within CP/M. There are from 20 to 100 calls, depending on which version of CP/M or MP/M you have. Each call number causes the operating system to do one of its intrinsic functions. The CP/M call that puts a character to the output port for the printer is 5:

```
putlpr (c)
char c;
{
    bios (5, c);
}
```

C's value as a mid-level language can be seen now. It saves you the work of assembly programming, which is the only other way to get to the printer.

It all seems so easy, once it has been explained! The system now saves the contents of the CPU (central processing unit) registers on the stack, puts the character in the proper CPU register, sends the character to the port, and pops the old register contents back off the stack and into the proper registers. All this, and it is transparent to the user. Assembly is at its best when it is avoided!

The function formfeed outputs the equivalent of a form feed to the function linepr, because many printers don't respond to a page-eject command.

"Page eject" is the same thing as a form feed, where the printer spits out an entire page in one shot. Since page ejects are device-dependent, the formfeed function simulates it by advancing the page one line at a time using line feeds.

```
formfeed ( )
{
   if (FF)
      putlpr (FF);
      else
         while (lineslft – – )
         putlpr ('\n');
   lineslft = PGLEN;
}
```

If FF is set to 0 because of the lack of a built-in page eject in the printer logic, the simplest of loops is entered, a while (do-until) loop. Here is where the equivalent of a page eject (form feed) is accomplished by a series of line feeds. As long as the variable lineslft shows that the number of lines left is not 0, the loop continues, and a newline is fed to the printer. At 0 the program exits the loop.

LISTED BUFFERED FILE OUTPUT WITH LINE NUMBERS

The last program of the chapter is almost a copy of the printer-driver program in Figure 6.5, except that it has an especially practical value to the programmer. It lists the contents of a file with line numbers. How many times have you typed the CP/M command

```
pip lst : = b:progname.ext [nt8]
```

in order to get a listing that is printed, tabbed, and numbered? Because compilers give error messages with references to specific line numbers, programmers must have a quick way to get a numbered hard copy of a developing program to facilitate locating the lines where the errors occurred. The program in Figure 6.6 does just that. I have called it N to make the invocation short:

```
n anyprog.c
```

That is all it takes to get a numbered listing with expanded tabs. Let's see what it looks like when the program invokes itself.

```
                filespec: N.C.
 1: /*
 2:        N.C
 3:
 4:        list file to printer with tabs expanded and
 5:        line numbers
 6:
 7:
 8: */
 9:
10: #include "bdscio.h"
11: #define FF 0X0c
12: #define PGLEN 66
13:
14: int colno, lineslft, lineno;
15:
16: main (argc, argv)
17: char **argv;
18: {
19:        char lbuf [BUFSIZ], obuf [BUFSIZ];
20:        char *fname, linebuf [MAXLINE];
21:        int c;
22:
23:        lineno = 1;
24:        clear ( );
25:        puts ("\n\n\n\n\t Line Print File\n\n ");
26:        if (argc != 2)
27:        {
28:            puts ("enter input file name\n");
29:            puts ("with file invocation");
30:            exit( );
31:        }
32:        if (fopen (argv [1], obuf) == ERROR)
33:        {
34:            printf ("cannot open %s", argv [1]);
35:            exit ( );
36:        }
37:
38:        fname = *++argv,
39:        sprintf (linebuf, "%28s%s\n","filespec: ",fname);
40:        linepr (linebuf);
41:        for ( ; ; )
42:        {
43:            if (! fgets (lbuf, obuf)) break;
44:            if (linepr (lbuf)) continue;
45:            if (lineslft > 2) continue;
46:            formfeed ( );
47:        }
48:        formfeed ( );
49: }
50:
51: linepr (string)
52: char *string;                 /*note the lvalue asgnmt*/
```

Figure 6.6: A Program to Print Source Files with Line Numbers and Expanded Tabs (continues)

```
53: {
54:     char c, ffflag, nstr [4];
55:     int i;
56:     ffflag = 0;
57:
58:     while (c = *string++)
59:       switch (c)
60:         {
61:         case FF:
62:             ffflag = 1;
63:             break;
64:         case '\n':
65:             putlpr ('\r');
66:             putlpr ('\n');
67:             printno (lineno++);
68:             putlpr (':');
69:             putlpr (' ');
70:             colno = 0;
71:             lineslft--;
72:             break;
73:         case '\t':
74:             do {
75:                 putlpr (' ');
76:                 colno++;
77:                 }
78:                 while (colno % 8);
79:             break;
80:
81:         default:
82:             putlpr (c);
83:             colno++;
84:         }
85:         if (ffflag) formfeed ( );
86:         return ffflag;
87: }
88:
89: putlpr (c)
90: char c;
91: {
92:         bios (5, c);
93: }
94:
95:
96: formfeed ( )
97: {
98:     if (FF)
99:         putlpr (FF);
100:         else
101:             while (lineslft--)
102:             putlpr ('\n');
103:     lineslft = PGLEN;
104: }
105:
106:
107: clear ( )
```

Figure 6.6: A Program to Print Source Files with Line Numbers and Expanded Tabs (continues)

Here's where we see what's new in this program:

```
51:   linepr (string)
52:   char *string;            /*note the lvalue asgnmt*/
53:   {
54:      char c, ffflag, nstr [4];
55:      int i;
56:      ffflag = 0;
57:
58:      while (c = *string++)
59:         switch (c)
60:            {
61:            case FF:
62:               ffflag = 1;
63:               break;
64:            case '\n':
65:               putlpr ('\r');
66:               putlpr ('\n');
67:               printno (lineno++);
68:               putlpr (':');
69:               putlpr (' ');
70:               colno = 0;
71:               lineslft--;
72:               break;
```

```
108: {
109:      putchar (0X0c);
110: }
111:
112: printno (n)
113: int n;
114: {
115:          int i, j;
116:          char s [6];
117:
118:          i = 0;
119:          do
120:             {
121:                 s [i++] = n % 10 + '0';
122:                 j = i ;
123:             }
124:          while ((n /= 10) > 0);
125:          s [i] = '\0';
126:          for (i = j ; i > -1 ; i--)
127:                 putlpr (s [i]);
128: }
129:
```

Figure 6.6: A Program to Print Source Files with Line Numbers and Expanded Tabs.

After putting the carriage-return/line-feed pair to the printer, the line number, which was initialized in the first executable line of code, is incremented and fed to the function printno. Next, the colon and blank characters are output, and the result is a number followed by a colon at the start of each line. The program execution goes on from this point as it did in Figure 6.5, but look carefully at this next portion of the code. A new problem has arisen because we are making this program print line numbers. See if you can isolate it.

```
73:            case '\t':
74:                do {
75:                    putlpr (' ');
76:                    colno + + ;
77:                    }
78:                while (colno % 8);
79:                break;
80:
81:        default:
82:                putlpr (c);
83:                colno + + ;
84:            }
85:        if (ffflag) formfeed ( );
86:        return ffflag;
87:    }
88:
89:    putlpr (c)
90:    char c;
91:    {
92:        bios (5, c);
93:    }
94:
95:
96:    formfeed ( )
97:    {
98:      if (FF)
99:          putlpr (FF);
100:            else
101:                while (lineslft − − )
102:                    putlpr ('\n');
103:        lineslft = PGLEN;
104:    }
105:
106:
107:    clear ( )
```

```
108:    {
109:        putchar (0X0c);
110:    }
```

Did you find the problem? The printer function putlpr ( ) cannot output an integer—or any number, for that matter. It needs a character. What we must do is convert the integer line number to a character. It's a bit more complicated than you would think at first glance.

The integer n is passed to the function printno and declared type integer. It doesn't have to be set to an lvalue, because it's going to be used as is—its value within the storage area won't be changed:

```
112:    printno (n)
113:    int n;
114:    {
115:        int i, j;
116:        char s [6];
```

A couple of counters, i and j, are declared type integer, and a character array of six characters is also declared. The array accommodates all the characters that can be held in an integer decimal, plus one for the null terminator.

Then the character string array s is incremented at each iteration:

```
118:        i = 0;
119:        do
120:        {
121:            s [i++] = n % 10 + '0';
122:            j = i ;
123:        }
```

Each character of the array is equal (assigned) to the remainder of the division of the number by 10, which is added to 48 decimal. In ASCII, 48 decimal corresponds to the character '0' (zero). The counter j is set to i. The next program line is one of the key lines in the function:

```
124:        while ((n / = 10) > 0);
```

Remember that n / = 10 is n = n/10. The loop tester divides the number by 10 (permanently), thereby decreasing the number of places by 1 place ($850/10 = 85$). If the result is greater than 0, the new n, a tenth (1/10) of what it used to be, is passed back up to the modulus operator s [i++] = n % 10 + '0';. The characters stored in the string array s [ ] are in reverse order, but they are there.

The next line puts a null terminator on the string:

```
125:        s [i] = '\0';
```

Now you have a backwards string. To get it to the printer in the right order, you must read it backwards. Remember j, the loop counter? The new for loop is set so that its index i (again) starts at the maximum number of the last index of the string variable. Thus initialized, it is checked to see if it is greater than 0, the last (or first) element of the array. Then it is decremented on each iteration:

```
126:        for (i = j ; i > -1 ; i--)
127:            putlpr (s [i]);
128:    }
```

The result is that the character array s [ ] is output backwards. Let's go through this again by taking an example and verbally following it through each step.

- Input the integer 324.

- Modulus division yields the remainder. 324/10 equals 32 with a remainder of 4. Therefore the result of the modulus division 324/10 is 4, which is stored as '4.'

- Now for the simple division by 10. Without the remainder, 324/10 equals 32. In this operation, the 3-digit number 324 has been permanently changed to the 2-digit number 32.

- Now we are dealing with the number 32. The result of the modulus division 32/10 is 2 (32/10 = 3 with a remainder of 2) which is stored as '2'. The string is now '42'.

- Now for the simple division by 10. 32/10 = 3 (without the remainder). 3 is the number we are dealing with now.

- The result of the modulus division of 3/10 is 3, stored as '3'. The string is now '423', the exact reverse of the input.

- The simple division of 3/10 is not greater than 0. Remember that the test for staying in the loop requires that the result of this simple division by 10 be greater than 0. Because it is not greater than 0, we exit the loop. The string '423' is printed backwards as 324, which is the integer we started with.

Before you compile this program and save it, notice that the line-numbering program has a minor deficiency. As the line numbers are incremented by each place, or power of 10, the text will be pushed to the right one more space.

```
8:      */
9:
10:     #include "bdscio.h"
```

.
.
.

```
99:     putlpr (FF);
100:       else
```

The listing starts to drift to the right, leaving a mildly unpleasant jogging of the text or program listing. What is needed is a consistent format for the number string that uses the same number of places, about five or six. The printno function in Figure 6.7 is designed to do just that.

This function creates an array of five characters, initializing it with five zeros in the positions 0–4. The do-while loop is the same as the last version, using the combination of integer modulus division and a simple division by 10.

When the do-while loop is exited, the last character in the string is set to the null terminator \0, as all strings must be. The final for outputs the string backwards. The result is numbers like

```
0099:
0100:
0101:
```

```
/*
    printno

    a function to convert integers to five-digit strings
    filled out with zeros to the left

*/

printno (n)
int n;
    {
        int i;
        char s [6];

        i = 0;
        strcpy (s, "00000");

        do
            s [i++] = n % 10 + '0';
        while ((n /= 10) > 0);

        s [i] = '\0';

        for (1 = 5; i > -1; i--)
            putlpr (s [i]);
    }
```

Figure 6.7: A Function to Convert Integers to Five-Digit Strings Filled Out with Zeros to the Left

Now compile and save the program in Figure 6.6, using the printno function in Figure 6.7. It should prove to be quite handy.

The key to buffered files is C's willingness to do the housekeeping. C maintains the buffers, filling and emptying them as the system requires without intervention by the programmer or operator. The programmer's only task is to remember the name assigned to the buffer. Although they are not identical, buffered files closely resemble stream or sequential files, particularly because they cannot, except in enhanced versions, be appended, and in no circumstances can they be randomly updated.

If random access is required, and high speed disk transfer is the goal of the programmer, the answer is raw files. Is there a price for this ability? Yes: raw files are very close to primitive file I/O, and the programmer must provide the necessary housekeeping to make them work. How this is done is the topic of the next chapter.

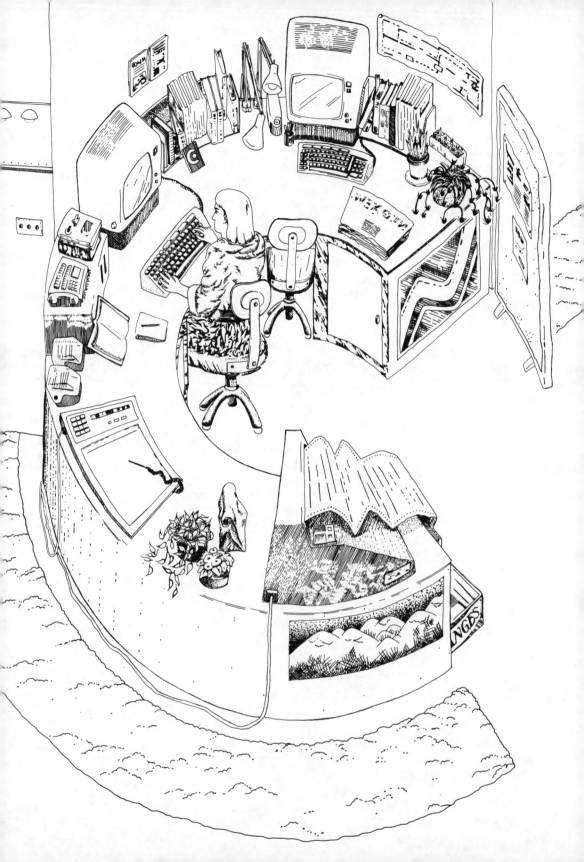

7:

Raw Files: Random I/O

Raw file I/O is the closest thing C has to random (direct) files. The description *raw* is apt, because raw file operations are just a bit above the system file primitives.[1] Data coming from or going to raw files are in blocks that are the same size as the system's logical record size. In UNIX the records are 512 bytes long; in CP/M they are 128 bytes long. Raw file functions do not buffer the data as do buffered file functions. The programmer must do any necessary buffering.

The open and creat Functions

Files in any language require a file descriptor or reference. In BASIC, a file is assigned a stream number; in Pascal, COBOL, and PL/I, internal names are assigned. In C, a file descriptor is assigned. The biggest difference between the C descriptor and that in other languages is that in C the value of the descriptor is unknown outside of the program. The file descriptor is assigned upon opening the file, and it is used in all references to the file. In the following two functions, the file descriptor (fd) is assigned:

```
fd = open (filename, mode)
fd = creat (filename)
```

The open function opens a file for I/O. In C, like other languages, I/O is relative to the program. That is, input comes *from* the file to the program, and output goes *to* the file from the program. Another way of saying this is that the file is *read* in input mode, and *written to* in output mode. A mode of 2 opens the file for update, which involves both input and output (reading from and writing to the file). The file name is a file specification with all the usual attributes of a file specification in the operating system, as in

```
b:myprog.dat
```

for a CP/M file. The file name, which must be an lvalue, can be passed to the program in the command line, as with buffered files.

The creat function operates in somewhat the same manner. It opens a file either by creating it "from scratch" or by deleting an existing file of the same name, if it exists, and writing over it. The file is implicitly open for output, i.e., writing. Both functions return the file descriptor, an integer, and if an error occurs, a -1 to signal the error.

Returning consistent error code is indeed a help to the programmer. It allows a comfortable exit from a potentially dangerous position:

```
if (open ("d:badprog.bum", 2) == ERROR)
{
    printf ("disk error in opening badprog.bum\n")
    exit ( );
}
```

With this sort of error handling, the program outputs its diagnosis of the failure, then settles down comfortably to calling up the operating system. The other alternative is simply to allow the program to crash, leaving the user with well-founded doubts about the programmer's ability. C does not have a built-in error-handling routine such as PL/I's exception handling or BASIC's ON ERROR, but most of C's functions return an error code that can be used either for a graceful exit from the program or a recovery within the program.

The following program fragment gets a good file name and exits the loop:

```
while (TRUE);
{
    puts ("input filename : ");
    gets (filename)
    if (open (filename, 0) == ERROR)
        continue;
    else
        break;
}
```

If an unusable file name is submitted, it asks for the name again. (Notice that with continue this can be done without the use of a backwards goto. Yes, even C has a goto.)

The write and read Functions

Once a file has been opened, the name of the game is to read from or write to the file. Reading from and writing to raw files cause immediate disk transfers. This is the first big difference between raw and buffered files. Buffered files store (buffer) information and fill or empty the buffers as the system requires. Raw files are primitive; the moment the program specifies reading from or writing to a file, immediate action is indicated.

The write function takes as arguments the file descriptor, the buffer (as an lvalue), and the number of blocks to be written:[2]

write (fd, buffer, number_of_blocks)

It returns an integer for the number of blocks actually read, a 0 for the end-of-file (EOF) mark, or a − 1 for an error. In the programs that follow you will see this statement:

while (nbr_read = read (fd, buffer, BUFSECTS))

This statement takes advantage of the fact that the read function does not return a 0 or − 1 until the end of the file is reached or an error occurs. Thus the statement performs its own test to exit, as it executes the read function within the while loop.

The structure of the read function is very similar to that of the write function:

read (fd, buffer, number_of_blocks)

It reads into the buffer the number of blocks specified from the file specified by the file descriptor. Now that's specific! Like the write function, read returns an integer for the number of records or blocks actually read, a 0 for the end-of-file mark, or a − 1 for an error.

PREPARATION FOR RANDOM FILE I/O

Now that you can open raw files for reading and writing, what do you do now? Raw files' "tall hat" is that you can *randomly* read and write them. There is a lot of refinement in buffered file I/O, but for all its refinement, this is a trick it just won't do. Buffered, stream, or sequential files, or whatever other languages call them, have this one big problem: they cannot be randomly accessed, and therefore they cannot be appended (updated).

The seek and tell Functions

The vehicles for random reading and writing are the tell and seek functions. The tell function tells the program where the file's record pointer is, and the seek function moves the record pointer to whatever location the program specifies. Here is a look at the seek function:

seek (fd, offset, code)

Our old friend, the file descriptor fd, lets the seek function know which file is to be dealt with. The offset tells the system how many records it wants to move the record pointer from the reference set by code. If code is 0, the seek function sets the pointer to the number of the record whose value is offset. If the code is 1, seek sets the pointer to its present value plus the offset. To reiterate, a 0 code prepares a record offset number of records for reading or writing starting from record zero. A 1 prepares a record offset number of records for reading or writing from where the pointer is at that time.

seek returns an integer value. If the record is out of range, it returns a − 1 for error. Never, *never* perform a seek function on a buffered file! It may work in Pascal MT +, but you'll be sorry if you try it in C. It simply won't work.

The tell function is short, sweet, and handy:

tell (fd)

The tell function returns as an integer the current position of the record pointer associated with the file descriptor fd. The number is the next block to be written or read.

A DISK-TO-DISK FILE PROGRAM

Before going on (and on) about file functions, I want to put the ones already covered to work. The program in Figure 7.1 is a disk-to-disk file copying utility that demonstrates both the read and write functions. It also shows raw files at their best—when they are making massive moves of records in remarkably little time.

Now to tear the code apart. The command-line passing of file names as arguments is accomplished by our old friends argv and argc in the "call" to the main block. The command line will look like this:

cpy oldprog.xxx newprog.xxx

A constant defined by the header file, BUFSECTS, is used by the program to set up a buffer area of 64 sectors (64 sectors × 128 bytes = 8 kilobytes):

```
#include "bdscio.h"
#define BUFSECTS 64
```

```
/*

                CPY.C

        a disk to disk file copy program

*/

#include "bdscio.h"
#define BUFSECTS 64

int fdi, fdo;
char buffer [BUFSECTS * SECSIZ];

main (argc, argv)
int argc;
char **argv;
{
    int nbr_read;

    clear ( );
    puts ("\n\n\n\n\t File Copy Utility\n\n\n\n");
    if (argc != 3)
    {
        puts ("The name of the source and destination files");
        puts ("\nmust be included in the command line");
        exit ( );
    }
    if ((fdi = open (argv [1], 0)) == ERROR)
    {
        printf ("cannot open %s", argv [1]);
        exit ( );
    }
    if ((fdo = creat (argv [2])) == ERROR)
    {
        printf ("cannot open %s", argv [2]);
        exit ( );
    }
    while (nbr_read = read (fdi, buffer, BUFSECTS))
    {
        if (nbr_read == ERROR)
        {
            puts ("file read error during copy");
            exit ( );
        }
        if (write (fdo, buffer, nbr_read) != nbr_read)
        {
            puts ("file write error during copy");
            exit ( );
        }
    }
    close (fdi);
    if (close (fdo) == ERROR)
```

Figure 7.1: A Disk-to-Disk File Copy Program (continues)

```
int fdi, fdo;
char buffer [BUFSECTS * SECSIZ];

main (argc, argv)
int argc;
char **argv;
```

C source code doesn't take up much space in memory, and a program of this size typically compiles into a compact 5 kilobytes of object code. In a normal 64K environment, 5 kilobytes are needed by the operating system and another 5 by the program. That leaves a safe 48 to 54 kilobytes available for storage assignments such as buffering, so the 8 kilobytes we are asking for is a minuscule amount. BUFSECTS could easily be enlarged to 380 or so, if you wanted to move really large files with a minimum of "disk thrashing."

After screening the command line to be sure that three file names are given, argv [1], the second file name (remembering that C almost always starts counting from 0), is used in the open statement:

```
{
    int nbr_read;

    clear ( );
    puts("\n\n\n\n\t File Copy Utility\n\n\n\n");
    if (argc != 3)
{
    puts ("The name of the source and destination files");
    puts ("\nmust be included in the command line");
    exit ( );
}
if ((fdi = open (argv [1], 0)) == ERROR)
{
    printf ("cannot open %s", argv [1]);
    exit ( );
}
```

```
            {
                puts ("disk error while closing");
                exit ( );
            }
            puts ("\n\n\n\n\t\t Copy complete");
        }

        clear ( )
        {
            putchar (12);
        }
```

Figure 7.1: A Disk-to-Disk File Copy Program

Notice that the file descriptor fdi (for input) is assigned by open ( ). The open function uses the 0 mode for input to the program. If the file can't be opened for any reason, for example, if it isn't there, or it doesn't have a disk in the object drive, a − 1 is returned, signaling an error. The program politely states on the console that the file cannot be opened, and then it exits.

It's a good idea to make your programs user-friendly by including "warm, furry buttons" such as this. By that I mean that you should include statements that let the user of the program know the status of the program. It's a courtesy that will be appreciated. If you want to alert the user to something (or if you feel just a bit mischievous), add the bell character:

```
putchar (0X7)
```

It wakes up the console operator to the fact that there has been an error.

The creation of the new file specified in the command line is accomplished by the creat function:

```
if ((fdo = creat (argv [2])) == ERROR)
{
    printf ("cannot open %s", argv [2]);
    exit ( );
}
```

It assigns the second file descriptor, fdo. Again, if the function fails, the program voices its objections and exits.

The next part gets into the heart of the program—the read function:

```
while (nbr_read = read (fdi, buffer, BUFSECTS))
{
    if (nbr_read == ERROR)
    {
    puts ("file read error during copy");
    exit ( );
}
```

In typical C fashion, the while loop statement does half a dozen tasks. Nested innermost in the while loop is the read function itself. It reads the entire file in one pass (if it does not exceed available heap memory), putting its contents into memory in a buffer, here called buffer. Nested at the middle level is the statement nbr_read = read (. . .). nbr_read is a dummy variable that holds the value returned from read ( ), waiting for the expected end-of-file mark or the dreaded − 1 error. The outer statement is the while loop itself, which iterates the file function read and quits when it finds the end of the file. In keeping with the tone of the rest of the program, it grumbles politely to the console and quits when it encounters an error.

Now that the plot has thickened, it's time to get into the real action:

```
if (write (fdo, buffer, nbr_read) ! = nbr_read)
{
    puts ("file write error during copy");
    exit ( );
}
```

The if statement houses the write function. Notice that the if statement is held within the block or loop created by while. The while statement clocks nbr_read as it passes through the loop, and its value must be matched by the number of blocks written in the write function. If write ( ) returns a different number, it signals an error. Otherwise, the entire contents of the file being copied are mirrored in the file being written, including the end-of-file mark.

The close Function

The last thing you *always* want to do is close the files:

```
}
close (fdi);
if (close (fdo) == ERROR )
{
    puts ("disk error while closing");
    exit ( );
}
puts ("\n\n\n\n\t\t Copy complete");
}
```

If the input file doesn't close, it is just a formality, because neither its contents nor its directory has been altered. However it is always good practice to close all files. This releases the file descriptor so that it can be used elsewhere. The output file is quite another story. Raw file I/O ensures that there is no need to flush buffers (there are none to flush), but the final system call (BDOS 16 in CP/M) must be made to close the file in the directory.

Output files (including update files) must be closed so that their disk directories will be written. Disk directories tell the system where the files are on the disk, and in the case of output files, they must be closed or the file directories will not be written. If that happens, you might as well kiss your file goodbye because the system will not be able to find it, and as far as the system is concerned, your file is gone.

The last line is another "warm, furry button." Once again, its sole purpose is to let the operator know that everything ran smoothly.

It is appropriate in a book on C (because C was developed with UNIX in mind) to note that the UNIX operating system is almost devoid of "warm, furry buttons" to make the program easy to use. That is because during I/O redirection through UNIX's intermediate files called pipes, "warm, furry buttons" cannot be used—the system, not the program, is in control. UNIX is not noted for being overly friendly. (There will be more on UNIX and pipes in Chapter 15.)

If you decide to compile and run the program in Figure 7.1, do a disk dump on both the file being read and the file that has been written, and you'll notice that the copy is a literal, byte-for-byte copy, nothing added and nothing lost.

A MINI MAIL LIST WITH RAW FILE I/O

It is time to get adventurous. Raw file I/O is not necessarily the best or easiest medium for transferring data from the console to a disk file, but throwing all caution to the wind, let's do it anyway. We'll create a small program to file names, addresses, and phone numbers, or a mini mail list program.

The first thing to do in creating a program is to pseudocode the program before attempting to code it. Pseudocoding is a compromise between English and programming language instructions, and it is used to plan and predefine the code and the algorithms. The first thing to do is to define the intent of the program:

1. Open a file for output.

2. Input the data from the console.

3. Output the data to the file.

Simple. Now for the pseudocode:

```
/*
        RAWWRITE.PSC
        Pseudocode for program to
read files from console and output them to raw file I/O

*/

declare 8K buffer

main
     declare bufptr
     declare number of records
```

Raw Files

```
initialize number of records to 0
set bufptr to buffer origin
clear screen
buffer = 0            /*fill buffer with zeros*/
return bufptr to buffer origin
write to console ("raw file I/O prog")
if argument count ! = 2
          write to console ("input file name")
          exit
     open output file
        if open error
           write to console ("open error")
           exit
     write to console ("enter 9 to exit")

     while first character is not "9"
        format_input (name, address, phone) into buffer
                /*format to 128-byte record*/
        store starting at bufptr
        increment bufptr 128 bytes
        increment number of records by 1

     if number of records written ! = number of records in buffer
        write to console ("write error")
        exit
     close file
        if close error
           write to console ("close error")
     write to console ("complete")
```

That was also simple. Pseudocode *any* program that you are writing from scratch. It saves time in the end, and programs are written ever so much more clearly when they have been planned in advance. It is an ideal opportunity to check out your program logic, as well. The actual program to file mailing list data is shown in Figure 7.2.

For no better reason than to show that it can be done, the file descriptor and the buffer are declared implicitly external:

```
#include "bdscio.h"
#define BUFSECTS 124
int fd;
char buffer [BUFSECTS * SECSIZ];
```

In fact, it is not a bad idea to declare the file descriptors and buffer, because if you add a function or two at a later date, it saves a lot of pointer passing. A really big buffer is declared, because you will create your own "heap" for storing the data. Remember, the heap[3] is a dynamic storage area that is in essence a second stack. The master plan is to store everything input into the program's memory buffer before putting it all to disk in one gigantic disk write. When you pay for high-speed memory, why not use it?

As with most of the file programs in this book, I take advantage of the command-line input of the file names:

```
main (argc, argv)
int argc;
char * * argv;
{
    int n_recds, c;
    char name [32], addr [82], phone [14];
    char *bufptr;
```

A memory refresher: the argument count (argc) and the pointer to the argument vector list (* *argv) should be declared between the main (argc, argv) line and the first opening brace of the main program block, because they are parameters passed from the command line. There are three string buffers for the names, addresses, and phone numbers, reasonably large enough to hold their intended contents and also just the right size to add

```
/*
                        RAWWRITE.C

        a program to input mailing list data from the
        console and buffer it in a file sized buffer
        before outputting it to a raw file of 128 byte
        sectors


*/

#include "bdscio.h"
#define BUFSECTS 124

int fd;
char buffer [BUFSECTS * SECSIZ];

main (argc, argv)
int argc;
char **argv;
{
    int n_recds, c;
    char name [32], addr [82], phone [14];
    char *bufptr;
```

Figure 7.2: A Miniature Mail List Creation Program Using Raw File I/O (continues)

```
        n_recds = 0;
        bufptr = &buffer;
        setmem (bufptr, BUFSECTS * SECSIZ, 0x20);
        clear ( );
        puts ("\n\n\n\n\n\tMini Mail List\n\n\n");
        if (argc != 2)
        {
            puts ("destination file must be included ");
            puts ("in the command line ");
            exit ( );
        }
        if ((fd = creat (argv [1])) == ERROR)
        {
            printf ("cannot open %s", argv [1]);
            exit ( );
        }

        for ( ; ; )
        {
            puts ("enter 9 to exit: ");
            c = getchar ( );
            if (c == '9')
                break;
            puts ("\n\n");
            puts ("enter  name: ");
            gets (name);
            puts ("\nenter address: ");
            gets (addr);
            puts ("\nenter phone: ");
            gets (phone);
            sprintf (bufptr, "%-32s%-82s%-14s", name, addr, phone);
            bufptr += 128;
            n_recds++;
            puts ("\n\n\n");
        }
        sprintf (bufptr, "%C", CPMEOF);
        n_recds++;
        if (write (fd, buffer, n_recds) != n_recds)
        {
            puts ("file write error");
            exit ( );
        }
        if (close (fd) == ERROR)
        {
            puts ("Disk error on closing");
            exit ( );
        }
        puts ("Disk write complete\n\n");
        puts ("end of execution");
    }

clear ( )
{
    putchar (12);
}
```

Figure 7.2: A Miniature Mail List Creation Program Using Raw File I/O

up to 128 bytes (the length of a CP/M record). A pointer to the "heap" is declared as well.

Now an explicit pointer to the buffer is set so that it can be incremented later:

```
n_recds = 0;
bufptr = &buffer;
setmem (bufptr, BUFSECTS * SECSIZ, 0X20);
```

This also could be done by subscripting, but using the pointer directly emphasizes the mechanics of heap addressing. The setmem function is used to fill memory. In this case the entire buffer area has been filled with blanks (020 hex) to ensure that no "garbage" will be in the buffer when it is read. (Previous computer activity may have left residual bits and pieces of data in memory.) The function works by putting as many characters into memory as the middle parameter SECSIZ specifies, using the characters called out by the last parameter, 0X20, and starting at the address pointed to by the pointer bufptr.

There is nothing new in the next section. It either gets the file names correctly or writes a message on the console, asking the operator to redo the command line.

Next you want a good, positive, quick way to exit the input phase of the program. Once in the main loop, a do-forever loop, the console operator is told, enter 9 to exit:

```
for ( ; ; )
{
    puts ("enter 9 to exit: ");
    c = getchar ( );
    if (c == '9')
        break;
```

You can use any character you want to exit the loop. I chose 9 because it is a convenient key for the operator to press, right nearby on the numeric key pad. The getchar function is used to obviate using the return key. The if statement tests to see whether the character input is indeed a 9. If it is, the loop is exited. If not, the loop is repeated.

Then we individually fill the name, address, and phone string buffers:

```
puts ("\n\n");
puts ("enter name: ");
gets (name);
puts ("\nenter address: ");
gets (addr);
puts ("\nenter phone: ");
gets (phone);
```

Now things begin to get a little tricky. A very large buffer is being formatted in 128-byte chunks:

```
sprintf (bufptr, "%-32s%-82s%-14s", name, addr, phone);
bufptr += 128;
n_recds++;
puts ("\n\n\n");
}
```

The sprintf function "prints" the "strings" to memory in an exact format. The program calls for name to occupy 32 bytes, left justified (denoted by the − symbol), followed immediately by 82 bytes, left justified, for addr, (address) and finally by 14 bytes, left justified, for phone. The sprintf function puts these into the buffer at the address pointed to by bufptr. Note that name, addr, and phone are pointers.

The pointer bufptr is incremented by 128 bytes at each input. n_recds, the number of records read from the console, is incremented by one at each iteration.

The rigorously formatted record fields are written to the disk file exactly as they are stored in memory. If a formatted read ( ) is performed, the individual record fields can be extracted easily.

When the main loop has been exited, the final record is written to memory, putting the CP/M end-of-file mark (^Z) as a character. Then the number of records is incremented for the last time:

```
sprintf (bufptr, "%c", CPMEOF);
n_recds++;
```

Like the final fireworks display on the Fourth of July, the entire buffer is written in one shot:

```
if (write (fd, buffer, n_recds) != n_recds)
{
    `puts ("file write error");
    exit ( );
}
```

When the program is run, the disk is only accessed twice, once to bring up the program and once more to file the entire buffer.

Run the program, input some data, and do a disk dump. Just as sure as smoke hurts floppies, the data will be rigidly formatted in 32-82-14 boundaries. There will be nothing else except the blanks placed in memory by the setmem function.

READING RAW FILES

Against all odds, we have succeeded in writing a data file of numbered addresses. A disk dump was used to read the data. For those who aren't fluent in reading Intel hex, however, a more readable form of output must be devised. The program in Figure 7.3 does just that.

What we need to do is to return the contents of the file created by RAWWRITE.C to high-speed memory and to read them back from high-speed memory in the exact way they were originally put in, so that they can be output in a form humans can read.

Except for a handful of integer variables destined to be indices, there isn't much new in the first ten or fifteen lines. The name buffers are the same as in RAWWRITE.C, as they should be if the file is going to be rebuilt. The action starts here:

```
clear ( );
puts ("\n\n\n\t Mini Mail List file read\n\n\n");
    .
    .
    .
    while (nbr_read = read (fd, buffer, BUFSECTS))
    {
        n = (n > nbr_read) ? n : nbr_read;
```

The while loop keeps the read function going until the entire contents of the disk file are transferred into memory. The while loop is exited when the end-of-file mark is read. We encounter a problem in logic at this point. The number of records read, nbr_read, must be saved, but it is set to zero upon encountering the end-of-file mark. To hold the maximum value, the

```
/*
                        RR.C

        a program for the reading of raw files
        created by RAWWRITE.C


*/

#include "bdscio.h"
#define BUFSECTS 128

int fd;
char buffer [BUFSECTS * SECSIZ];
```

Figure 7.3: A Program to Read Raw Files (continues)

```
main (argc, argv)
int argc;
char **argv;
{
    int nbr_read, i, j, k, n;
    char *bufptr;
    char name [32], addr [82], phone [14];

    n = k = 0;
    bufptr = &buffer;
    setmem (bufptr, BUFSECTS *SECSIZ, 0&x0);
    clear ( );
    puts ("\n\n\n\t Mini Mail List file read\n\n\n");
    if (argc != 2)
    {
        puts ("the name of the source file must\n");
        puts ("be included in the command line");
        exit ( );
    }
    if ((fd = open (argv [1], 0)) == ERROR)
    {
        printf ("cannot open %s", argv [1]);
        exit ( );
    }
    while (nbr_read = read (fd, buffer, BUFSECTS))
    {
        n = (n > nbr_read) ? n : nbr_read;
        if (nbr_read == ERROR)
        {
            puts ("file error during read");
            exit ( );
        }
    }
    for (i = 0 ; i <= n ; i++)
    {
        for (j = k ; j < (k + 127) ; j++)
        {
            putchar (buffer [j]);
        }
        k += 128;
        puts ("\n\n");
    }

    close (fd);
    puts ("\n\nfunction complete");
}

clear ( )
{
    putchar (12);
}
```

Figure 7.3: A Program to Read Raw Files

ternary operator ? : is invoked. The assignment statement translates into this: If the statement in parentheses is true, that the dummy variable n (the number of lines actually read) is greater than nbr_read, then n is equal to n. If n is not greater than nbr_read, it is equal to nbr_read (If n > nbr_read, then n = n ELSE n = nbr_read).

The next section is where the output occurs:

```
if (nbr_read == ERROR)
{
    puts ("file error during read");
    exit ( );
}
}

for (i = 0 ; i < = n ; i++)
{
    for (j = k ; j < = (k + 127) ; j++)
    {
        putchar (buffer [j]);
    }
    k += 128;
    puts ("\n\n");
}
```

A pair of nested loops regulates the output. The outer loop clocks the records, while the inner loop puts out the characters one character at a time. The outer loop increments the counter for the inner loop 128 bytes at a time (the length of the record). The variable k is the vehicle for resetting the text in the inner loop after each pass through the outer loop.

The inner loop ticks off in 128-byte increments from 0 to 127. The loop counter j self-increments while its boundaries are tested by the expression j < = k + 127. The end result is that each 128-byte record is output one record at a time with each record followed by two line feeds. With each loop iteration, another record followed by two line feeds is output until the buffer is exhausted. The value n, saved with the ternary operator, sets the outer loop limit to the exact number of records read.

Now we have the final "warm, furry button":

```
close (fd);
puts ("\n\nfunction complete");
```

RANDOM FILE I/O

That takes care of raw file read and write functions. But where is the random access that was promised? After all, if read ( ) and write ( ) are supposed to be capable of random reading and writing, why not use them for that purpose? The program in Figure 7.4 does just that.

Because the initial portions of the program are about the same as their predecessors, I will jump over the beginning part of the code.

Random Writing

The action starts when the record number is requested. The file has already been read through, to find out how many records are in it. It is now compared with the input number to see whether the number the operator has input is out of range:

```
puts ("enter record number to be written");
scanf ("%d", n)

if (seek (fd, n, 0) == ERROR)
{
    printf ("seek %d out of range\n", n);
    continue;
```

The number of the record having been stored in n, it is passed to seek ( ) along with the file descriptor and the mode 0. The mode 0 offsets the

```
/*
                            RW.C

                a program to update mail list type data
                by random write using the seek function


*/

#include "bdscio.h"

int fd;
char buffer [SECSIZ];

main (argc, argv)
int argc;
char **argv;
{
        int n_recds, c, n;
        char name [32], addr [82], phone [14];
        char *bufptr;

        n_recds = 0;
        bufptr = &buffer;
        setmem (bufptr, SECSIZ, 0x20);
        clear ( );
        puts ("\n\n\n\n\n\tMini Mail List\n\n\n");
```

Figure 7.4: An Update Program for the Mail List Using the seek *Function for Random I/O
(continues)*

```
if (argc != 2)
{
    puts ("destination file must be included ");
    puts ("in the command line ");
    exit ( );
}
if ((fd = open (argv [1], 1)) == ERROR)   /*open for output */
{
    printf ("cannot open %s", argv [1]);
    exit ( );
}

for ( ; ; )
{
    puts ("enter 9 to exit : ");
    c = getchar ( );
    if (c == '9')
        break;
    puts ("\n\n");
    puts ("enter record number to be written");
    scanf("%d",n)
    if (seek (fd, n, 0) == ERROR)
    {
        printf("seek %d out of range\n", n);
        continue;
    }
        puts ("enter name : ");
        gets (name);
        strcat (name, "\n");
        puts ("\nenter address : ");
        gets (addr);
        strcat (addr, "\n");
        puts ("\nenter phone : ");
        gets (phone);
        strcat (phone, "\n");
        sprintf (bufptr, "%-32s%-82s%-14s", name, addr, phone);
        if (write (fd, buffer, 1) != 1)
        {
            puts ("file write error");
            exit ( );
        }
        puts ("\n\n\n");
    }
    if (close (fd) == ERROR)
    {
        puts ("Disk error on closing");
        exit ( );
    }
    puts ("Disk write complete\n\n");
    puts ("end of execution");
}

clear ( )
{
    putchar (12);
}
```

Figure 7.4: An Update Program for the Mail List Using the seek Function for Random I/O

record pointer from the origin or beginning of the file. Now the record pointer is set to access the nth record.

Next comes a new wrinkle. A line feed or newline is appended to each field to aid in separating the fields later:

```
}
puts ("enter name : ");
gets (name);
strcat (name, "\n");
puts ("\nenter address : ");
gets (addr);
strcat (addr, "\n");
puts ("\nenter phone : ");
gets (phone);
strcat (phone, "\n");
```

Then the three separate buffers, name, addr, and phone, are formatted and stored in the main buffer, buffer:

```
sprintf (bufptr, "%-32s%-82s%-14s", name, addr, phone);
```

Now for the write function:

```
if (write (fd, buffer, 1) ! = 1)
{
    puts ("file write error");
    exit ( );
}
```

The file record specified by n and pointed to by the seek function is written to disk. That's what we've been waiting for—a random write.

The program is completed by closing the file, providing for a closing error message and a "sign-off."

```
    puts ("\n\n\n");
}
if (close (fd) == ERROR)
{
    puts ("Disk error on closing");
    exit ( );
}
puts ("Disk write complete\n\n");
puts ("end of execution");
```

Random Reading

So far raw files have been handled in every way but one—random reading. The chapter won't be complete without it, so let's take a look at Figure 7.5.

The for loop, a do-forever loop, houses the main logic of the program:

```
for ( ; ; )
{
    puts ("enter 9 to exit: ");
    c = getchar ( );
    if (c == '9')
        break;
    puts ("\n");
    puts ("enter record number to be accessed: ");
    puts ("\n\n");
    gets (ch);
    nbr = atoi (ch);
    if (nbr > n)
    {
        puts (" record out of range: reinput\n\n ");
        continue;
    }
    seek (fd, nbr, 0);
```

```
/*

                            SK.C

          a program for reading raw C files
          created by RAWWRITE.C
          using the seek function to search for records


*/
#include "bdscio.h"
#define BUFSECTS 128

int fd;
char buffer [BUFSECTS * SECSIZ];

main (argc, argv)
int argc;
char **argv;
{
    int nbr_read, i, n, nbr;
    char *bufptr;
    char c;
    char buf1 [128];

    n = 0;
    bufptr = &buffer;
    setmem (bufptr, BUFSECTS *SECSIZ, 0&x0);
```

Figure 7.5: A Program To Read Raw Files Created By RR.C Using the seek Function
   (continues)

```
        clear ( );
        puts ("\n\n\n\t Mini Mail List file read\n\n\n");
        if (argc != 2)
        {
            puts ("the name of the source file must\n");
            puts ("be included in the command line");
            exit ( );
        }
        if ((fd = open (argv [1], 0)) == ERROR)
        {
            printf ("cannot open %s", argv [1]);
            exit ( );
        }
        while (nbr_read = read (fd, buffer, BUFSECTS))
        {
            n = (n > nbr_read) ? n : n += nbr_read;
            if (nbr_read == ERROR)
            {
                puts ("file error during read");
                exit ( );
            }
        }
        printf ("file %s had %d records\n\n", argv [1], n);
        for ( ; ; )
    {
        puts ("enter 9 to exit: ");
        c = getchar ( );
        if (c == '9')
            break;
        puts ("\n");
        puts ("enter record number to be accessed: ");
        puts ("\n\n");
        scanf("%d",n);
        if (nbr > n)
        {
            puts (" record out of range: reinput\n\n ");
            continue;
        }
        seek (fd, nbr, 0); /*set recd ptr to recd nbr */
        read (fd, buf1, 1);

            for (i = 0 ; i <= 127 ; i++)
                {
                putchar (buf1 [i]);
                }
        puts ("\n\n");
    }
    close (fd);
    puts ("\n\nfunction complete");
}

clear ( )
{
    putchar (12);
}
```

Figure 7.5: A Program To Read Raw Files Created By RR.C Using the seek Function

The request to quit breaks you out of the loop when the character 9 is input. The record number requested is compared with the maximum number of records available. If it is out of range, the continue brings the execution back to where the record number is input. When all the conditions have been tested and met, the do-forever loop is exited, and the record pointer is set to the requested number by the seek function.

The record is then read once again, one character at a time, and its contents are passed to the buffer buf1.

FILE FUNCTIONS FOR RAW AND BUFFERED FILES

You have now been introduced to randomly reading and writing raw files. Before closing the chapter, let's look at the remaining file I/O functions.

The rename Function

The rename function renames the file specified in the first argument to the name given by the second argument. It is very similar to CP/M's REN command. Both names must be lvalues or string array members. An integer value is returned, a 0 for success and a −1 for error.

        rename (oldname, newname)

The unlink Function

The unlink function deletes (removes) the file filename from the system. Use this function cautiously.

        unlink (filename);

These two functions, rename and unlink, come in handy with buffered files, but they can be used with raw files too. They allow you to update the files by reading the file to a new file, modifying or appending it, and then erasing it and renaming the new file to the same name as the old one. The effect is that of updating the existing file.

The fabort Function

The fabort function frees the file descriptor fd for reuse by C. It does not close the file, however, so if the file is opened for reading (input), it is not a major problem. If the file is opened for writing (output), you lose the file. Use this function cautiously.

A LOOK BACK AT DISK FILES

Looking back at C file systems, you have both buffered files and raw files to contend with. You need to determine which one to use and why.

Raw files take up extremely little memory, and can be processed with lightning speed. They can be read and written to randomly, and they are the only type of file in C that can be updated directly. With a lot of attention to housekeeping, raw files can also read or write random files created by other languages. That's the good news.

The bad news is that raw files are labor-intensive for the programmer, because they are only a bit more sophisticated than the file primitives they invoke. The programmer must do a great deal of work to make the program do the necessary housekeeping that is taken for granted in other languages.

Buffered files are relatively slow to process, and in many versions they can't be appended or updated. That's the bad news. The good news is that they are sophisticated and do nearly all of the housekeeping tasks for the programmer. For temporary files, text files, and, for that matter, for any nonbinary file of non-fixed length that doesn't require updating, buffered files can't be beat.

8:

Structures and Unions

STRUCTURES

One of the more powerful concepts in computer languages is the structure. Structures are lifesavers in "real-world" programming. As we all know, this is not a perfect world, and the data we have to deal with seldom comes in nice, tidy little categories that all fit conveniently into the same data type. Structures allow associated data to be handled as a single entity, and the data do not have to belong to the same data type.

A good example of associated data is an account. The information stored as account information is useless if separated, yet it seldom belongs to the same data type. Let's look at the information contained in a typical account:

Account
    Account name
    Account number
    Address
    Street
    City
    State
    Zip
Phone
Account balance

Here, in noncomputer terms, is a data structure. The entirety of the account is a structure. The address is a structure as well, but it is inside the more comprehensive structure of the account. The data cannot be stored as an array, because they don't belong to the same data type, but they can be stored as a structure. (Even more intriguing, structures themselves can be array elements.) Take a closer look at the various data types in the previous typical account informally represented as a structure.

ACCOUNT STRUCTURE

Account Information	Data Type
Account name	Character
Account number	Integer
Address	Structure
Street	Character
City	Character
State	Character
Zip	Integer
Phone	Character
Account balance	Float

A number of languages support structures of some sort. PL/I has an extremely versatile structure, Pascal has one called *record*, and even COBOL has one. C's structure is called struct, and it is powerful and diversified.

If you have had exposure to structures in other languages, a word of caution: syntactically, C's structure is quite different. Be prepared to part with preconceived ideas of structure syntax. When it is first declared, C's structure acts as a template for memory. It does not allocate any storage, but it is more or less a blueprint for allocating storage. Here is a simplified version of the account structure in perfectly good, syntactic C:

```
struct account
    {
    char name [32];
    int act_nbr;
    char address [64];
    char phone [12];
    float act_bal;
    } ;
```

The keyword struct informs the C compiler that account is data type struct. The braces hold the contents of the structure. The semicolon closes the structure. The braces do not have to line up, but having braces aligned is a great way to ensure that every left brace has a matching right brace.

The storage area has been defined with the structure. Now you can tell C to go ahead and allocate the storage:

```
struct account payables;
```

This declares a structure of the type specified by account, named payables. It has storage allocated, 114 bytes to be specific.[1]

C allows for structures of arrays or arrays of structures, in just about any combination imaginable. To declare an array of structures, the following syntax is used:

```
struct account payables [1000];
```

This allocates an array of 1000 account structures named payables.

How are the individual elements of the structure reached? First, there's a name for everything: account is a *structure tag*. name, act_nbr, address, and so on are the *structure members*. payables is the *structure name*. To refer to a specific member, the member should be modified by the structure name. For example:

```
payables.name
```

or

```
payables.act_nbr
```

The member also can be modified by a pointer reference, but more on that later.

C, being the clever language that it is, also allows the structure name to be assigned while declaring the structure tag and structure members:

```
struct account
    {
    char name [32];
    int act_nbr;
    char address [64];
    char phone [12];
    float act_bal;
    } payables ;
```

The last statement, } payables ;, is the structure assignment.

Don't be carried away by the convenience of this easy method of assignment. It only works well if one structure name is being assigned to the structure. Beyond that, it tends to lead to confusion. The compiler can keep track of almost anything, but the programmer and maintainer of the code cannot.

The members of a struct can belong to any data type, including arrays or other structures. It therefore follows that structures can be nested, as shown below:

```
struct account
    {
    char name [32];
    int act_nbr;
    struct address cust; / * Note nested structure * /
    char phone [12];
    float act_bal;
    } payables ;

struct address / * This is the structure nested above in struct acct * /
    {
    char street [32];
    char city [16];
    char state [2];
    int zip;
    } cust ;
```

Note the structure member struct address cust; in struct account. This shows the syntax of structure nesting.

I haven't talked a lot about initialization. In UNIX 7 C you can initialize variables upon their declaration, but few 8-bit C compilers implement the full set of UNIX 7 C. One of the sacrifices of small compilers is nearly always initialization. The above notwithstanding,

```
struct address cust = {"1745 Main St", "Bullfrog", "Nv", 89475};
```

is the way it is done. Fortunately, almost every 16-bit compiler supports not only initialization but the rest of the features of UNIX 7 C.

Structures and Functions

One of the limitations of C's structure (as well as Pascal's) is that it cannot be passed freely. If a structure is to be acted on by a function, it cannot be passed as a single parameter. The individual elements (members) can be passed by value, but it defeats the utility of the structure to handle its pieces rather than the whole. If the structure, tag, name, and members are all external to the entire code, there is no problem (other than having to declare it static if it is to be protected from being read by other programs). But there is also the pointer. If the pointer to the structure name is passed to the function as the function declares the struct, then bingo!—you have it by the address. For example:

```
disk_file (&payables)
    .
    .
    .
}

disk_file (pp)
struct account *pp
{
    .
    .
    .
```

The pointer to the structure payables is passed to the function disk_file as its parameter (argument). It is received as pp (pointer to payables) and declared before the block of the function as a pointer. A friendly warning: be rigorous about the syntax—you'll be sorry if you aren't.

ARRAYS OF STRUCTURES

You will often read that one language or another is "powerful." What is meant by power? One definition is the ability of a language to perform a great deal of work with relatively little code (that leaves out COBOL). By this definition, C is very powerful. Its ability to create arrays of structures illustrates this power. In the following example, the account structure is an array of 1000 account structures named **payables**:

```
struct account
    {
    char name [32];
    int act_nbr;
    char address [64];
    char phone [12];
    float act_bal;
    } payables [1000];
```

Referencing the members of an array of structures requires some very special syntax. We learned that references to a specific member of an array of structures should be modified by the structure name. References to the member can also be modified by a pointer. Think of the member as the noun and the pointer as the adjective:

```
ptr->name
```

Here the structure member (account) is modified by the pointer to a specific member (name). It also can be written as

   (*ptr).name

(*ptr) is in essence the structure name because the unary operator yields the contents of the address, which in this case is the tag.[2] It therefore acts the same as

   payables.name

The operators ( ), . , ->, and [ ] are at the top of the list in precedence; therefore the expression *ptr must be enclosed in parentheses (to get the indirect operator * to operate before the structure member operator .).

Programming With Structures

That's enough theory for a while—it's time to put structures to work. The program in Figure 8.1 is an exercise in multidimensional arrays, arrays of structures, and structures themselves. So as not to overwhelm you with too many concepts at once, particularly the concept of pointer modification, the program has been written in two versions. The first, S1.C, places the structure assignments external to the program to eliminate the need for structure modifiers. The second version, in Figure 8.2, uses pointer modifiers profusely.

The purpose of the program is to calculate the day of the year on a scale from 1 to 366, of a conventional date (month, day, year) input by the operator. The program creates a two-dimensional array of the days of the months, one for leap years and one for non-leap years. It then uses the date input by the operator to calculate the day of the year. January 1, 1983 is day one of the year. December 31, 1983 is day 365.

Now let's tear it apart and see what makes it tick:

```
struct date {
    int day;
    int month;
    int year;
    int yearday;
    char mo_na [8]; /* name of month */
            } d ;
```

A structure with the tag date is defined by this declaration. Its members are type integer with the exception of the character array mo_na. You can see how easy it is to have a structure containing arrays. The tag date itself does not allocate permanent storage. A structure with the structure

```
/*
                    ST.C

        an exercise in structures, arrays of structures,
        multidimensional arrays, and array initialization

*/

    struct date {
        int day;
        int month;
        int year;
        int yearday;
        char mo_na [8]; /*name of month*/
              } d ;

    struct month_na {
        int mon;
        char *name [8];
                  } m [13] ;


    int leap;

main ( )
{
    init_m ( );
    clear ( );
    puts ("\n\n\n\n\t Date Conversion Program\n\n");
    for ( ; ; )
    {
        puts ("month : ");
        scanf ("%d", &d.month);
        if (d.month < 1 || d.month > 12)
        {
            puts ("month must be 1 to 12");
            continue;
        }
        strcpy (d.mo_na, m [d.month].name);
        printf ("%s\n", d.mo_na);
        puts ("day : ");
        scanf ("%d", &d.day);
        puts ("year : ");
        scanf ("%d", &d.year);
        if (d.year < 1900 || d.year > 2000)
        {
            puts ("this century!!");
            continue;
        }
        leapy ( );
        d.yearday = day_of_year ( );
        printf ("The day of the year is %d\n\n", d.yearday);
    }
}
```

Figure 8.1: An Exercise in Structures, Arrays of Structures, Multidimensional Arrays and Array Initialization (continues)

```
day_of_year ( )
{
    int i, dy;
    int dt [2] [13];

    dt [0] [0] = 0;   dt [0] [1] = 31; dt [0] [2] = 28;  dt [0] [3] = 31;
    dt [0] [4] = 30;  dt [0] [5] = 31; dt [0] [6] = 30;  dt [0] [7] = 31;
    dt [0] [8] = 31;  dt [0] [9] = 30; dt [0] [10] = 31; dt [0] [11] = 30;
    dt [0] [12] = 31;
    dt [1] [0] = 0;   dt [1] [1] = 31; dt [1] [2] = 29;  dt [1] [3] = 31;
    dt [1] [4] = 30;  dt [1] [5] = 31; dt [1] [6] = 30;  dt [1] [7] = 31;
    dt [1] [8] = 31;  dt [1] [9] = 30; dt [1] [10] = 31; dt [1] [11] = 30;
    dt [1] [12] = 31;

    dy = d.day;
    for (i = 1 ; i < d.month ; i++)
        dy += dt [leap] [i];
    return dy;
}

clear ( )
{
    putchar (12);
}

init_m ( )
{
    int i;

    strcpy (m [0].name,  "");
    strcpy (m [1].name,  "January");
    strcpy (m [2].name,  "February");
    strcpy (m [3].name,  "March");
    strcpy (m [4].name,  "April");
    strcpy (m [5].name,  "May");
    strcpy (m [6].name,  "June");
    strcpy (m [7].name,  "July");
    strcpy (m [8].name,  "August");
    strcpy (m [9].name,  "September");
    strcpy (m [10].name, "October");
    strcpy (m [11].name, "November");
    strcpy (m [12].name, "December");

    for (i = 0 ; i <= 12 ; i++)
        m [1].mon = i;
}

leapy ( )
{
    leap = 0;
    if (((d.year -- 1900) % 4) == 0)
        leap = 1;
}
```

Figure 8.1: An Exercise in Structures, Arrays of Structures, Multidimensional Arrays and Array Initialization.

name of d is declared at the end of the declaration of date. Notice the syntax: } d ;. It assigns the actual storage to a struct of type date, and the structure tag is date.

This structure and the next structure are declared implicitly external to the main block, and are therefore global to the program.

The second structure is tagged month_na:

```
struct month_na {
    int mon;
    char *name [8];
                } m [13] ;
```

It is a structure of the names of the months and their position in the year. The statement

```
    } m [13];
```

declares an array of 13 structures of type month_na. The name of the array is m.

Then the integer leap is declared:

```
    int leap;
```

It is a flag to signal whether the year given is a leap year or not.

On opening, the program initializes the array of month names m by calling the function init_m. After clearing the screen, the program then requests the month, and the function scanf scans the input for a decimal integer, which it stores at the address of d.month:

```
puts ("\n\n\n\n\t Date Conversion Program\n\n");
for ( ; ; )
{
    puts ("month : ");
    scanf ("%d", &d.month);
    if (d.month < 1 || d.month > 12)
    {
        puts ("month must be 1 to 12");
        continue;
    }
    strcpy (d.mo_na, m [d.month].name);
    printf ("%s\n", d.mo_na);
```

scanf must be handed a pointer to the name of the variable it is dealing with. The member d.month is tested to see whether it is a reasonable number. If it isn't, the program grumbles month must be 1 to 12, and the continue statement brings the execution back to the loop.

strcpy copies m [d.month].name (a character array which is a member of the struct in an array of structures of type month_na) to d.mo_na (which is also a character array and is a member of the structure d. Having copied a member of one structure to another, the printf function puts the name of the month on the screen.

Then the day of the month and the year are requested and input through the scanf functions:

```
puts ("day : ");
scanf ("%d", &d.day);
puts ("year : ");
scanf ("%d", &d.year);
if (d.year < 1900 || d.year > 2000)
{
    puts ("this century!!");
    continue;
}
```

The year input is tested by the if statement to see whether it is a reasonable response. If it isn't, the operator is reminded that the year input must be in this century, and the continue statement avoids a backwards goto by throwing the execution of the program back to the loop.

All the data in the program are global, so a call to the leapy function sets the leap year flag one way or the other:

```
leapy ( );
d.yearday = day_of_year ( );
printf ("The day of the year is %d\n\n", d.yearday);
    }
}
```

The day_of_year function calculates the day of the year and assigns the calculation to the member d.yearday. The next printf displays the results.

Going into the functions themselves shows how the calculation is made:

```
day_of_year ( )
{
    int i, dy;
    int dt [2] [13];
```

The day_of_year function starts out by declaring a loop index i and another day variable dy. A two-dimensional array dt of 2 by 13 is declared to house the number of the days in each month. As you can see below, the 0 element has no days in it, so the months will be numbered 1 through 12.

The array is "initialized" by the following mass assignment:

```
dt [0] [0] = 0;    dt [0] [1] = 31; dt [0] [2] = 28;   dt [0] [3] = 31;
dt [0] [4] = 30;   dt [0] [5] = 31; dt [0] [6] = 30;   dt [0] [7] = 31;
dt [0] [8] = 31;   dt [0] [9] = 30; dt [0] [10] = 31; dt [0] [11] = 30;
dt [0] [12] = 31;
dt [1] [0] = 0;    dt [1] [1] = 31; dt [1] [2] = 29;   dt [1] [3] = 31;
dt [1] [4] = 30;   dt [1] [5] = 31; dt [1] [6] = 30;   dt [1] [7] = 31;
dt [1] [8] = 31;   dt [1] [9] = 30; dt [1] [10] = 31; dt [1] [11] = 30;
dt [1] [12] = 31;
```

A few of the larger compilers of C, and of course the full set, initialize variables at declaration. The one I used here does not. Notice the row-major assignment of the array elements, which fills first the rows, then the columns. The two arrays are identical *except* for February. Therefore, the second array, dt [1] [ ], is the leap year array.

The next step is to initialize dy to the number of days in the month that has been input in the main block: which occurs in the dy = d.day; statement:

```
dy = d.day;
for (i = 1 ; i < d.month ; i++)
    dy += dt [leap] [i];
return dy;
}
```

For as many months as the number that also has been input, less one, the for loop reads the days in the month array and increments the days (dy) by the number of days in each respective month. The leap flag is set in the third-to-last executable line of code, and whether leap is 0 or 1 determines which row of the array is to be read.

The initialization of the structure array m is accomplished by the following 13 assignment statements:

```
init_m ( )
{
    int i;

    strcpy (m [0].name, "");
    strcpy (m [1].name, "January");
    strcpy (m [2].name, "February");
    strcpy (m [3].name, "March");
    strcpy (m [4].name, "April");
    strcpy (m [5].name, "May");
    strcpy (m [6].name, "June");
    strcpy (m [7].name, "July");
    strcpy (m [8].name, "August");
```

```
strcpy (m [9].name, "September");
strcpy (m [10].name, "October");
strcpy (m [11].name, "November");
strcpy (m [12].name, "December");
```

Notice the array subscripting:

```
m [1].name
```

not

```
m.name [1]
```

If this were PL/I, the syntax m.name [1] would be perfectly acceptable, but in C the *structure* name must be subscripted. m.name [1] would refer to the second element of the string name of array element zero. This would be a blank when we want January.

The for loop then initializes the month numbers. Through the 13 passes, the month number m [i].mon is initialized to its own index:

```
for (i = 0 ; i <= 12 ; i++)
    m [i].mon = i;
}
```

The leap year function initializes the leap year flag to 0 (FALSE):

```
leapy ( )
{
    leap = 0;
    if (((d.year – 1900) % 4) == 0)
        leap = 1;
}
```

It then gets the last two digits of the year input and modulus divides them by 4. Notice the parentheses in the expression ((d.year – 1900) % 4). The subtraction must take place before the modulus operator takes over. The rules of hierarchy are in action here. The operator % has precedence over the subtraction operator – . If there is no remainder, it is a leap year, and the leap flag is set to 1 (TRUE).

Pointer Referencing of Structures

The program in Figure 8.2 is the same as that in Figure 8.1, but this time the structures are not external to the code and are dealt with through pointers. There is a big difference in the way the structure members are referenced in the functions. Before the program is torn apart and examined step by step, look at it in its entirety. Note the pointer references before the member names.

```
/*
                    S2.C

        an exercise in structures, arrays of structures,
        multidimensional arrays, and array initialization
        through pointer referencing


*/

    struct date {
        int day;
        int month;
        int year;
        int yearday;
        char mo_na [8];
                };

    struct month_na {
        int mon;
        char *name [8];
                    };

    int leap;

main ( )
{
    struct date d;
    struct month_na m [13];

    init_m (&m);
    clear ( );
    puts ("\n\n\n\n\t Date Conversion Program\n\n");
    for ( ; ; )
        {
            puts ("month : ");
            scanf ("%d", &d.month);
            if (d.month < 1 || d.month > 12)
            {
                puts ("month must be 1 to 12");
                continue;
            }
            strcpy (d.mo_na, m [d.month].name);
            printf ("%s\n", d.mo_na);
            puts ("day : ");
            scanf ("%d", &d.day);
            puts ("year : ");
            scanf ("%d", &d.year);
            if (d.year < 1900 || d.year > 2000)
            {
                puts ("this century!!");
                continue;
            }
```

Figure 8.2: An Exercise in Structures, Arrays of Structures, Multidimensional Arrays and
Array Initialization through Pointer Referencing (continues)

```
        leapy (&d);
        d.yearday = day_of_year (&d);
        printf ("The day of the year is %d\n\n", d.yearday);
    }
}

day_of_year (pd)
struct date *pd;
{
    int i, dy;
    int dt [2] [13];

    dt [0] [0] = 0;   dt [0] [1] = 31; dt [0] [2] = 28;  dt [0] [3] = 31;
    dt [0] [4] = 30;  dt [0] [5] = 31; dt [0] [6] = 30;  dt [0] [7] = 31;
    dt [0] [8] = 31;  dt [0] [9] = 30; dt [0] [10] = 31; dt [0] [11] = 30;
    dt [0] [12] = 31;
    dt [1] [0] = 0;   dt [1] [1] = 31; dt [1] [2] = 29;  dt [1] [3] = 31;
    dt [1] [4] = 30;  dt [1] [5] = 31; dt [1] [6] = 30;  dt [1] [7] = 31;
    dt [1] [8] = 31;  dt [1] [9] = 30; dt [1] [10] = 31; dt [1] [11] = 30;
    dt [1] [12] = 31;

    dy = pd->day;
    for (i = 1 ; i < pd->month ; i++)
        dy += dt [leap] [i];
    return dy;
}

clear ( )
{
    putchar (12);
}

init_m (pm)
struct month_na *pm;
{
    struct month_na *pstrt;
    int i;

    pstrt = pm;
    strcpy ((pm++) -> name,  "");
    strcpy ((pm++) -> name,  "January");
    strcpy ((pm++) -> name,  "February");
    strcpy ((pm++) -> name,  "March");
    strcpy ((pm++) -> name,  "April");
    strcpy ((pm++) -> name,  "May");
    strcpy ((pm++) -> name,  "June");
    strcpy ((pm++) -> name,  "July");
    strcpy ((pm++) -> name,  "August");
    strcpy ((pm++) -> name,  "September");
    strcpy ((pm++) -> name,  "October");
    strcpy ((pm++) -> name,  "November");
    strcpy ((pm) -> name,    "December");

    pm = pstrt;
    for (i = 0 ; i <= 12 ; i++)
```

Figure 8.2: An Exercise in Structures, Arrays of Structures, Multidimensional Arrays and Array Initialization through Pointer Referencing

In some respects it doesn't look like the same code as the program in Figure 8.1. This is because the structures are declared outside of the main, but the structs are only a template of what they will look like once they have been assigned. Notice the last two symbols in the declaration };, which indicate that no real assignment has been made:

```
struct date {
    int day;
    int month;
    int year;
    int yearday;
    char mo_na [8];
            };

struct month_na {
    int mon;
    char *name [8];
                };
```

Now we find the lines where the storage of the two structs is assigned:

```
main ( )
{
    struct date d;
    struct month_na m [13];
```

The structure named d is declared as type date and the structure named m is declared an array of 13 structures of type month_na. These two declarations assign the actual storage.

Now, when the month names are initialized, the address of the structure m is passed to the function:

```
init_m (&m);
```

Because the structures are local to the main, init_m has no way of knowing that the structures even exist without a pointer to the address of m.

The month, day, and year are requested and stored in the appropriate addresses of the structure members. These lines are identical to those in Figure 8.1. The next difference occurs when parameters are passed to the leapy and day_of_year functions:

```
leapy (&d);
d.yearday = day_of_year (&d);
```

Both of these functions are passed the address of the structure d by assigning a pointer &d.

pd, the pointer to d, is received by the function and declared as a pointer before entering the block of the function:

```
        printf ("The day of the year is %d\n\n", d.yearday);
    }
}
day_of_year (pd)
struct date *pd;
{
```

The bulk of the day_of_year function is identical to the one in Figure 8.1, but there is one major difference in referencing the structure member. At the end we see the statement

```
dy = pd -> day;
```

We can no longer use the "tag syntax" as we did in Figure 5.1, since the tag cannot be passed to the function. If we want to change the data, the only way to access it is by passing a pointer. The struct pointer operator -> points to a particular member of the structure. In the full set of C, member names of different structures can be the same. If there were a structure of type date named e, e.day would be different from d.day. By changing the value of the pointer pd, pd -> would have different values, depending on the address assigned to the pointer pd.

In a few lines, we will do a lot of pointer arithmetic, and the value of the pointer pm will be altered. To preserve the origin of the array of structures m, a pointer pstrt is declared:

```
            dy += dt [leap] [i];
        return dy;
    }
init_m (pm)
struct month_na *pm;
{
    struct month_na *pstrt;
```

Then pstrt is set to the origin of the array month_na (original value of the pointer pm):

```
    int i;

    pstrt = pm;
```

The string literal "blank" is copied to the structure member name by the function strcpy:

```
    strcpy ((pm++)->name, "");
```

The pointer pm is incremented *after* name is addressed. Because the unary incrementation operator ++ is a step lower in the hierarchy ladder than the pointer operator ->, the expression pm++ must be parenthesized so it is incremented after the system makes the pointer assignment. Note that it is pm++, not ++pm, which would cause it to increment first.

There is not only no *need* to increment the pointer on the last assignment, there is also no place to increment it to:

```
        .
        .
        .
    strcpy ((pm++) -> name, "November");
    strcpy ((pm) -> name, "December");
```

A strong warning: don't ever set a pointer off to "never-never land." Not only will it wreak its vengeance on the CPU, it also will set the logic in your terminal into a fit of schizophrenic paranoia, leaving everything in the system locked up tighter than the gold in Fort Knox.

The m structure pointer then is returned to its original value:

```
    pm = pstrt;
```

In the for loop the member mon is set to the value of the loop index, using the same method of incrementing the pointer:

```
    for (i = 0 ; i <= 12 ; i++)
        (pm++) -> mon = i;
```

As a matter of good programming practice, the pointer again is returned to the origin, pstrt. (Don't try to save an extra line of code or 30 seconds by not picking up the loose ends. If the program were appended at a later date, the first incrementing of the pointer would send it off to Valhalla if it were not reset to the origin of the structure.)

Then a pointer to d, called pd, is passed to the function leap. The pointer is declared immediately:

```
    }

    leapy (pd)
    struct date *pd;
    {
```

The pointer pd is used now to modify year:

```
        leap = 0;
        if (((pd -> year - 1900) % 4) == 0)
            leap = 1;
    }
```

Let's conclude this example with a few notes on programming philosophy. The program in Figure 8.2 could be compressed into 75 percent of the space used by placing multiple operations on a single line and initializing the structures and arrays within the declarations. That would also *not* be good programming practice, particularly for applications programming. Source code must be read by people as well as by the compiler. As programmers, we owe it to ourselves and to other programmers to make the code as understandable as possible. Back in the days of the IBM 1620, with 20K of wired "core" memory, bit saving was a necessity. Today it is unnecessary, and it wastes programming time. The only exception is at the system level, where the overhead (storage requirements) of an operating system, word processor, or compiler crowds the available memory. When doing that sort of programming, be prepared to comment the code liberally. Kernighan and Plauger state boldly on the second page of their book, *The Elements of Programming Style:* "Write clearly—don't be too clever."

UNIONS

The union is a data type designed to hold objects of differing sizes and types. It is a sort of garbage can for unknowns. There is a strong similarity between unions and structures. Both are aggregate data types, and both can contain scalars, unions, arrays, structures, pointers, and so on. The usual purpose of the union is to house data whose type is anticipated but unknown. For example, if a numeric value is to be received, but its data type is unknown, the following union is prepared to house it:

```
union numeric
    {
    int in;
    float fl;
    double dbl;
    } nbr ;
```

The union numeric will now accept anything numeric from 16 bits up to 64 bits.

The syntax of the union is the data type declaration union followed by the union tag, in this case numeric. As in structures, the variables in, fl, and dbl are the members of the union, and the variable nbr, appearing between the end brace and the terminating semicolon, is the union name. The members of the union are accessed as

```
union_name.member
```

or, from the above example,

    nbr.in

The members can also be accessed as the member name modified by a pointer reference:

    pu -> in

The nesting of unions and structures can present a syntactic dilemma in accessing. Take the two structures from Figure 8.2 and incorporate them in a union:

```
union s2
    {
    struct *date;
    struct date
        {
        int day;
        int month;
        int year;
        int yearday;
        char mo_na [9];
        } d ;
    struct *month_na;
    struct month_na
        {
        int mo;
        char *name [9];
        } m ;
    } cal [100] ;
```

What the union cal has accomplished here is an array of type union which will house either the struct date, the date, or the struct month_na.

The union cal, once declared as type s2, creates an array whose element has sufficient room to hold either data of type month_na or type date.

To access a member of the union s2, the following syntax is used:

    cal [idx].m.name [0]

This statement enters the union cal and goes to the array element of cal type s2 specified by the index idx, then goes to the structure m and its member name and gets the first letter of the month name. Symbolically, it looks like this:

    union_name.struct_name.member

A classic use of a union is the header union used by C to define storage for the storage allocator alloc ( ) (the alloc ( ) function is covered in Chapter 13):

```
union header
   {
   struct
      {
      union header *ptr;
      unsigned size;
      } s ;
   } ;
```

This union houses a structure s which is a node. The node contains the size of the block of storage to be assigned, and a pointer to the next node.

Nodes are parts of *data structures*. (This should not be confused with the type struct, which is only a component of data structures in the larger sense.) We have come to the edge of this area of computer science, but we will go no further in this text. When you get into data structures, you get into such subjects as binary trees, B trees, linked lists, and the like. Data structures deal with the allocation and accessing of heap and array storage. They are a science in themselves and have been the subject of many a book. If you are interested in pursuing this subject further, two very good books are *Sorting and Searching* by Donald E. Knuth, and *Data Structures and PL/I Programming* by Moshe J. Augenstein and Aaron M. Tenenbaum.

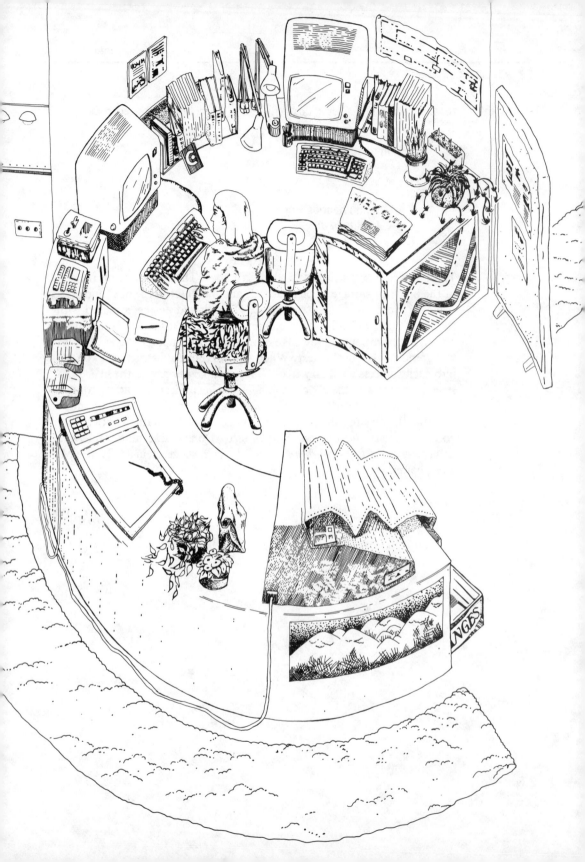

9:

An Overview and Definition of the Language

In the last several chapters, C has been covered piece by piece, from having it come up and say "hello" all the way to file I/O and data structures. It has been a fast and furious trip. Although the language has been defined in bits and pieces, now that you have some concrete knowledge of C, it is time to take a more comprehensive look at the C language as it exists today.

C is available in versions running under CP/M ranging from tiny-c and Small-C to the sets that are fully compatible with UNIX 7. There are C packages ranging in price from $17 to over $600. We will examine many of these versions.

Some C packages are most suitable for hobbyists, but there are also compilers that allow serious C programming. Three compilers have been used to write commercial utilities and compilers themselves. The utilities written in BDS C include operating systems (MARC) and system overlays such as MicroShell.

A strict definition of the C language can be found in Appendix A: "C Reference Manual" of Kernighan and Ritchie's *The C Programming Language*. C's subsets are also valid sets of C, however, as long as they do not change the original definition of the C language.[1] Large function libraries like BDS C's provide a new standard by which to judge C.

The core of C has no I/O other than getchar, putchar, and a few functions. It seems a contradiction for so powerful a language to have so little provision for I/O, but C was created with the UNIX operating system in mind. UNIX has powerful input and output capabilities, including redirection. Redirected I/O allows the operator to direct the flow of data from file to terminal to printer, and so forth, in any reasonable combination.

On the other hand, C's capacity for creating and executing functions has led to an enviable function library, challenged only by the full set of PL/I. This ability to "customize" your own C makes it potentially the most creative language around. To get the I/O capability you need, you need to write the drivers yourself (or copy them from someone like Leor Zolman, who has written many fine drivers and graciously makes them public). Or you can use a utility like MicroShell, which provides the I/O capability for you.

Back to the essentials—here are some C specifics.

IDENTIFIERS

Names or identifiers in C are from six to eight characters in length. Most 8-bit versions accept eight characters. C1-C86, a 16-bit version, accepts long variable names. C recognizes all numeric and alphabetic characters (lowercase letters have a different ASCII representation from uppercase characters). The underscore is also a recognizable character. Most compilers handle names longer than eight characters, but they do not recognize the characters beyond the eighth:

        accounts_payable

and

        accounts_receivable

are all the same to the compiler (but not to the accountant!).

COMMENTS

Comments must be enclosed within the slash/star, star/slash pair /* */, and cannot be nested.

WRITING SYTLE

C is a free-style language. Commands are not restricted to one line. The carriage-return/line-feed pairs in the source code mean nothing to the compiler (BASIC users take note!). A complete command is terminated with a semicolon. It is considered good style in C (as in Pascal and PL/I) to make the best possible use of white space for clarity:

```
if (a <= b)
    funct (a);
else
    funct (b);
```

KEYWORDS

The following identifiers are keywords and are reserved by C. They cannot be used as variables, function names, or constants.

auto	extern	short
break	float	sizeof
case	for	static
char	goto	struct
continue	if	switch
default	int	typedef
do	long	union
double	register	unsigned
else	return	while

COMPILER CONVENTIONS

In a sense, a compiler is a computer language instruction translator. It translates from an English-like set of instructions to an intermediate code, which is usually a form of assembly language. The purpose of the intermediate code is to provide a language for the linker to translate into direct machine language. If you think that this sounds like a difficult task, you are right. It is extremely difficult to make a reliable, efficient compiler and still have it small enough to operate within reasonable memory bounds. By the way, this is why compilers for computers with larger memories and disk capacities seem to offer more and do more. For example, as a rule of thumb 16-bit compilers offer a fuller set of the language and more sophistication than 8-bit compilers.

The compiler needs all the help from the programmer and the program it can get. It reads one "word" at a time and deals with it. The "words" are called tokens. It must examine each token and test that against its own "vocabulary." If the token is a keyword, the compiler will issue a set of appropriate instructions. If it is an operator, it will act accordingly and issue the set of instructions corresponding to the operation. If "words" are enclosed in quotes, the compiler will treat them as strings. What is left must either be an identifier (a variable name) or a constant. Tokens are separated by white space.

The programmers's task is to write code that is understandable to the compiler. This involves following acceptable syntax rules and observing established conventions that the compiler can "live" with.

CONSTANTS

Constants are those values with assigned storage that do not change their value throughout the program. By convention, many are defined by the preprocessor command, #define. There are several classes of constants, as outlined below.

Integer Constants

Integer constants are program-defined constants with integer values. Internally they will be stored as machine-dependent integers. short, signed integers range from − 32768 to 32767, short unsigned integers range from 0 to 65535, long unsigned integers are numbers like 16777215, and so forth. In the C programming language, integer constants can be in decimal (base 10), hexadecimal (base 16), and octal (base 8). Hexadecimal numbers are represented like this: 0,1,2,3,4,5,6,7,8,9,A,B,C,D,E,F,10 . . . and so on. To represent number constants in C, use conventional notation for decimal:

>   32767

In hex the number must be preceded by a 0X or 0x:

>   0XFFF

and in octal it must be preceded by a 0:

>   077777

Floating Constants

Floating constants consist of an integer part, a decimal part, and an optional E or e followed by a signed or unsigned integer exponent. A float constant does not have to have a decimal point. The following are all "legal" float constants:

>   65536
>   30e6
>   − 6.5536E − 6
>   987654321.0

long Constants

long constants are hex, octal, or decimal integers followed by an L or l. They are not implemented in most 8-bit versions of C.

Character Constants

A character constant is any character enclosed within single quotes, such as '0'. It is taken by C to represent the numeric value of the system's character set. For example, '0' is the same as ASCII 030 hex.

   The backslash, in combination with other characters, allows placing the following printable and unprintable character constants into the output stream.

\n	newline
\b	backspace
\f	form feed (new page)
\'	single quote
\0	null
\t	tab
\r	carriage return
\\	backslash (\)
\ddd	octal bit pattern (e.g. \02)[2]

STRINGS

A string is any sequence of characters (including nonalphabetic characters) enclosed by double quotes; for example, "This is a string." Strings are character arrays. They are stored with one more character than the actual characters input, to allow room for the string terminator, \0. It takes a strike of the return (enter) key to enter any input from the keyboard, with the exception of some versions of getchar ( ), which will take one and only one character. As a result, a carriage-return/line-feed pair (r\n\) is entered into the buffer. C removes them from the input string, and if the data are to be stored as a string, replaces the return with a null (\0).

STORAGE CLASSES AND DATA TYPES

Storage classes and data types are discussed in Chapter 3.

OPERATORS

Operators are discussed in Chapter 2.

STATEMENTS

Statements are the executable code in C. Statements can be single or compound. Compound statements are preceded by a left brace and followed by a right brace. Some Cs allow the block delimiters to be begin and end. These versions are atypical, intended for limited keyboards that do not have curly braces.

Expressions followed by a semicolon cause the expression to be evaluated and the results discarded. For this reason, expressions such as

    y – x;

serve no useful purpose without assignments and function calls. In an assignment statement, an expression is evaluated, and the result is assigned to a variable. A function evaluates the expression and does something with the result, such as passing the value of the expression as a parameter. The lesson to be learned here is that you must use expressions in assignment statements or functions if they are to be useful.

A lone semicolon is a null and does nothing other than act as required punctuation in special cases—for example, in the do-forever loop. A do-forever loop is a loop with no built-in termination, such as

    while (TRUE)

or

    for (; ;)

or

    do {
        .
        .
    } while (TRUE)

Because the loop has no terminator it will iterate forever. "Do-forever" loops always have a statement within the loop to direct program flow out of the loop when some specific condition occurs. It is particularly handy to use when you don't know beforehand how many iterations will be required.

Conditional Statements

The simple if

    if (expression) statement

The expression is evaluated to see if the result is nonzero (TRUE). If it is, the statement is executed. (Do not make the mistake of using the assignment operator = in an if expression when the logical == is intended. The assignment operator = would always produce a nonzero result.)

The if else

```
if (expression) statement else statement
```

If the expression produces a nonzero result (is TRUE), the first statement is executed. Otherwise, the second statement is executed. A null else can be used to balance nested if-else statements.

Compound ifs

if and if-else statements can be chained and/or nested in any reasonable combination. else statements in nested if statements are associated with the closest if. Repetitive ifs tend to make code confusing, particularly if there are many associated ifs, as in the following:

```
if red
    goto stop;
if yellow
    goto pause;
if green
    goto go;
```

It's better to handle them this way:

```
if red
    goto stop;
else
    if yellow
        goto pause;
    else
        go;
```

Both do the same task. Frequently a case will do the job even better.

The switch

```
switch (expression) statement;
```

The switch statement causes control to be transferred to any one of multiple statements, depending on the value of the expression. The expression must either be integer or be converted to integer. If the expression matches the value associated with the case labels following the switch, execution transfers immediately to the statement following the switch. If not, the execution of the program goes to the next statement, unless a default label is present, in which case execution is transferred to the statement following the default label.

The case

```
case constant-expression: statement(s);
```

The case is (in essence) a label for the switch statement to go to. The case value must be an integer constant. It can only occur following a switch statement. The statement(s) following the case can be multiple. If there are multiple statements, they are referred to as the statement list. Note that execution will drop down to the next case unless a break terminates the statement list.

Here's an example of a statement list from Leor Zolman's printer driver.

```
case '\n':
    put lptr ('\r');
    put lptr ('\n');
    printno (lineno ++);
    .
    .
    .

    break;
case '\t';
    .
    .
    .
```

The default

The default follows the case list, and if no case match has occurred, it executes. It can only appear once within a case.

```
switch (integer_expression)
    {
    case constant1:
        statement1;
        .
        .
        .
        statementn;
        break;
    case constant2:
        statement;
        break;
```

```
        case constantn:
           statement;
           break;
        default:
           statement(s);
        }
```

The while

The while is one of the three available forms of looping in C. It has the form

```
        while (expression) statement;
```

As long as the expression is evaluated to be nonzero (TRUE), the statement(s) following is executed. The expression is tested *before* the statement is executed.

The do

The do loop has the form

```
        do statement(s) while (expression);
```

The statement is executed repeatedly until the expression is evaluated to be zero (FALSE). The test takes place *after* the execution of the statement.

The for

The for is a loop structure with an index. It has the form

```
        for (expression_1 ; expression_2 ; expression_3)
           statement(s);
```

or

```
        for (initialization ; test ; incrementation) statement(s);
```

expression_1 is evaluated once, at the beginning of the loop iteration. expression_2 is evaluated on each iteration; if it is nonzero, the loop continues. expression_3 is evaluated on each iteration: it is usually a loop index to be incremented or decremented. An equivalent form would be

```
        expression_1
        while (expression_2)
           {
           statement;
           expression_3;
           }
```

The break

The break causes an immediate exit from the containing do, for, while, or switch. Program execution resumes at the statement following the statement block exited. If the statement is nested, execution transfers from the nested statement housing the break into the next statement block. See Zolman's printer driver, on page 106, for an example.

The continue

The continue causes the program to halt execution at the continue and return immediately to the loop statement:

```
while ( . . . )
{
    expression_1;
    if ( . . . )
        continue;
    expression_2;
}
```

In the above example, expression_1 is executed. If the if expression evaluates to nonzero (TRUE), the continue causes the program execution to return to the while loop for testing and then return to expression_1, without seeing expression_2.

The goto

The goto statement has the following form:

```
goto identifier;
```

This causes the immediate transfer of program control to the statement following the label or identifier.

The label

A labeled statement has the form

```
label: statement;
```

It acts as the target of a goto. A label is a form of an identifier and for this purpose they are one and the same.

The return

The return statement causes the program to exit from the containing function and return to the calling block. It has the form

```
return;
```

or

```
return (expression);
```

If the expression is present, it is evaluated and coerced to the data type of the function before being returned. Look at an example of this below.

```
double power (x,n)
int n;
float x
    {
    float xf;
    for (xf = 1; n > 0; --n)
        xf * = x;
    return (xf);
}
```

This example takes integer and float as parameters and returns double. Remember, there is an implicit return at the end of each function.

SPECIAL FEATURES

There are a number of powerful operators that tend to get lost among the descriptions and definitions of the C syntax. They are too handy to be treated as "miscellaneous," so I call them special features.

sizeof

sizeof acts as a function, even though it is a unary operator. It returns as an integer value the size of the expression or variable enclosed in the parentheses following it, and it has the form

```
sizeof (expression)
```

casts

In C, as in many languages, some data conversions are done automatically while other conversions are not automatic and have to be forced (coerced). The cast is the operator that *coerces* the value of the expression it operates on to the data type specified in parentheses. It has the form

```
(type_name) expression
```

For example, if a floating-point number were to be divided by the loop index, it would be divided by an integer,[3] when what is wanted is float division. To coerce the index into float, a cast is used:

```
for (i = 1 ; i <= limit ; i++)
    result = float_nbr / (float) i;
```

A classic use of a cast is

```
sqrt ((double) n)
```

The function sqrt requires that a double-precision number be passed to it. The cast (double) n converts n to a double-precision number.

Those of you who are experienced programmers will appreciate the following uses of cast.

An exemplary use of the cast is to convert the character pointer to allocate the desired data type required by the program:

```
(int *) alloc (n....)
```

casts can get a bit complex, as in

```
(struct a *(*)( ))
```

This coerces a pointer to a function returning a pointer to the structure a. The cast is discussed further in Chapter 14.

PRECOMPILER COMMANDS

The precompiler handles a number of chores before the actual compilation of the program takes place. The precompiler does all the substitution of constants with their actual value, includes all files that the header line requested, does mass substitution of functions defined by macros, and then allows the compiler to translate the "program" (source code) into intermediate code which the compiler proper can deal with.

If you ever doubt for a minute the power of a precompiler, consider the language RATFOR, which is a precompiler translating RATFOR code into FORTRAN code. RATFOR is a very C-like language that neither looks nor acts anything like FORTRAN. The RATFOR "compiler" is in fact a preprocessor, which translates beautiful structured C-like RATFOR into the worst-looking, ugliest FORTRAN imaginable. The catch is that the FORTRAN code runs incredibly well and rapidly, and it allows the use of strings, unheard of in FORTRAN. Thus the power of the precompiler.

The precompiler pass of compilation is the first pass. It recognizes the control character # and reads the command following it, modifying the program accordingly. Here are the commands:

```
#define identifier token string
```

This command replaces each occurrence of the identifier with the token string. In practice, it is used to define constants within the program. When the program is transported to another environment, all that needs to be changed is the token string. This allows all the constants to be changed within the program by making only one physical change to the program.

#undef identifier

This command "undefines." It removes the most recent definition of the identifier so that it can be redefined later.

#include "filename"
#include <filename>

This command appends the text file filename to the front of the program file. It obviates retyping the contents of the file filename for each program requiring the file.

#ifdef identifier

This command causes a conditional precompilation. If the identifier is true (nonzero), then all the code from #ifdef to #endif is acted upon.

#endif

This marks the end of the conditional precompilation begun by #ifdef.

#if expression

This command includes the code after the statement if the expression is TRUE (nonzero).

#else

This command includes or excludes the code after it, depending on the logic of #if expression.

C, as defined in this chapter, in Chapter 2 on operators, and in Chapter 3 on data types and storage classes, is what is considered "C itself." The remainder, the functions, are considered to be "external" to C. Yet how can any person seriously considering learning C as a programming language not consider the entirety of C, including particularly the large group of functions? It is this wealth of functions that has taken C from the language defined by Kernighan and Ritchie to the larger and ever more extensible language we have today. It is these functions that are the subject of the next chapter.

Part Two

The C Functions

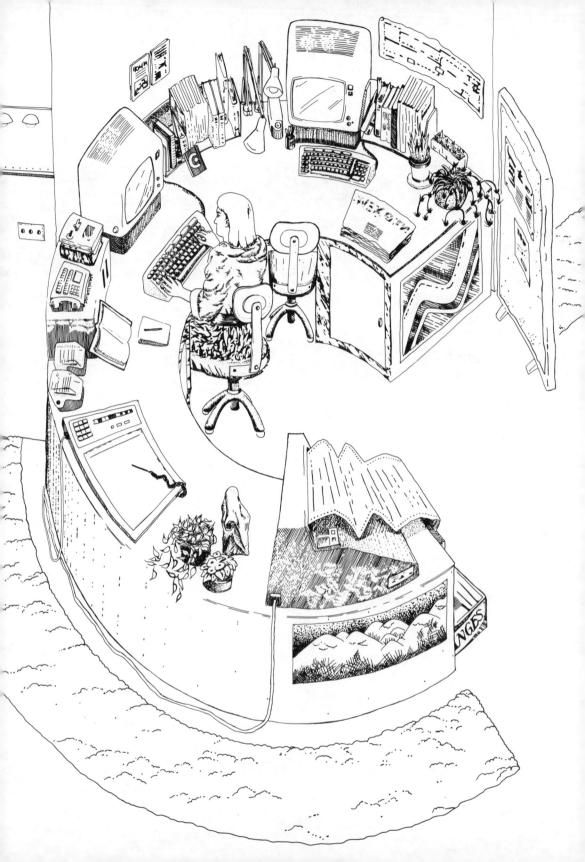

10:

An Introduction to the C Functions
and Function Libraries

Unlike PL/I or FORTRAN, C has not been standardized by ANSI (American National Standards Institute) or any other standards organization. *The C Programming Language,* by Brian W. Kernighan and Dennis M. Ritchie, is the major reference for the C language, because it is written by two of the creators of the C language. The specific definition of the language appears in Appendix A of that book, entitled *The C Reference Manual.* If you look through it, you will find that functions are not included. They are said to be external to the definition of the language. Nonetheless, the functions enumerated in *The C Programming Language* can be quite useful as a guide in determining how closely a particular C package conforms to the original definition of C. The version of C provided by Bell Labs with Version 7 of the UNIX operating system is considered the standard set of C.[1]

The following chapters provide a general overview of C functions available today in the various 8-bit and 16-bit C compilers running under UNIX, CP/M, MS-DOS, MP/M, and related systems. Sixteen C compilers have been examined for this text. When looking at the 8-bit versions of C, remember that all 8-bit Cs technically are *subsets* (a subset being anything less than the full set). All of these subsets still take the definition of C from Kernighan and Ritchie. But because they are subsets and because, being 8-bit, they do not run under UNIX, they have idiosyncrasies of their own. Also, bear in mind that the computer industry is not static, but constantly changing. With the advent of the "personal computer," the standard 8-bit micro with its 8-bit data bus and 16-bit address word is being replaced by computers with a 16-bit data bus and a 24- to 32-bit address word. Sophisticated math processors such as Intel's 8087 further expand the micro, bringing it closer to the mini. That is what the immediate future holds, but let's examine what exists at present.

There are a lot of versions of C out there, and their diversity is evident when their library functions are compared. Unlike other languages, functions in C are not an inherent part of the language. They are housed in a *function library*, and as a group they are referred to as library functions. Thus, when you buy a C compiler, an entire library of functions is included. The functions are readily accessible, and are included in the program only as needed, to permit efficient compilation. Why burden the compiler with an assortment of trigonometric functions, for example, when you are compiling an accounting program? Some versions of C have more functions in their libraries than others, and a quick look at the function library can tell you a great deal about a C compiler. The number of functions you need to use varies with the program application. Some program applications only require a few functions, but other applications need to have a large variety of functions on hand. The versions of C whose functions are described in the following chapters are listed below:

> Kernighan and Ritchie's definition of the language (K & R)
> Digital Research C (DRC)
> Computer Innovations C (CI-86)
> Lattice C
> BD Systems C
> Q/C
> CW/C
> C/80
> Aztec II C
> InfoSoft C
> DeSmet C
> tiny-c
> SuperSoft C
> Whitesmiths C
> Telecon Systems C
> C-Systems C

I have listed the functions common to most versions of C, but omitted most of those that are unique to one or two versions. C is an emerging and extensible language. New library functions inevitably show up with each new version.

The descriptions of the functions given here are provided as a reference only, so don't expect them to substitute for any manual. Because functions vary from version to version and from one compiler author to another, you may find different parameters associated with each function in the various compilers. You should always use the language manual for the version you are using as the definition of your C, and bear in mind that the final arbiter of the language is the compiler itself and its specific function library.

Unlike most other languages, the source code of the library functions is generally furnished on the installation or distribution disk of the language supplied by the vendor. If you can't figure out how a function works, you can list the source code, which is usually quite helpful in clarifying the function in question. Most functions are easy to understand and have been explained in detail by Kernighan and Ritchie. Others—alloc, for example—can be a bit cryptic unless you are familiar with lists and data structures.

One of the joys of the C language is the ease with which functions can be added to the function libraries. Functions can also be rewritten, a relatively common practice among hard-core C programmers. You must always bear in mind that many C functions, such as SuperSoft's, have been copyrighted and have the full protection of copyright law. Most functions are in the public domain, however, and they are there to be used gratefully by all.

Eight-bit versions of C have followed the functions outlined by Kernighan and Ritchie as faithfully as can be expected given their limitations, but there are some limitations that remain on many 8-bit compilers. C, as defined by Kernighan and Ritchie, was designed to run on machines with a minimum word length of 16 bits. This is especially apparent when you encounter such machine-dependent features as long and short integers (because they require more, or wider, CPU registers). Nevertheless, some compiler authors (Leor Zolman of BD Systems, for one) have successfully brought C down to the 8-bit machine, tailoring it to the smaller storage capabilities of the micro. Some of the functions in the 8-bit versions have been simplified. Some functions have even been improved. Moreover, many useful functions have been added. BDS C has been around for so long that it has acquired a certain validity of its own.

For a great many C users and the C Users' Group, it is the *only* C. A great deal of software has been written in BDS C. Many compiler publishers, such as Computer Innovations (16-bit) and SuperSoft (8-bit), have taken great pains to ensure a high degree of compatibility with both the Kernighan and Ritchie set of C and BDS C. In fact, most programs compiled in BDS C or SuperSoft C are compatible, needing only the header changed in the source code.

There is quite a variety among C compilers, which are discussed in detail in Chapter 16. The 8-bit version of Whitesmiths C is as close to the full set as can be found in an 8-bit implementation today. It has *two* function libraries, one that emulates UNIX 7 C, and another that is uniquely its own.

There are a number of small-scale implementations of C, most of them based on tiny-c, which has both a compiler and an interpreter version. Among its offspring are Small-C, Small-C Plus, CW/C, Q/C, InfoSoft C, and C/80. Most of them will handle type integer only.

Among the larger 8-bit Cs are SuperSoft C, Telecon Systems C, and Aztec II C. Some of them support float as well as integer.

As for 16-bit versions of C, those used for this book are Digital Research's C, which is billed as UNIX 7 C with no excuses; CI-86 by Computer Innovations, whose heart is UNIX with just a few atypical functions; Lattice C (also very close to UNIX); Telecon C; and DeSmet C, a surprisingly full set of C for a very low purchase price.

LIBRARY FUNCTIONS AND FUNCTION LIBRARIES

Every installation disk of C has a library of standard functions. They comprise the reservoir for all those C functions that form the "standard" C package. Most versions of C provide the libraries in both source code and relocatable code. The relocatable code has already been compiled into an intermediate code that later will be linked along with the compiled main program to form the final program object code, the command file.

After programming for a while in C, you will notice that you tend to rewrite specific functions which you have created (or borrowed) over and over. The thought will cross your mind: "Why isn't this function a part of the library? It should be." The practice is to include frequently used functions in your own personal library. This can be accomplished in a number of ways, two of which are described below.

Adding the Function to the Main Library Source Code

One method is to use the text editor to bring up the source code for the function library. The new functions are added by typing them in. Then you have to recompile the library source code. Now when the library is linked by the linker, the new functions can be incorporated by the linker into the object code. Do not attempt this technique casually. You should

C Library of Functions

familiarize yourself with the library source code before attempting to add to or modify it.

Adding Functions via a Librarian

Many C packages include a *Librarian*. The Librarian is a utility that allows the programmer to manipulate the intermediate library code. With the Librarian, functions can be transferred, appended, renamed, and deleted. Library utilities vary greatly, so read the documentation carefully before attempting to modify the library.

Writing Library Functions

C library functions don't look very different from the C functions you have already included in your programs. The only noticeable difference (and it is not mandatory) is that the entire function is declared by its data type. For example:

```
int min (a,b)
{
    return (a <= b) / a : b;
}
```

The function to return the lesser of two integers, min, examines the values input as parameters a and b. By use of the conditional expression, min returns a if it is less than or equal to b; otherwise it returns b. Notice that the entire function is declared integer by

```
int min (a,b)
```

which means that the value returned by min will be integer. Another example:

```
int isupper (c)
char c;
{
    return c >= 'A' && c <= 'Z';
}
```

Again the function is declared integer, since the value returned will be TRUE (1) or FALSE (0). The statement

```
c >= 'A' && c <= 'Z'
```

is in essence Boolean, in that it can only give a true or false reply. It is that reply that will be returned. In the description of the string functions in Chapter 12, isupper ( ) is described.

The lines

```
int isupper (c)
char c;
```

constitute the actual code of the function up to and including the declarations of the parameters. This should help you understand what the function receives and returns.

The operators and statements are the heart of C. The arms of C are the functions. These functions have transformed C from a small and somewhat restricted language to a large and nearly universally accepted language. The addition of function libraries and of individual functions to these libraries can change the entire nature of an installed C package. With the addition of transcendental functions and the ensuing trigonometric, logarithmic, and power functions, C becomes a number cruncher. A library with a picture function to create formatted numeric output as part of its printer driver could turn C into a ready-made business applications language.

The modification of function libraries and the creation of your own header files will both extend the C language. Utilizing these two techniques will enable you to make your own unique and powerful version of C. Because C is an extensible language, it is malleable—it can be molded to suit individual needs and requirements.

THE FUNCTIONS

The following chapters discuss the various functions by category. File functions have been omitted because they have been covered in Chapters 6 and 7. Chapter 11 deals with system-specific functions, including those unique to UNIX 7 C. Chapters 12 and 13 concern string functions and memory management functions, respectively. Chapter 14 will present mathematical and miscellaneous functions.

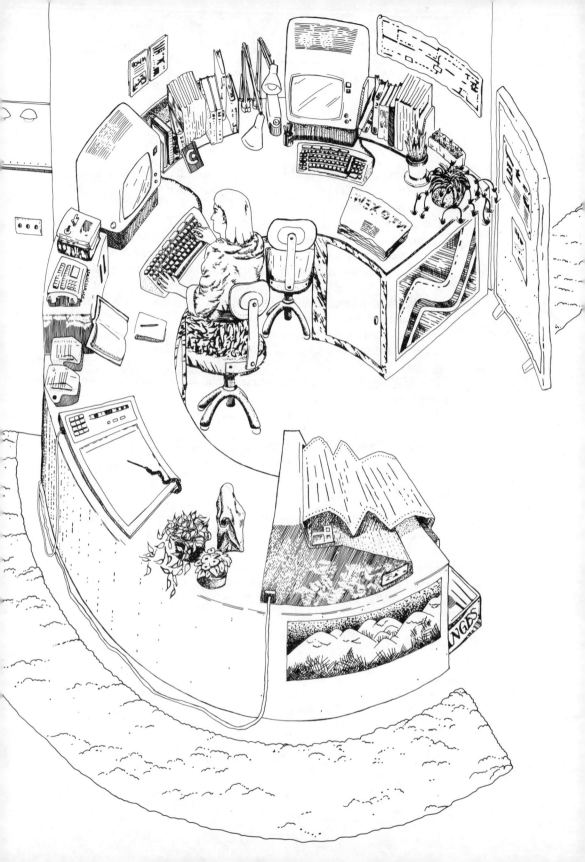

11:

System-Specific Functions

A number of functions exist specifically to interact with the host operating system. The reason that C is called a systems language is because of the ease with which it can interface with operating system primitives,[1] the mark of a true systems language. This is such a valuable feature of the C language that I want to discuss some of the options at length. If you are coming from a high-level language such as BASIC or Pascal, you may not be aware of the scope of systems-level programming. It's a whole different world, offering much more programming power.

Consider a program to write a form feed to a remote printer so that the tear line on the paper will always be positioned just above the print head:

```
/*
        FF.C #1
*/

main ( )
{
    bdos (5,12);
}
```

That is the entire program in C. The program line bdos (5,12) is a direct system call, which we will discuss shortly. Without the use of a direct system call, the program has to look like this:

```
/ *
     FF.C #2
 * /
main ( )
{
int fd;
char *pfile [5]
    strcopy (pfile, "LIST:");
    if ((fd = fopen (pfile), "w")) == 0)
    {
        printf ("Printer not ready\n");
        exit ( );
    }
    fputc ('\f', fd);
    close (fd);
    }
```

Both of these programs accomplish the same task—sending a form feed (page eject) to the printer. They are very different in both appearance and length.

The second program (FF.C #2) has to invoke a number of functions, and this adds a great deal of code. The end result is a compiled program of eight kilobytes to do what could have been done with much less code. The first program (FF.C #1) takes the direct route. Here's where system calls come in handy. The direct system call, bdos (5,12), tells the operating system to perform a BDOS 5 function. BDOS 5 passes a single character to the line printer. The character being passed is an ASCII 12, a form feed.

BDOS FUNCTIONS

Thus, some operations you program can be performed much more efficiently by using the CP/M and MP/M basic disk operating system (BDOS). It is the fastest way to get in touch with the operating system. The function call to BDOS is bdos ( ). BDOS operates by placing the appropriate system call number in the appropriate CPU register, which for this call is the C register. The additional value for this call is placed in the D (8080) or DX (8086) register.

```
int bdos (c,de)
    int c, de;
```

BDOS allows direct BIOS calls. It calls the CP/M absolute location 0X5 after setting the (8080) C register to the value c. The value returned is the same machine word that is found in the HL register pair. The H and L registers are a CPU register pair (Z80, 8080) usually reserved for addresses and returning addresses to calling functions.

Originally there were less than 30 CP/M BDOS functions. The advent of MP/M and Concurrent CP/M caused the list to grow greatly, and it is well on its way to containing a couple of hundred functions. The listing below contains the first 36 functions, from basic I/O through random files. These calls depend on the version number of CP/M.

 0 Warm boot

 1 Console input

 2 Console output

 3 Reader input

 4 Punch output

 5 List (printer) output

 6 Direct console I/O

 7 Get I/O byte

 8 Set I/O byte

 9 Print string

10 Read console buffer

11 Get console status

12 Return version number

13 Reset disk system

14 Select disk

15 Open file

16 Close file

17 Search for first (match file in directory)

18 Search for next (continue to match file in directory)

19 Delete file

20 Read sequential

21 Write sequential

22 Make file

23 Rename file

24 Return log-in vector

25 Return current disk

26 Set direct memory address

27 Get address of allocation vector

28 Write-protect disk

29 Get read-only vector

30 Set file attributes

31 Get address of disk parameters

32 Set/get user code

33 Read random

34 Write random

35 Compute file size

36 Set random file record

Not all versions of C use the BDOS functions per se. Whitesmiths C uses a function called CPM which looks like cpm (bc, be, hl). The HL register is used only by CDOS, an offspring of the original CP/M, Version 1.3. There are also variations on the theme, such as BDS C's bios (n,c) and bios (n, bc, de).

These calls to CP/M and CP/M-like operating systems all operate in the same manner, placing the appropriate integer call to the proper register, placing the data byte (if any) in its register, and then calling the system address to get the disk operating system (DOS) to perform the desired results.

THE SYSTEM FUNCTION

Systems-level programming in CP/M is relatively complex, because it assumes an understanding of assembly language, the CPU registers, and the CP/M absolute jump addresses. Using C to do systems-level programming makes an intimate knowledge of assembly and so forth unnecessary. Most CP/M system calls can be made with only a minimal knowledge of the CP/M operating system. UNIX, on the other hand, requires *no* knowledge of assembly programming—UNIX's approach to system calls is far simpler. The system call function is system, and it operates by placing a character string describing the desired system command as the argument to the function, as in the following example:

'system ("date");'

This is UNIX's date function. You type "date" and the date (mm/dd/yy) is returned from the system clock. The system calls in UNIX are highly specific to the local UNIX operating system, and the system manual should be consulted before making any system calls.

Some of the more standard UNIX calls are the status inquiries:

du   Lists a summation of the space utilized by the files within the file structure hierarchy.

tty   Lists the name of the terminal (port) to which the user's terminal is attached.

who   Lists the individuals logged into the system.

ps   Reports on active system processes.

pwd   Lists the working directory name.

As the micros approach the minis in sophistication, the distinctions between the two classes of computers diminish. The 8-bit micro still abounds, but 16-bit micros are more and more common. Recent versions of CP/M operating systems, like Concurrent CP/M and MP/M, are progressively more UNIX-like, particularly as enhanced by original equipment manufacturers. For example, Gifford Computer Systems has a fine implementation of MP/M called MP/M 8-16. It has many UNIX-like features including individual shells[2] to direct each user area. UNIX-like utilities, such as MicroShell, which offers many extensive UNIX Shell features, are already available for CP/M and MP/M use. Thus, the CP/M family of operating systems is gradually becoming more UNIX-like. Digital Research has its own C for systems-level development, and all future development work will be done in C, thus putting future operating systems and utilities in the same development language as UNIX. It also facilitates a changeover to the 68000 series of processors already realized with CP/M 68K and numerous 68K versions of UNIX. As the operating systems of the micros become more and more like the operating systems of the minis, it is intriguing to ponder what the future will bring. The main advantage of the micro has always been price. If the day comes when super micros can compete with minis, it is interesting to speculate whether some of the mini operating systems will adapt to become more micro-compatible.

UNIX AND UNIX LOOK-ALIKE
SYSTEM FUNCTIONS

Most of the functions in this section are miscellaneous functions. They have two things in common: they are UNIX functions and they interact with the system. Many of them are supported by CP/M as well.

The access Function

The access function checks to see if the calling program can access a specific file. Although under CP/M any file is theoretically accessible if it exists, it may not be accessible if it is declared a system file. The function returns zero if access is allowed. Otherwise it returns a − 1, signifying error.

```
int access (name, mode)
    char *name;
    int mode;
```

The access function checks for four different modes of access:

4 Check read access

2 Check write access

1 Check execute access

0 Check directory path access

CP/M versions ignore argument 0.

The ch Family of Functions

All multiuser systems, and many single-user systems, offer file and record protection. Further protection is offered for access to the entire system as well as for specific disk drives. Some even offer protection to individual record fields. The ch family of functions allows the user to change file protection modes.[3]

chmod

The chmod function changes the access status (permissions) on system files.

As a system call (in UNIX) it is executable only by the "owner" of the file or by the "super-user," the system manager.

```
int chmod (name, mode)
    char *name;
    int mode;
```

chown

The chown function changes the owner identification of a file.

```
int chown (mode, owner, group)
    int mode;
    int owner;
    int group;
```

The exit Functions

No matter what process has been written and called, its execution must eventually come to an end, at which point control is returned to the operating system. The exit function is not as simple as you might think. It is not enough simply to return to the system. Open files must be closed, and memory allocated by the program must be deallocated. If buffered (stream) files have been used, they must be flushed to assure that all the data has been written to disk before disk files are closed.

The ideal situation would include the option of deliberately leaving files opened to "chain" one program to another without losing data. This is possible, and as a result two exit functions are provided, exit and _exit.

exit

The exit function passes control back to the operating system after closing all the open files. Most versions empty stream-file buffers as well. This function receives system-dependent arguments under UNIX. Most versions return no value, but some UNIX-like versions can return a non-zero value to indicate abnormal termination.

```
int exit (value)
    int value;
```

_exit

The _exit function returns control to the operating system without closing open files or flushing file buffers.

```
_exit (value)
    int value;
```

In normal programming conditions, the exit function is used. However, the _exit function is useful for debugging, because it leaves the program data untouched when the program is terminated. The _exit function also allows for "chaining" one program to another, in the sense that BASIC programs are chained with common (a MicroSoft Version 5, BASIC command, that allows a program to run another program, keeping variables common to both programs). Obviously, the programmer must ensure that the data are passed and retrieved.

Password Protection Functions

When programs and processes operate within a multiuser environment, conflict between users is inevitable. As simple a task as updating a record can be a problem when you consider that another user could be accessing that record while it is being updated. For problems such as this, systems and languages interact by locking files and records, in order to prevent untimely access. Another potential problem in a multiuser environment is unwanted entry to processes or data by people who have no "need to know." Deliberate sabotage, for whatever reason, is also possible. To prevent unauthorized access to the process, the operating systems (UNIX, MP/M, etc.) and the C language will protect passwords.

getpass

The getpass function issues the prompt prompt to the screen. It then reads in the password without echoing the keyboard input on the console. The password is a conventional null-terminated string of a maximum length determined by the system (eight in CP/M, MP/M, and UNIX). The function then returns a pointer to the password.

```
char *getpass (prompt)
  char *prompt;
```

Error Message Functions

When you have finally debugged your new program and it compiles, you breathe a sigh of relief. However, that's no guarantee that the program will run. Often you run your newly compiled program only to have it stop in midexecution because of some mistake you made in your code. These errors are called run-time errors. Most languages automatically put error messages on the screen in response to these run-time errors, to let you know where you goofed. Leor Zolman's BDS C has some amusing error messages, such as "totally confused." The humor in BDS C's error messages is one of the few things that can make you laugh when a program falls down (computer parlance for stopping in midexecution). Unfortunately, most error messages are humorless. "Read beyond eof" is the usual fare. Often they are irritatingly cryptic, like "Error 43 in line 12," which doesn't even give you a clue as to what type of error you made. Thus you have to look up Error 43 in the manual, in addition to finding your error in the code. Running your new program and having it fall down is frustrating enough. But an error message that is poorly stated, nondescriptive, or just plain cryptic is really frustrating. If Alexander Pope will forgive me, to err is human; to get a decent error message is divine. Few people who have seen it can forget CP/M 1.8 and 2.2's "BDOS error on A:".

perror

Standard error (stderr) is the C standard file dedicated to outputting reasonable error messages in the event of the program failing. The function perror does the actual writing of the message to stderr.

```
perror (sptr)
  char *sptr;
```

The perror function retrieves the last error from the external variable errno, which contains the last error returned from the operating system. Non-UNIX implementations simulate errno. The error messages returned by the function correspond to the error number. The argument sptr is a pointer to the the string to be printed.

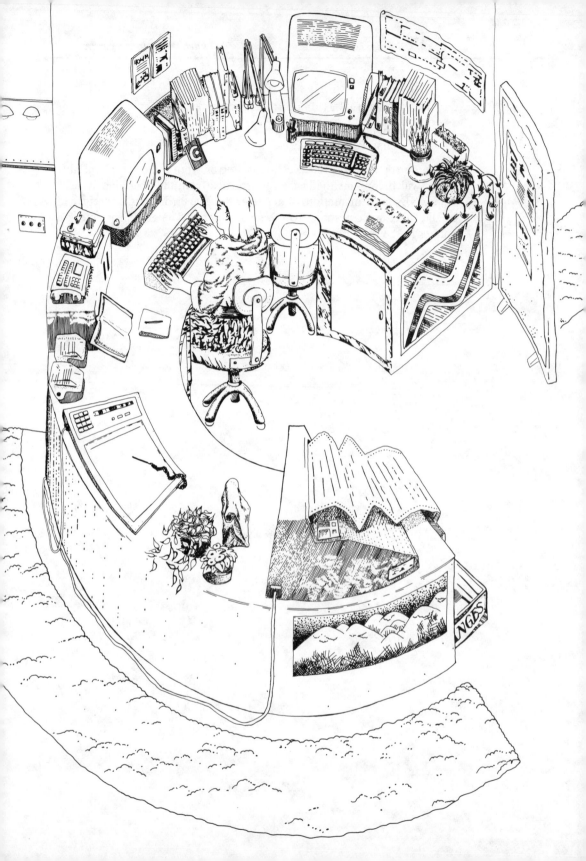

12:

String Functions

A language can be judged by its string functions, because the ability of a computer language to handle strings largely determines its usefulness (with the exception of very specialized programming applications). The reason FORTRAN has failed to hold its place as an applications language is that it has no string functions, lacking even the data type string. RATFOR (rational FORTRAN) was designed to overcome FORTRAN's string-handling shortcomings and to force structure into the language. RATFOR source code is very much like C source code. This is not a coincidence—C was the model for RATFOR.

There is another important point about a language's ability to handle strings, the significance of which may not be obvious at first. A language that handles a string only as a string has intrinsic disadvantages. In order to examine or manipulate a single character in the string, you are forced to rely on special functions to tear the string apart, such as BASIC's LEFT$, RIGHT$, and MID$, or PL/I's substring. C doesn't have this problem because it only handles one character at a time. A group of characters—a string—must be handled as an array of type character. The original Jensen and Wirth (ISO) set of Pascal also handles strings as arrays of type character, but that is where the similarity to C ends. Pascal does not provide for entering a string from an output device as a string, nor does it specify the length, nor demarcate the end, of a string. A string in C is automatically terminated by the null, a \0, by the system. As a result, the end of a string is obvious. Most important, C has exceedingly fine and varied functions and macros to input strings into the system. The gets function gets a string precisely as entered. The scanf functions format string input as effectively as PL/I, and that is very well indeed.

THE *AT* FUNCTIONS

The purpose of the atoi, atof, and atol is to convert alphanumeric (character) data to some form of numeric data type.

atoi

In the following example, the atoi function returns an integer value corresponding to the value of string. Most versions ignore leading blanks or other white space but allow a leading sign (+ or −). Conversion in the AT functions continues until all digits are exhausted.

```
int atoi (string)
    char *string;
```

atof

Like atoi, the atof function converts the ASCII portion of the string that is its argument, but atof returns as its value type double (double-precision floating point). Leading blanks are ignored but signs are not.

```
double atof (string)
    char *string;
```

atol

The function atol converts string to long integer in the same manner as atoi. atol examines its argument and converts each recognizable digit until all have been converted.

```
long atol (string)
char *string;
```

THE INDEX FUNCTION

The string function index is in a class by itself. index is a true string function in its universality. It exists as index in PL/I and pos in extended Pascal. BASIC has no equivalent. The index function tells you the first position in which a particular alphanumeric character exists within a string. It is particularly useful in finding a substring (a string within a string) by locating the first occurrence of its initial character.

```
char *index (string, chr)
    char *string;
    char chr;
```

There is a converse function called rindex that finds the last occurrence of the target character.

C's version of the index function returns a pointer to the location of chr within string. Notice that the argument string is a pointer to the string, a subtle distinction. All strings are character arrays, so if the variable name of the array is used, it is a pointer to the string. If the character does not exist, the function returns a zero.

THE STR FUNCTIONS

C strings, being character arrays, have one large problem. Because C deals with only one character at a time, strings are not single entities but groups of characters. That means that they cannot be assigned to one another the way they can in other languages. Expressions like string1 = string2 are illegal in C. A similar condition exists in Pascal for the same reason. In Pascal one string can be assigned to another only if they are "conformant" arrays, arrays with the same dimensions and a specific function declaration. C overcomes this problem by having a number of specific string functions all prefaced with str.

strcat

The strcat function concatenates (appends) one string to another. As in almost all string functions, string1 and string2 must be pointers to the strings (character arrays) to be appended. The strcat function returns a pointer to the first string.

```
char *strcat (string1, string2)
    char *string1, string2;
```

Some versions return nothing and have this form:

```
int strcat (string1, string2)
    char *string1, *string2;
```

This is a subtle but important distinction. char *strcat allows such expressions as ret = strcat (string1, string2);, where ret is a pointer to the concatenated string created by the function with the declaration char *ret;.

strncat

The strncat function is similar to strcat, except that it concatenates only a specified number of characters from the second string, string2.

```
char *strncat (string1, string2, n)
    char *string1, *string2, ret;
    int n;
```

strcomp

As we've discussed, in C strings cannot be compared directly, just as they cannot be assigned directly, because C deals with only one character at a time. As a result, the expression if (string1 == string2) is illegal. Fortunately, a string function is provided to overcome the problem of comparing arrays of character. The function strcomp compares the two strings passed to it as arguments, string1 and string2. It returns − 1 if string1 is the lesser (i.e., lower in the ASCII collating sequence), 0 if the strings are equal, and 1 if string1 is greater than string2.

```
int strcomp (string1, string2)
    char *string1, string2;
```

strncomp

The strncomp function works the same as the strcomp function, except that it compares the two strings for length, indicated by n number of characters. This is a powerful function in that it acts as a substring function as well.

```
int strncomp (string1, string2, n)
    char *string1, *string2;
    int n;
```

strcpy

In C it is illegal to assign one string to another using the assignment operator. Consequently, the strcpy command is used to "copy" one string to another. Failure to use strcpy, or, more precisely, attempting to use a string-to-string assignment by way of the conventional assignment operator, is one of the most common errors made by new C programmers.

The strcpy function makes a copy of string2 at the string buffer address pointed to by string1.

```
char *strcpy (string1, string2)
    char *string1, *string2, *ret;
```

In the above version ret is the pointer to the first string; in the version below, string1 is.

```
int strcpy (string1, string2)
    char *string1, *string2;
```

strncpy

A variation of the strcpy function is the strncpy function. This function operates the same as strcpy, but it counts only n characters.

```
char *strncpy (string1, string2, n)
  char *string1, *string2;
  int n;
```

strlen

No self-respecting programming language can exist without some form of a string-length function. C's is strlen. This function returns the length of the string pointed to by the pointer string.

```
unsigned strlen (string)
  char *string;
```

FORMATTED I/O STRING FUNCTIONS

The family of formatted string functions deserves special attention. They are an exceptionally powerful tool and save programmers a lot of time and effort. Without these functions, performing the tasks they enable you to do would be nearly impossible. The common feature of formatted I/O functions is the following expression:

```
(format, arg1, arg2,....argn)
```

Here format is a string expression with embedded escape characters. The formatted string function substitutes the arguments for the escape characters in the sequence of the argument list. The escape characters specify the format, which is similar to FORTRAN's or PL/I's format, but with quite a different approach. The output string length and justification are controlled by the escape sequence. The escape or conversion characters convert the arguments:

d   Decimal notation

o   Octal

x   Hexadecimal

u   Unsigned decimal

c   Single character

s   String (a null-terminated C string)

e   float or double to be converted to exponential

f   float or double to be converted to decimal

g   Use %e or %f, whichever is shorter (as in FORTRAN)

The length of the converted arguments and justification are controlled numerically, for example:

%32s	Prints a string of 32 characters right justified, with leading blanks if the input string is less than 32 (33 with \0 included).
% – 32s	Prints the string left justified and padded to the right with blanks if it is shorter than the specified 32.
32.12s	Prints a field of 32 with the string occupying the rightmost 12 positions, preceded by 20 blanks.
– 32.12s	Prints a 12-character, left-justified string within a 32-character field; the last 20 characters of the main field are blanks.

In use, the formatted functions look like this:

printf ("account name %s and number %d\n", actna, actnbr);

FORMATTED OUTPUT—THE PRINTF FAMILY

There are formatted I/O functions to read to or from the console as well as disk and memory. They are among C's most powerful functions. Formatted output is handled by the printf family.

printf

The printf function directs its output to stdout, the standard output (console). Its purpose is to format the output string in accordance with the format specifications embedded within the string and substitute the variables following the string. The format string holds the conversion specifications (escape characters). The number of escape characters or conversion specifications must match the number and type of the arguments. The printf function converts each argument to the format specified in the format string. Most versions of this function return no value, but the versions closest to pure UNIX 7 C (like DRC) return either the number of characters output or, if an error occurs, – 1.

int printf (format, arg1, arg2,...,argn)

fprintf

The fprintf function is the buffer—or stream—output version of the printf function. It allows formatted data to be sent to any file (or device). Because it is a stream file function, the file must be opened in the ASCII mode.

stream is the stream pointer to the file that was opened for output, or to the special values stdout (standard output) or stderr (standard error). With the exception of the added argument stream, the syntax is the same as printf.

```
int fprintf (stream, format, arg1, arg2, ... , argn)
    FILE * stream;
    char * format;
```

Most commonly, the fprintf function is used to format the output to buffered files. The function allows precise formatting and eliminates the task of reformatting the output when the data is again retrieved from the file on its final output. Like printf in the most UNIX-like versions, the function returns the number of characters output. It returns a − 1 on error.

sprintf

The sprintf function formats the function's output before printing it to memory. string is the buffer where the output of sprintf is to be stored. Like all the printf family of functions, the arguments argn are formatted in accordance with the format specification format.

```
int sprintf (string, format, arg1, arg2, . . . , argn)
    char * string;
    char * format;
```

The most UNIX-like of the sprintf functions returns a pointer to the string buffer where the data has been sent. Most versions return nothing. This is no hardship, however: a programmer who is able to specify (declare) the string certainly will be able to get a pointer to the string buffer.

The sprintf function formats the function's output before printing it to memory. The usefulness of this function is often lost on the first reading. The ability to format output as it is being written into memory is the same as when it is being written to a disk file. Once stored in the desired format, there is no need to reformat the data on output.

C has great power to manage memory through the memory allocation functions alloc, calloc, and malloc. Storage can be allocated and freed at the need or whim of the programmer. With this sort of dynamic memory allocation, an entire world of data structures opens up to the programmer. One-way and two-way linked lists, circular linked lists, binary tree structures, and all sorts of sophisticated memory management techniques are available to the programmer just for the effort of learning them. However, to use this ability efficiently, the programmer must first format the data being stored.

Whether data being stored goes to disk file or to memory, the data should always be thought of as a record. The individual values, whether they were constants or variables in the program, are record fields when being stored. The reason for this is that if data is stored as received, it will be packed end to end. The three fields

Edward J. Erxleiben
1 Main Street
San Dimas, CA 91741

will be stored like this:

Edward J. Erxleiben1 Main StreetSan Dimas, CA 91740

It is not impossible to sort out a mess like the above record, but nearly! If the name field, street field, and city/state fields are formatted into fixed lengths with trailing blanks, they can be separated easily when the record is read. If the additional spaces that are added to each field are undesirable, a newline can be appended to each field as the record is stored. Whichever option is used or created, the formatted output functions sprintf and fprintf are there to do the job.

FORMATTED INPUT—THE SCANF FAMILY

Remember the original ground rules of input/output in C: all I/O is character data. What exactly does this mean? The characters come and go from and to stdin (standard input) and stdout (standard output) as unsigned short integers. In the case of ASCII the integers are in the range of 0 to 127 (base 10). Because all input is character data, how can numeric values be entered?

The scanf family of functions is the answer to the problem. The format expected is specified by the function within the program, and when the data are entered, they are converted from character to the specified format by the scanf functions. Like the printf family, scanf comes in three versions: scanf, fscanf, and sscanf.

The scanf function is used with standard input (the keyboard), fscanf with file input, and sscanf with memory input. The scanf family of character-formatting functions use essentially the same conversion characters as printf.

scanf

The scanf function reads the input from stdin, the standard input, and converts the data obtained through the arguments by way of the format string.

```
scanf (format, arg1, arg2, ... ,argn)
   char *format;
   something *args;
```

When using scanf and the scanf family of functions, a major point to consider is that the arguments *must* be pointers. They can be pointers of any type appropriate to the format, but they must be pointers. For string data, the conversion is almost automatic because the name of the string is in reality a pointer to the first element of the character array housing the string. With all other data types, *including* pointer, care must be exercised to be sure that the value used as an argument is a *pointer* to the argument and not the value itself. If the data type is pointer, the value must be a pointer to a pointer. When constructing data structures such as lists and trees, each stored record is called a *node*. Each node contains one or more pointers. These pointers point to the next or last node. When storing them, remember to set a pointer to the pointer. Then you store it by passing it as an argument to the appropriate scanf function.

fscanf

The fscanf function reads characters from the input stream from a file opened for ASCII I/O whether it is a disk file or a device. It then interprets them in accordance with the control (escape) characters in the format string and stores them at the address specified by the arguments. It should now be apparent why the arguments must be pointers.

```
int fscanf (stream, format, arg1, arg2, .. , argn)
   FILE *stream;
   char * format;
   something *args;
```

sscanf

The sscanf function reads and formats its input the same way scanf does. In the case of sscanf, the input comes from a string stored in memory. The string is usually the same string buffer that sprintf wrote. Again, the arguments must be pointers, as must the string and the format.

```
int sscanf (string, format, arg1, arg2, .. , argn)
   char *string;
   char *format;
   something *args;
```

sscanf is useful in reading dynamic memory created by the alloc family of functions. The function is usually used with the help of sprintf, but not always. When transferring your code from pseudocode to C, you should consider the fact that you will have to format the data eventually. It is probably easier in the long run to format it when it goes into the buffer than when it comes out.

THE *TO* STRING FUNCTIONS AND CHARACTER FUNCTIONS

When you program long enough, you become used to the fact that inevitably something must be converted to something else. Related to the AT family (atoi, atol and atof), the TO family converts from uppercase to lowercase and lowercase to uppercase. They are among the easiest of C functions to write, usually consisting of a single line of executable code.

tolower

The function tolower returns the lowercase equivalent of c if it is uppercase. If it is not uppercase, it returns the character.

```
int tolower (c)
    char c;
```

toupper

The function toupper returns the uppercase equivalent of c if it is lowercase; otherwise it returns the character (argument).

```
int toupper (c)
    char c;
```

THE *IS* FAMILY OF FUNCTIONS

The IS family of functions tests the characters that are the functions' arguments to see if they are some specific class of character. There are over a dozen and a half IS functions existing in one compiler or another. These functions are useful for writing filters. Any program that must test the I/O stream for a particular class of character can make good use of these functions.

The general form of the functions is this:

```
int issomething (c)
    char c;
```

Depending on the implementation, the form may be this:

```
BOOL issomething (c)
    char (c);
```

The function returns 0 if the argument is a member of the class in question. It returns a 1 if the argument is not a member of the class in question. Many programmers and compiler writers who have come to C from Pascal have come to enjoy the convenience of Pascal's data type BOOLEAN. The data type has only two members, T for true and F for false. As a convenience, some versions of C have a class BOOLEAN as well. TRUE is defined as 1 and FALSE as 0 when using BOOL.

Here is a synopsis of some of the IS functions:

isalnum (c)	Tests for alphanumeric characters.
isalpha (c)	Tests for alphabetic characters.
isascii (c)	Tests for ASCII characters.
issatty (fd)	Tests the file descriptor to see if it is a terminal.
iscntrl (c)	Tests for a control character.
isdigit (c)	Tests for a digit.
isfd (fd)	Tests to see if fd is a valid file descriptor.
isheap (ptr)	Returns TRUE if the pointer points to a data area returned from malloc.
islower (c)	Tests for lowercase alphabetic characters.
isnumeric (c)	Like isdigit, tests for a valid digit.
isprint (c)	Tests for printable characters.
ispunct (c)	Tests for punctuation characters.
isspace (c)	Tests for a white-space character.
isupper (c)	Tests for uppercase alphabetic characters.
iswhite (c)	Tests for white space, like isspace.

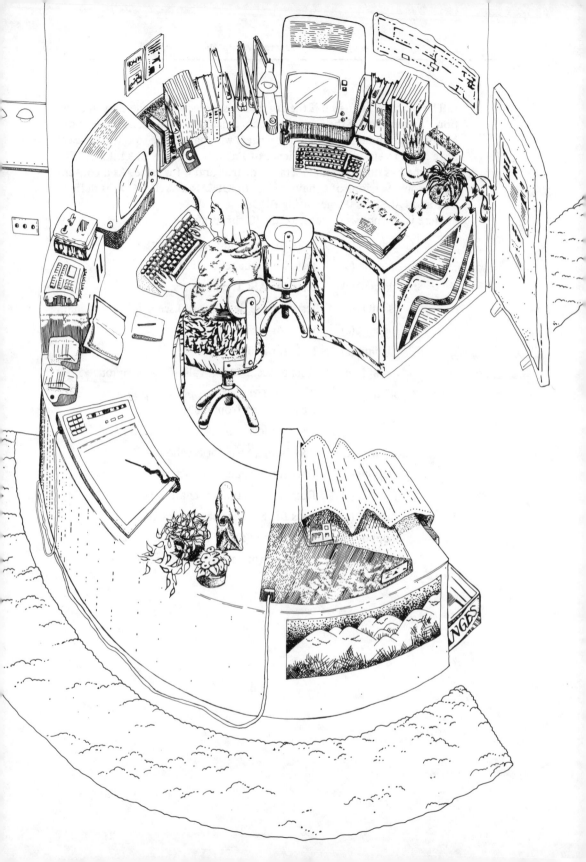

13:

Memory Management, Numeric, and Miscellaneous Functions

MEMORY MANAGEMENT

If a program is to handle data, it must be able to manage memory. Simple scalar variables and constants are stored at specific locations in memory, in an area called the data area or data segment, which is directly above the program or code area. A form of aggregate storage is allocated for arrays, which are stored there as well in some versions, but primarily for arrays of scalars.

The *stack*, the area where the CPU directly accesses memory, is located at the very top of high memory. The stack gets its name from the fact that variables are pushed onto the stack and popped off at the convenience of the direct register functions. There are no addresses, and therefore no pointers, within the stack. Like dishes stored on a shelf, the first ones in are the last ones out. The stack never handles mass storage (for the same reason that we would not attempt to stack 65,535 dishes in a single stack on a single shelf). Stack storage is used, for example, when a DOS function call, which uses most of the CPU registers, is about to be made. The contents of the registers are pushed onto the stack before the call is made, to preserve the register contents. Once the call has been made, the old register contents are popped off the stack and loaded back into the registers.

Directly above the program data area but well below the stack is the *heap*. Both the stack and the heap may increase in size. The stack grows down towards the heap, and the heap grows up towards the stack. The area separating them is most often called the *moat*, and is usually a few kilobytes in width. In programming languages like BASIC, FORTRAN, and COBOL there is no heap. Pascal, PL/I, and C use heap storage.

The alloc Family of Functions

The alloc family of functions requests space from the the operating system, specifically from the heap. The request for storage is not a simple matter of asking for a piece of contiguous storage. Not only may alloc be used directly by more than one call to the function, but other functions may call alloc as well. As a consequence, alloc may be called from many different points in the program, thus cutting up the heap. The heap may also be freed, by the free function. alloc must then look for the next open storage area within the heap. In practice, alloc allocates blocks of storage in the order of increasing addresses (remembering that the heap grows *up* while the stack grows *down*).

alloc

The alloc function allocates a region or block of size bytes in length on the heap.

        char *alloc (size)
            unsigned int size;

Some versions fill the allocated area with zeros. All versions return some sort of error when there is no more space left to allocate, either 0, −1, or printing a message to the console and exiting to the system. Running out of heap space is a "macro-disaster." If the entire stack has been allocated, then an enormous amount of data will be lost when the program crashes. The K & R versions of this function return 0 on failure. This allows you to save the data by creating a salvage routine. For example:

        if (alloc (BLOCK_SIZE) == 0)
            savedat (block);

There is more to the alloc family of functions than just alloc. malloc allocates heap storage, calloc allocates storage for arrays, and realloc changes the block size.

malloc

The malloc function sets aside a region of the heap of size bytes in length. The region is not filled with zeros. The starting address is returned if the function is successful. A 0 is returned if the attempt to get a block of memory fails.

        char *malloc (size)
            unsigned int size;

It is wise to remember that if the storage is not filled with zeros (or blanks), as it will not be with malloc, whatever computer garbage that was in memory before the program was called will still be there, whether it be fragments of text, source code, or the compiler. Accessing garbage-filled data can cause unpredictable results. The programmer must guard against this by deliberately filling allocated memory with zeros or blanks before putting in new data.

calloc

The calloc function allocates contiguous memory or elements by element_size. It is useful for arrays and array-like structures where continuity of memory is required. Some versions automatically fill memory with zeros. The starting address of the area is returned by the function unless the space is not available, in which case a 0 is returned.

```
char *calloc (elements, element_size)
    unsigned int elements;
    unsigned int element_size;
```

realloc

Once the size of the area or block has been created by alloc, calloc, or malloc, it is not absolute. The function realloc can diminish the size of the allocated area. The realloc function increases or decreases the size of the block of (heap) memory to the size specified by size while preserving the address and contents of the beginning of the block.

```
char *realloc (old_bk, size)
    char *old_bl;
    unsigned int size;
```

If a second call to alloc, malloc, or calloc were made, in order to increase the size of the heap area devoted to your data, the data stored there would be destroyed, thus the usefulness of realloc.

The realloc function returns the address of the newly allocated region (which is the same as the old block). It returns a zero if the attempt to create a new block is unsuccessful.

free

Allocating storage for dynamic memory is only half the battle. To take full advantage of memory being dynamic, the heap must be capable of being freed. The free function is used to free a portion of storage within the heap previously allocated by alloc, malloc, calloc, or realloc. The storage returns to the heap, making it available for further heap activity. The pointer that is the argument to free is the starting address of the region allocated. This function returns nothing in most versions.

```
int free (pointer)
    char *pointer;
```

The brk and sbrk Functions

brk

The alloc family of functions works within the heap allocating storage while free frees it. Once all the available storage has been used, then what do you do? What you need then is a function to get more storage from the system to use for the heap. The functions brk and sbrk work within the system to extend the heap. The brk function sets the upper bounds of the program to an absolute address.

```
RESULT brk (ptr)
    char *ptr;
```

The sbrk function extends memory as necessary.

In UNIX terminology, the upper bound of the program is called the break. The brk function extends the upper bounds of the program to the address pointer by the pointer ptr. The brk function returns a 0 if successful, a −1 (error) if not.

sbrk

The sbrk function extends the program storage area by size number of bytes. It then returns a pointer to the extended area.

```
char *sbrk (size)
    unsigned int size;
```

Most C implementations do some very heavy housekeeping to be sure that as the heap storage grows upward into memory it will not overwrite the stack, which is of course growing down towards the heap. As mentioned earlier, many of the functions are "incestuous" in that they call other functions. malloc calls sbrk when there is insufficient memory in the heap.

Non-UNIX Functions

A number of the versions of C inundating the market have unique memory management functions that, although not original UNIX 7 C, are useful nonetheless. The following are some of the available non-UNIX functions:

rbrk   Resets the memory break point to its original point of origin.

ubrk   Seeks an area of a specific size and returns a pointer to it.

evnbrk   Like sbrk, except the pointer is always an even value (the rightmost bit is zero).

topofmem   Returns a pointer to the byte beyond the program's external data area.

wrdbrk   Like all the brk functions, wrdbrk returns a pointer to an area of a specific size. The difference is that wrdbrk uses a size specified by an unsigned integer, and therefore cannot free any of its memory.

NUMERIC FUNCTIONS

A programming language's maturity can be accurately judged by two criteria: its string-handling ability and its ability to handle floating-point math. C has a rich and ever-growing set of numeric and transcendental functions. Although these sets of functions are no match for FORTRAN's, they are large enough to be the envy of Pascal's function libraries, allowing C to work very well as an applications language.

An examination of some of the math functions illustrates this point. Because C was created on the DEC PDP 11 series of minicomputers, the language used very wide numeric "words" (16 to 32 bits is the standard word size for minis, and the usual length for type long and type float is 32 bits. The usual length for type double is 64 bits).

Early versions of C for 8-bit micros were restricted by the inability of 8-bit CPU registers and 16-bit addressing words to handle double. Integer was therefore the standard–and only–numeric type in 8-bit Cs. With Intel's 8086/8087 processors and Motorola's 68000 (68K), the limitations of 16-bit words were eradicated. The 8087 math processor chip, which handles 80-bit words, is designed to coprocess with the 8086 CPU, enabling the micro to compete with the maxis. Even without the aid of the math processors, 16-bit processors deal in 32-bit words, and double-precision numbers are in the range of 64 bits, which is more than enough accuracy for the majority of computations.

C's floating-point math functions all automatically convert the arguments into double precision and return type double. This guarantees that the

returned results of a function will not be unnecessarily truncated. Trigonometric functions in C accept the arguments in radians, as they do in most
languages. (Note that in many versions, particularly UNIX 7 C, the header
file math.h must be "included" to take advantage of the math functions.)

Trigonometric Functions

atan

The atan function returns the trigonometric arc tangent of the argument
val. val is returned in radians.

```
double atan (val)
   double val;
      or
   float val;
```

tan

The tan function returns the trigonometric tangent of the argument val
(which must be expressed in radians).

```
double tan (val)
   double (val);
      or
   float (val);
```

Other Trigonometric Functions

The remainder of the trigonometric functions are straightforward and self-
descriptive, all taking their arguments in radians:

double sin (val)	Returns the sine
double cos (val)	Returns the cosine
double asin (val)	Returns the arc sine of the argument
double acos (val)	Returns the arc cosine of the argument

Logarithmic Functions

Aside from the trigonometric functions, the balance of the C double-
precision functions deal with logarithms, powers, and roots, which in the
mathematical sense are different sides of the same coin. The log functions
return either the natural log (base e) or common log (base 10).

log

The log function returns the natural log of the argument value.

```
double log (value)
    double value;
```

log10

The log10 function returns the common log of the argument value.

```
double log10 (value)
    double value;
```

Power and Root Functions

pow

The pow function returns the value of x raised to the y power. The function returns 0 if both x and y are 0 or if y is negative and is not an integer.

```
double pow (x, y)
    double x;
    double y;
```

sqrt

The sqrt function returns the square root of the argument val. The function will return 0 if the argument is negative.

```
double sqrt (val)
    double val;
```

More and more brand new versions of C are appearing at this writing. At the same time, established versions of C are expanding and refining their capabilities. As a result, more float functions are bound to appear, which is good news for users of 8-bit versions of C.

MISCELLANEOUS FUNCTIONS

The most prolific author in history is "anonymous" and the most frequently used category is "miscellaneous." In this section we deal with the inevitable miscellaneous category of functions.

Sort Functions

Sort routines come in all flavors and sizes. Sorting is so important in handling data that entire books have been devoted to the subject (for example,

Sorting and Searching, by Donald E. Knuth). Simple bubble sorts do a reasonable job of sorting variables stored in an array if the amount of data is very small. The Shell sort and the slightly more sophisticated Shell-Metsner sort are efficient enough to handle slightly larger amounts of data. If you need to sort much larger groups of data, you need the sophistication of quick sort. The price of sophistication is that the quick sort is not the easiest algorithm either to grasp intellectually or to code.

qsort

C has a built-in sort function called qsort. It is a quick sort:

```
int qsort (base, number, size, compare)
    char *base;
    int number;
    int size;
    int *compare ( );
```

The programmer supplies a vector of elements and a function to compare the elements within the vector. base is the base address of the element vector. number is the number of elements to sort. size is the size of the elements (in bytes). compare is the address of the comparison function.

Process Assignment Functions

tty

It is useful, particularly in a multiuser environment, to be able to determine which console a process is assigned to. The ttyname function enables the program to get the filename of the console or device assigned to an open fd (file descriptor).

```
char *ttyname (fd)
    int fd;
```

The ttyname function returns a pointer to the null-terminated string that is the file name of the device associated with the file descriptor used as the argument to the function. For example, in CP/M, if the program were using the console (stdin) for its I/O, the ttyname function would return a pointer to CON:.

Random Number Generators

Random number generators are alleged to generate random numbers. They in fact generate pseudo-random numbers, because whatever the seed fed to the generator, it always produces the same corresponding number.

To generate anything close to a random number by the usual tortuous route of passing a seed through a number of transcendental functions and returning the leftmost part of the result, the seed itself must be random.

srand

Random number generators must be *seeded,* that is, they require a number to be input to the function, which the function will alter and then output. The srand function seeds the random number generator with the argument seed.

```
int srand (seed);
    int seed;
```

rand

The rand function returns a pseudo-random number once rand has been initialized by the function srand.

```
int rand ( );
```

The swab Function

Although there are 200 to 300 unique C functions just among the 16 or so versions reviewed for this book, the last function we will discuss in this chapter is similar to a memory function in that it copies the contents of one area of memory to another.

swab

The swab function copies nbytes of data from the source buffer, whose address is pointed to by from, to the destination buffer pointed to by to. In 16-bit, 32-bit, and 24-bit addresses, memory is allocated in even-numbered increments. The number of bytes, nbytes, must therefore be an even number, to avoid overlapping memory boundaries.

```
int swab swab (from, to, nbytes)
    char *from;
    char *to;
    int nbytes;
```

The DRI C version of swab swaps the high with the low order bytes. This function allows the 8080 family of Intel processors to transfer data within memory to the 68000.

Part Three

Practical Applications

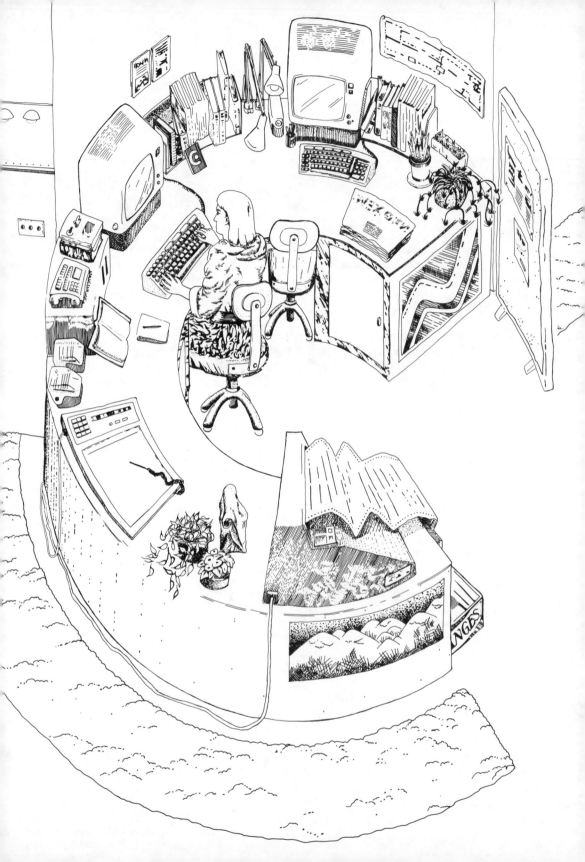

14:

Number Crunching

Number crunching, the mathematical manipulation of numbers, always has been the forte of high-level languages. FORTRAN was born for no other purpose; its name is derived from FORmula TRANslator. C began as a mid-level language, and as we know it today, as UNIX 7 C, it has enviable power as a manipulator of numbers.

DATA TYPES FLOAT AND DOUBLE

The first hint of C's power to calculate is the presence of floating-point single-precision (type float) and floating-point double-precision (type double) numbers. Floating-point single-precision numbers are generally 4-byte (32-bit) numbers, while floating-point double-precision numbers are generally 64-bit numbers. Their internal representations depend on both the machine and the compiler used. Typically, single-precision numbers devote three bytes to the mantissa, while double-precision numbers devote seven bytes. The last byte is used for the exponent. The scale and precision are usually transparent to the user, because the user needs to know only that float will handle most of the floating-point and exponential-notation problems.

Double precision is used where very large, very small, or extremely accurate numbers are needed. When numbers are raised to powers, particularly to the third power and larger, double should be used to prevent underflow[1] or overflow to the result of the exponentiation.

It is particularly important to note that all floating-point arithmetic in C is carried out in double-precision (Kernighan and Ritchie, Appendix A, 6.2). All C functions use double rather than float. Therefore, if there is any doubt in your mind whether to use float or double, use double. Also remember that C functions return double, not float. If you want float returned from a standard number function, you will have to declare the function as float.

Both float and double can be input or output as "straight" decimal or as exponential. The I/O will be determined by the format used in scanf ( ) and printf ( ), not by the data type:

Program Statement	Data Type	Output
printf ("%f", large)	float	decimal
printf ("%lf", huge)	double	decimal
printf ("%e", large)	float	exponential
printf ("%le", huge)	double	exponential

Note the use of the l (el) modifier for long float or double.

float takes on the familiar form of a decimal number or a number with exponential notation. Here are π and *e:*

$\pi = 3.1415927$

$e = 2.7182818$

Exponential notation has the form

11.5e + 6

For the curious, this number is the torsional modulus of carbon steel. Exponential notation relieves you of the problem of losing precision with very large or very small numbers, and assures that the right number of zeros is added. The above number, known as G among mechanical engineers, would be written by a computer as

11500000

when what a human would want to see is

11,500,000

Another problem with very large or very small numbers is truncation. A little later in this chapter a coil spring will be designed, and a small number will have to be taken to the third and fourth power. If the number were .012 (and it often is) its cube would be .000001728. The machine will more than likely represent the number as .000002 if float rather than exponential is used, a loss of 11 percent accuracy. Consequently, the use of exponential (scientific) notation is important in scientific and mathematical programs, as you can see.

USING THE *CAST*
FOR DATA TYPE COERCION

Another proof of C's usefulness for numeric manipulation is the cast operator. Each language has its rules for converting data within an expression. To avoid unpredictable results, the safest rule is to declare all numbers to be of the same type whenever possible. (There are times when doing so is impossible, as when dividing a floating-point number by the loop index.)

When unable to do so, you must force, or *coerce*, the change of data types. In its simplest form, a number can be coerced by assigning it to a variable of the type desired, as in the following example:

```
int inbr;
float fnbr;

puts ("input integer : ");
scanf ("%d", &inbr);
fnbr = inbr;
printf ("\nthe number is % – 9.2f\n", fnbr);
```

The data type always will be that of the lvalue. In this case inbr is coerced to the data type float by being assigned to fnbr. This type of coercion is confusing, in that it generates an extra line of code and creates another variable, making the code hard to follow. You never want to create what Dr. Hogan calls "write-only" code (programs written so that they run, but are impossible to read). To avoid this problem, perform coercion by using the cast operator. The expression

```
(float) inbr
```

is a cast. The type name, here float, is parenthesized and precedes the expression to be converted. Taking the example above, the line

```
printf ("\nthe number is % – 9.2f\n", (float) inbr);
```

uses the cast to convert the integer inbr to float without using an intermediate variable.

FORMATTING NUMBERS

Since you have already seen printf ( ) and scanf ( ) used, this is a good time to look at them again, particularly scanf ( ). BASIC and other high-level languages input numeric data almost automatically by data type. In BASIC, for example, the statement

        INPUT "ENTER NUMBER"; NBR

expects a single-precision number. C's low-level I/O functions are getchar ( ) and putchar ( ). Their very names tell you that they aren't going to accept a floating-point number. To avoid a proliferation of functions such as getdec ( ), getfloat ( ), and getdouble ( ), as well as to allow formatted I/O, the formatted print and scan functions were created. The scanf function "scans" the standard input for data conforming to the formats in its control statements. It then puts these data, in the proper format, into its arguments:

        scanf (control, arg1, arg2,... argn)

Its form allows you to put the expected data format into the control statement, and the data will be put into the addresses specified by the arguments. The arguments must not be variables; rather, they must be the pointers to addresses of the variables. So the sequence

        puts ("input name and number");
        scanf ("%s, %d", name, &nbr);

uses "%s, %d" to format a string and an integer respectively, and it assigns the data to the pointers name and &nbr. Remember that a string-array variable name, such as name, *is* a pointer and does not have to be preceded by the address operator &. The integer variable nbr is not a pointer, and therefore *must* be preceded by & to become a pointer.

Here's a quick review of the conversion characters for formatted input:

    d   Decimal integer

    o   Octal integer

    x   Hexadecimal integer

    h   Short integer

    c   Single character (same as %ls)

    s   String

    f   Float

It's important to remember that the types d, o, and x must be preceded by the letter l (el) if they are pointers to type long rather than type integer.

The type f (or float) must also be preceded by the letter l if it is to be double precision.

Formatted output functions such as printf use similar conversion characters, with the addition of the following:

u   Unsigned integer

e   Exponential notation ($\pm$ i.ddddddddd E$\pm$ xx, where i = integer, d = decimal fraction, x = exponent)

f   float ($\pm$ iiiii.dddd)

g   Use e or f, whichever takes fewer bytes, as in FORTRAN

Type e (exponential) must be preceded by the letter l if it is to be double precision.

The conversion characters may be modified by the use of a minus sign to signify left justificaton; otherwise, output defaults to right justification. A number preceding the character specifies the width of the output field and a decimal fraction .dd, the width of the string output of decimal fractions. The conversion sequence

%–64.12s

will output 12 characters left justified in a field of 64 characters, like this:

abcdefghijkl   *

The spaces from the l to the * are all blanks. More pertinent to numbers, the conversion sequence

%–9.3f

will output a left-justified, floating-point number of a scale of nine with a decimal fraction of three numeric characters, like this:

123456.789

STANDARD DEVIATION

Now is as good a time as any to put formatted output to use. In statistics, standard deviation formulas are used to measure deviation of data from a calculated mean or average. While the computations for standard deviation are not particularly complex, they are tedious, and well suited for programmed calculators or computers. The standard deviation formula calculates how much the elements of a sample deviate from the average or mean. The spread, or asymmetry, of the sample is the variance. The average is called the sample mean.

The algorithm for a program to compute standard deviation is as follows:

```
do forever
    input number (to array)
    sum (total) number(s)
    test for break
    end do
average = sum / number of entries

do while numbers in array
    x = array number − average
    square = square + x_squared
    end do

variance = square / number of entries less one
variance = 100 * variance + 5 / 100
standard deviation = ((square root (variance)) * 100 + 5 / 100
print number of entries, average, standard deviation, and variance
```

The program to calculate standard deviation appears in Figure 14.1. Now to tear it apart. Here for the first time is a new character in our "cast of characters," double:

```
double nbr [MAXINT], sum, sqr, avr, var, stddev, x;
```

double declares that all the variables following it are to be floating point, double precision. A number of these variables could just as well be float (single precision). Because you do not want to have to coerce them later, it is best to declare them as double now.

The next line is a multiple assignment:

```
sum = sqr = n = 0;
```

Because C performs assignments from right to left, a multiple assignment like this is not only legal but downright handy.

Next you enter what is essentially a do-forever loop, by looping from one to MAXINT (MAXINT is the language's maximum integer, which is also the maximum number of entries allowed):

```
putchar (CLEAR);
puts ("\n\n\n\tStandard Deviation\n\n\n");
puts ("input −9999 to exit \n");
for (i = 1 ; i <= MAXINT ; i++)
{
    puts ("\nnumber :");
    scanf ("%f", &nbr [i]);
```

Notice the convention of putting everything defined as a constant in uppercase. This makes finding constants and understanding them easier. The
scanf function is looking for a floating-point number to put in the address
&nbr [i]. Again, remember that scanf ( ) requires that the argument be an
address or pointer to the variable that holds the number.

```
/*

                    SD.C

        standard deviation, average, and variance

*/

#include <stdio.h>
#define CLEAR OXOc
#define MAXINT 128
main ( )
{
    int i, j, vara, n;
    double nbr [MAXINT], sum, sqr, avr, var, stddev,x;

    sum = sqr = n = 0;
    putchar (CLEAR);
    puts ("\n\n\n\tStandard Deviation\n\n\n");
    puts ("input -9999 to exit \n");
    for (i = 1 ; i <= MAXINT ; i++)
    {
        puts ("\nnumber :");
        scanf ("%f", &nbr [i]);
        if (n [i] == -9999)
            break;
        sum += nbr [i];
    }
    n = i;
    avr = sum / ((double)n);
    for (i = 1 ; i <= n ; i++)
    {
        x = nbr [i] - avr;
        sqr += x * x;
    }
    var = sqr / ((double)n - 1);
    vara = (100 * var + 5) / 100;
    stddev = ((sqrt(var)) * 100 + 5) / 100;

    puts ("\n\n\n\n");
    printf ("number of entries : %d\n\n", n);
    printf ("average : %f\n\n", avr);
    printf ("standard deviation : %f \n\n", stddev);
    printf ("variance : %d", vara);
}
```

Figure 14.1: A Program to Compute Standard Deviation, Average, and Variance

Then the number input is tested for the flag – 9999 to see if the operator wants to terminate input:

```
if (n [i] == -9999)
    break;
sum += nbr [i];
```

The numbers are added, and the sum of all the numbers input is put into sum. The += operator saves the tedium of writing sum = sum + nbr [i].

Because the index i is going to be reinitialized, the value is saved to n, the number of entries, and therefore the number of items in the sample:

```
}
n = i;
```

Now the cast operator shows up for the first time:

```
avr = sum / ((double) n);
```

n, the number of numbers entered, is an integer. It *must* be of type double to divide the double-precision variable sum. The cast

```
(double) n
```

performs the conversion without creating an intermediate variable.

```
sqr += x * x;
```

C has no exponentiation operator like BASIC's X ^ N or FORTRAN's X**n. There are power functions such as

```
sqr = pow (x,2)
```

but it takes less time to type x*x, and the program will run much faster if it doesn't have to call an internal routine, which in turn will have to call log functions. (The pow function does come in handy for higher powers, where the arithmetic gets complex.)

The next line is the calculation of the variance:

```
var = sqr / ((double) n - 1);
```

It uses the cast operator again. The expression ((double) n – 1) is enclosed in parentheses to ensure that the entire expression will be used as the divisor. Extensive use of parentheses is no crime, and it shows both the reader of your code and the compiler exactly what you want it to do. Whether n is coerced first and then 1 subtracted or the subtraction calculated first and then coerced is not important, so you don't need another set of parentheses.

```
vara = (100 * var + 5) / 100;
stddev = (( sqrt(var)) * 100 + 5) / 100;
```

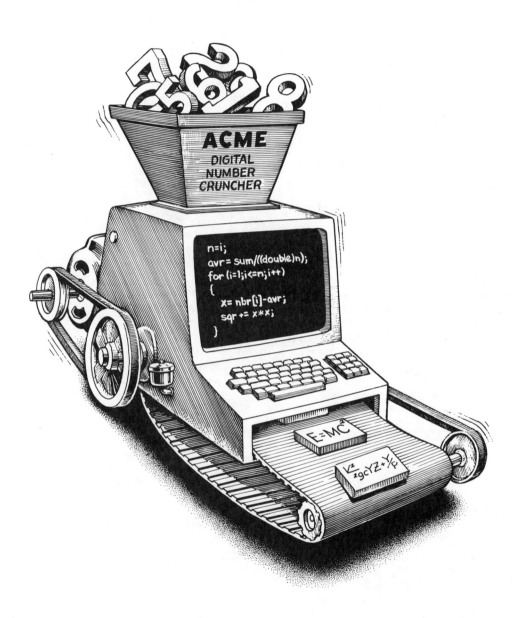

Number Crunching

Notice the use of the square root function sqrt ( ). Many functions like these are not part of the defined body of the C language; they depend on the implementation. Always check your manual to see what functions are available.

Last is the formatted output:

```
        puts ("\n\n\n\n");
        printf ("number of entries : %d\n\n", n);
        printf ("average : %f\n\n", avr);
        printf ("standard deviation : %f \n\n", stddev);
        printf ("variance : %d", vara);
    }
```

Note that double-precision numbers are output as f (float) and integers as d (decimal integer).

AN ENGINEERING APPLICATION

The program in Figure 14.2 deals with the calculation of the design criteria of coil springs. This is a tedious, iterative task performed routinely by mechanical engineers, and it is ideally suited for small computers. Although somewhat oversimplified, it is a typical "real world" programming example.

The first step in the program is to define π and G:

```
        #define PI 3.14159
        #define G 11.5e + 6
```

```
/*
 *
 *                         Spring.C
 *
 *
 *      a program to calculate helical compression springs
 *
 *
 ********************************************************************/
#define PI 3.14157
#define G   11.5e+6
#define CLEAR 0X0c
#include libc.h
#include math.h
```

Figure 14.2: A Program to Calculate Helical Compression Springs (continues)

```
main ( )
{
    double inputn, mstress, wire_d, o_d, ncoils, load, rate;
    double stress, height, c, k, ncoils, freelen, travel, mload;
    double wd3, wd4, d3;
    int reply;

start:
        putchar (CLEAR);
        puts ("\n\n\n\n\n\tHelical Compression Spring Program\n");
        puts ("\n\n\nwire dia : ");
        scanf ("%lf", &wire_d);
        puts ("\noutside diameter : ");
        scanf ("%lf", &o_d);
        puts ("\nnumber of coils : ");
        scanf ("%lf", &ncoils);
        puts ("\nspecified load :");
        scanf ("%lf", &load);
        puts ("\nspecified height :");
        scanf ("%lf", &height);

    wd3 = pow (wire_d, 3);
    printf ("wd3 = %7e\n",wd3);
    wd4 = pow (wire_d, 4);
    d3  = pow (o_d - wire_d, 3);
    c = (o_d - wire_d) / wire_d;        /*coil to wire d ratio*/
    k = (4 * c - 1) / (4 * c - 4) + .613 / c;   /*Wahl factor*/
    stress = 8.0 * (o_d - wire_d) * k * load / (PI * wd3);
    if (stress > 500000)
    {
        printf ("\n\nStress = %-9.0f\n\n", stress);
        puts ("continue (0) or retry (1) ");
        scanf ("%d", &reply);
        if (reply)
            goto start;
    }
    rate = G * wd4 / (8.0 * (d3 * ncoils));
    freelen = load / rate + height;
    travel = freelen - ((ncoils + 2) * wire_d);
    mload = travel * rate;
    mstress = 8.0 * (o_d - wire_d) * k * mload / (wd3 * PI);

    printf ("\n\n\nstress at working height %7e \n",stress);
    printf ("Wahl factor %-4.2f\n", k);
    printf ("Max load %-4.1f\n",mload);
    printf ("Travel %-4.2 in \n", travel);
    printf ("total coils %-4.1f \n", ncoils + 2.0);
    printf ("rate %-7.3f free length %-6.2f\n", rate,
            freelen);
    printf ("stress at closed height %7e\n", mstress);
}
```

Figure 14.2: A Program to Calculate Helical Compression Springs

G, the torsional modulus of elasticity of carbon steel (music wire), is 11,500,000 psi. Scientific (e) notation makes this number manageable by cutting it down to 11.5e + 6.

The header inclusions are particular to the version of C used, this one being Aztec C:

```
#define CLEAR 0X0c
#include libc.h
#include math.h
```

The only exception to the rule is the ubiquitous and nebulous <stdio.h>.

At the beginning of the main block, it looks as if nearly everything has been wildly declared double precision:

```
main ( )
{
    double inputn, mstress, wire_d, o_d, ncoils, load, rate;
    double stress, height, c, k, ncoils, freelen, travel, mload;
    double wd3, wd4, d3;
    int reply;
```

In fact, double is used deliberately to avoid underflow errors when small wire diameters are being used. This program will execute in a second or two, once all the input is in. No appreciable time is saved by the use of float rather than double in this case. On the other hand, if you were calculating a payroll, you most certainly would notice the additional time required to process 64-bit numbers.

The next line is something new:

```
    start:
```

I haven't made use of the label yet, so here it is. Line numbers in BASIC, FORTRAN, and Pascal are labels, numeric labels to be exact. They provide a target, a place to go, for branching statements and GOTOs. Labels in C and PL/I are character. Not only do they give a program execution a place to goto but it goes there in style. Whereas GOTO 150 is nondescriptive, goto end_loop tells where and why. Character gotos are self-documenting and thus contribute to program clarity.

The goto unconditionally redirects program execution. Its use has been under heavy attack for a decade because it is associated with unstructured programming. On the other hand, it is fallacious to assume that code lacking gotos is automatically structured. It is far more realistic to reserve the use of gotos for those algorithms that cannot be clearly redirected any other way. If calculated stresses are high, we can use this label to come back to. That would also make the goto a "comefrom" (computer humor).

The first thing the spring designer will input is a "guesstimate" of the spring wire diameter (wire_d):

```
putchar (CLEAR);
puts ("\n\n\n\n\n\tHelical Compression Spring Program\n");
puts ("\n\n\nwire dia : ");
scanf ("%lf", &wire_d);
```

The scanf function is told to look for a long, float number (a double-precision number) and store it in the address &wire_d. As mentioned before, the argument to scanf ( ) must be a pointer.

Similarly, the outside diameter, number of coils, and force (load) at a specified height are input:

```
puts ("\noutside diameter : ");
scanf ("%lf", &o_d);
puts ("\nnumber of coils : ");
scanf ("%lf", &ncoils);
puts ("\nspecified load : ");
scanf ("%lf", &load);
puts ("\nspecified height : ");
scanf ("%lf", &height);
```

Spring design is an iterative process, and, as a rule, the first few passes are estimates. Numbers like the wire diameter and number of coils must be compromised to get a workable spring.

The wire diameter then must be cubed and raised to the fourth power. The mean (average) diameter of the spring coil d must be cubed as well. The power function is used to accomplish this:

```
wd3 = pow (wire_d, 3);
wd4 = pow (wire_d, 4);
 d3 = pow (o_d - wire_d, 3);
```

The expressions that follow are long, in the sense that they occupy nearly the whole line they are printed on. For this reason, the intermediate variables wd3, wd4, and d3 are assigned. This makes the code easier to follow than it would be if the functions were jammed into the expressions.

A coil spring is in reality a torsion bar that has been wrapped into a helix or coil. Being wound tightly affects the torsional rate of deflection, so a factor to calculate the change of rate is used. This is the Wahl factor (named after A.M. Wahl, the author of both the formula and a fine book on springs):

```
c = (o_d - wire_d) / wire_d; /*coil to wire d ratio*/
k = (4 * c - 1) / (4 * c - 4) + .613 / c; /*Wahl factor*/
```

Take particular note of the parentheses and the order of notation. Precedence is a key factor when writing code involving calculations in any language. This is particularly true in C, because C has so many operators.

This is the formula for k, the Wahl factor, in algebraic notation:

$$k = \frac{4c-1}{4c-4} + \frac{0.613}{c}$$

C works left to right through the expression, doing the subtraction expressions in parentheses first, then coming back to divide the first expression in parentheses by the second. The number 0.613 is divided by c before the result is added to the result of the first two expressions. The table of associativity and hierarchy in Chapter 2 is an absolute necessity until you can do this sort of thing from memory.

Next, the stress at the extreme fiber of the wire is calculated. This part is often a headache for the designer, since stresses will usually be too high on the first design try.

```
stress = 8.0 * (o_d – wire_d) * k * load / (PI * wd3);
```

Algebraically, the formula is as follows:

$$stress = \frac{8PDk}{\pi D^3}$$

where D is the mean diameter of the wire, P is the load, and k is the Wahl factor. The mean diameter is calculated by subtracting the wire diameter from the outer diameter (o_d – wire_d). The expression is executed from left to right, doing the expressions within the parentheses first and then coming back and doing the remaining multiplications and divisions in order.

The next step is to test stress to see whether it exceeds 500KSI (500,000 pounds per square inch, in engineering notation). Usually it will be much lower:

```
if (stress > 500000)
{
    printf ("\n\nStress = % – 9.0f\n\n", stress);
    puts ("continue (0) or retry (1) ");
    scanf ("%d", &reply);
    if (reply)
        goto start;
}
```

If it does exceed 500KSI, the option is given to either continue, developing a highly overstressed spring, or go back and do it right. Note the goto, directing execution back to the label start if the operator decides to try again.

Once stress is determined, the spring rate (pounds per inch deflection) is calculated:

```
rate = G * wd4 / (8.0 * d3 * ncoils);
```

Algebraically, the formula is as follows:

$$rate = \frac{GD^4}{8ND^3}$$

where N is the number of coils. Note: the expression 8.0 * d3 * ncoils must be evaluated before it is used to divide the rest of the expression—thus, the parentheses.

Now the free length, spring travel, maximum load, and maximum stress are calculated:

```
freelen = load / rate + height;
travel = freelen - ((ncoils + 2) * wire_d);
mload = travel * rate;
mstress = 8.0 *(o_d - wire_d)* k * mload / (wd3 * PI);
```

Next, we get into formatted output:

```
printf ("\n\n\nstress at working height %7e \n",stress);
```

Here stress is output in exponential notation with a precision of seven decimal places.

Now the Wahl factor is output as a left-justified, floating-point number of two decimal digits and a precision of four:

```
printf ("Wahl factor % - 4.2f\n", k);
```

The default precision would have been six. The next five lines output the results of the computations.

```
    printf ("Max load % - 4.1f\n",mload);
    printf ("Travel % - 4.2 in \n", travel);
    printf ("total coils % - 4.1f \n", ncoils + 2.0);
    printf ("rate % - 7.3f free length % - 6.2f\n", rate, freelen);
    printf ("stress at closed height %7e\n", mstress);
}
```

And though I am sure it will surprise some, you can see that C can be a formidable number cruncher as well as a systems-level language. For a language that started out as a systems language, it does admirably well in applications. To perform as a first-class number processor, C needs only a good library of mathematical and transcendental functions, which is furnished with many compilers and is available in the public domain as well.

To make the spring program fully practical, trap the body of the code within a "do-forever" and provide a reasonable escape. In normal use, a number of iterations will be required to get a usable spring.

THE SIEVE OF ERATOSTHENES

Before leaving this chapter on number crunching, I want to include the Sieve of Eratosthenes. I'm including it because it has become a benchmark program used to time the computational speed of languages, compilers, and machines. An integer-only program that can be run on the smallest subsets of C, it works by setting up an array of all possible numbers up to

```
/*
                        Sieve of Eratosthenes
                benchmark program from an article by Jim Gilbreath
                in BYTE Magazine, September, 1981, p. 186.
                             ********
*/

#define TRUE 1
#define FALSE 0
#define SIZE 8190
#define SIZEPL 8191

char flags [SIZEPL];
int i,prime,k,count,iter;

main ( )
{
        printf ("Hit return to do 10 iterations: ");
        getchar ( );

        for (iter = 1; iter <= 10; iter++) {
                count = 0;
                for (i = 0; i <= SIZE; i++)
                        flags [i] = TRUE;
                for (i = 0; i <= SIZE; i++) {
                        if (flags [i]) {
                                prime = i + i + 3;
                                k = i + prime;
                                while (k <= SIZE) {
                                        flags [k] = FALSE;
                                        k += prime;
                                }
                                count++;
                        }
                }
        }
        printf ("\7\n%d primes.\n",count);
}
```

Figure 14.3: The Sieve of Eratosthenes

8,191, then filtering out all the numbers that are not primes. Knowing that 1, 2, and 3 are prime numbers, it filters out all multiples of 2 and 3. Going to the next generated prime number, it continues to remove all multiples of 2, 3, and so on, until nothing is left but prime numbers. The program appears in Figure 14.3.

This program has been copied many times by many people, and it will continue to be a benchmark for some time to come. Running at 4 MHz, it will compute all the primes to 8,191 in about 15 seconds. Try the same thing on any BASIC interpreter—when you have all day to watch it run. It should be about as exciting as watching paint dry.

Part Four

Implementations of C

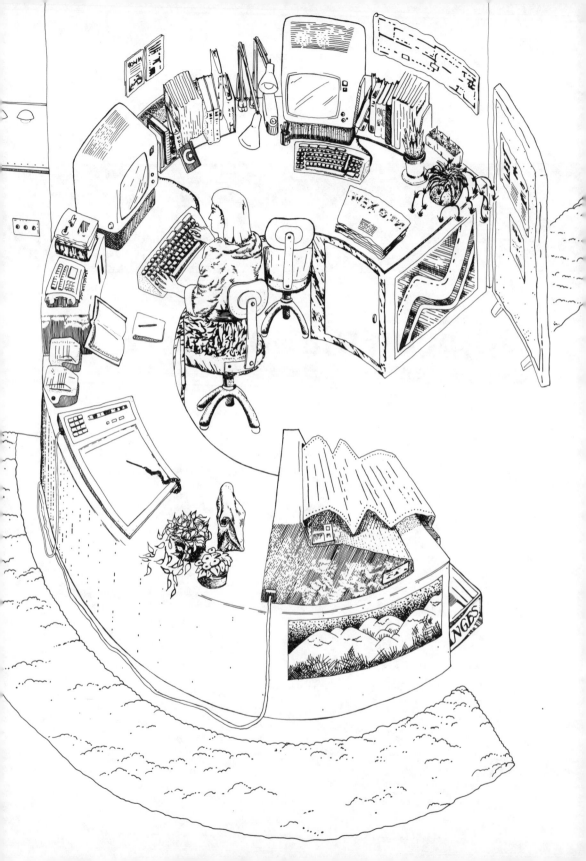

15:

C in a Shell—The UNIX Environment

Born quietly at Bell Labs, UNIX was the creation of Ken Thompson and a handful of dedicated geniuses. Unlike any other operating system in design or philosophy, UNIX came to the attention of the computing world at large in the late 1970s. It is an innovative operating system in concept and design. Oriented towards the computer professional, it is neither "user-friendly" nor suitable for casual computer users. Nevertheless, the effects of UNIX on computing in general are already being felt in the industry.

There is only one true UNIX, the Bell Labs version. All others are UNIX emulators and licensed versions. To run anything close to UNIX you need a "supermini" computer like a DEC PDP 11-70 or the larger DEC VAX, but many operating systems for micros are incorporating some of UNIX's features.

UNIX has a unique way of doing things as an operating system, and UNIX can even be a "state of mind" once you get used to it. The micro user can get a feel for UNIX through several UNIX-like systems and UNIX-emulating utilities available for use on micros. New microcomputer operating systems are incorporating UNIX features, and a number of software packages enhance existing operating systems by giving them UNIX features.

I wrote this book on three separate CP/M and MP/M computers, and enlisted two or three more for UNIX and MS-DOS background. Much of the book deals with C programs using full I/O, and therefore the programs are quite independent of the operating system. A few use system calls, and those programs are bound to the operating system (in most cases CP/M) unless the call is changed. A good number of programs, those using only the console (stdin, stdout) for I/O, are intended for UNIX and UNIX-like environments. To develop those programs, and the filters and Shell programs, I brought a number of UNIX-like software packages into my system, and the one I came to depend on was Rick Rump's MicroShell.

MicroShell is very close to the UNIX Shell, and an extremely handy utility. Because UNIX is available to so few, and MicroShell is available to so many, I will make many references to MicroShell; the UNIX Shell will often be dealt with in terms of MicroShell, which operates in the CP/M environment.

Throughout C's early development, C and UNIX were inseparable. UNIX was written in C, and C was written under UNIX. They were more than a team—they were a "marriage made in heaven." However, once outside of Bell Labs, it was only a matter of time before C found its way into other operating systems and was eventually tailored to fit CP/M environments.

A DISCUSSION OF OPERATING SYSTEMS

It's time to discuss operating systems. We have talked about computer languages throughout the book, but they don't function alone. They operate within the environment of the operating system. The operating system coordinates the operations of the computer—it is the interface between the people, the programs and the computer hardware.

The primary concerns of the operating system are memory management and the handling of I/O, which in today's computers involves heavy reliance on the use of secondary storage such as floppy disks and hard disks. Secondary storage is any place where data is stored or manipulated outside of high-speed memory, and without it, computers are little more than programmable calculators! In CP/M, an entire portion of the operating system is responsible for disk I/O, the DOS or disk operating system. Many operating systems are named for this activity, because so much of the system is devoted to it. MS-DOS, DOS, TRSDOS, and TurboDOS take their names from DOS, to name just a few.

Because disk I/O is not the only responsibility of the primary operating system, another portion of the system handles the remainder of I/O. In

CP/M this part of the system is referred to as BIOS (Basic Input/Output System). It not only handles the terminal, keyboard, printer, modem, paper tape punch (another anachronism of pre-floppy storage), and so forth, it does a portion of the disk I/O as well. This portion of the operating system must be present in high-speed memory at all times. If it is not, nothing happens, in which case your terminal is useless—you might as well use it for a planter.

Another very important function of the operating system is to act upon the direct commands to the system from the console (or, more precisely, the console operator). Because requests are put in as console commands, a *command line interpreter* is required. In CP/M this job is handled by the CCP, the console command processor. In UNIX a great deal more is expected of the command line interpreter, and a marvelous facility called the Shell handles the job. We will be looking at the UNIX Shell in some detail in this chapter, and we will also take a look at UNIX-like utilities that emulate some of the features of UNIX, but operate within a CP/M environment.

The last part of an operating system is the collection of tools and utilities that become the niceties of the system. If an operating system were to be compared to a jackknife, the DOS and the BIOS would be the blades and the command line interpreter the handle. The remaining programs, tools, and utilities are like the myriad gadgets on a Swiss Army knife. Not only are they not always used, sometimes their usefulness is questionable. The absolutely necessary tools and utilities are those that keep track of the files, and copy and modify them. In CP/M this is the job of STAT and PIP, the status program and peripheral-interchange program. Here, as in most uses of the word *files*, the meaning goes far beyond disk files, referring to data going to and from any device attached to the computer. STAT, PIP, and the other tools and utilities are not resident in high-speed memory. They are called by the user as needed.

Micro Power—A Variety of Operating Systems

Single-user, single-tasking operating systems such as CP/M used to be the norm for micros. CP/M was the first operating system for micros, and it still dominates the 8-bit market. It is probably safe to say that the 16-bit market is dominated by PC-DOS, the operating system of the IBM PC. Like CP/M, PC-DOS is a single-user, single-tasking operating system. However, multiuser, multi-tasking operating systems such as MP/M are becoming more and more common for micro use. MP/M can handle several users running different processes simultaneously.

Multiuser operating systems are just one way the micro's power is increasing. There is another type of operating system that allows 8- and 16-bit processes to be run simultaneously on single-user systems, and there are single-user, multi-tasking operating systems such as Concurrent CP/M. This is representative of what is available today for the micro, but it wasn't always this way.

Where It All Began for the Micro

In 1973, just as Bell Labs was first releasing UNIX licenses to universities and distributing UNIX to various nonprofit institutions, Gary Kildall, then a software consultant for Intel, developed CP/M, primarily to take advantage of the obviously promising future of the floppy disk. Intel, the creator of the 8008 and 8080, and Shugart, the manufacturer of floppy disk drives, were young companies then. In 1973 the micro was born. Imsai came out with the 8080, Shugart had perfected the floppy disk drive, and Kildall wrote the operating system to put it all together. It was a cooperative effort that changed computing forever.

UNIX

Compared to CP/M or even MP/M, UNIX is a veritable giant. On the other hand, it is not the behemoth of operating systems that CP-5 and CP-6 or IBM's OS and DOS are. UNIX is a multiuser operating system like MP/M. The following sections highlight some of the features of UNIX.

The Shell Command Language

The Shell is the interface between the user and the system. It handles foreground and background tasks—those that are transparent to the user and occur while the computer is doing a number of things at once. The instructions the user wishes completed are acted upon immediately. The Shell does command chaining, grouping commands on a single line to be acted upon successively. It takes care of input/output redirection, a concept unique to UNIX. It also does batch control files, a chore associated with mainframe operating systems.

Languages

UNIX comes complete with a number of languages. First and foremost, it has C. Not just C alone, but C with every utility you could imagine. The UNIX package also has FORTRAN, BASIC, RATFOR, and Pascal. COBOL is provided with the operating system XENIX, a UNIX-emulating operating system.

System Development Tools

UNIX is written in C. To make system programming possible, an assembler, a debugger, and a utility called YACC is provided, which is a compiler compiler (just in case you feel like writing your own language or rewriting one you already have).

Text Support

The tools provided for text processing are staggering for the micro user, who seldom needs to get beyond Electric Pencil, WordStar, and Spellguard. Besides the inevitable editor, there is a spelling program, SPELL, a utility to hunt and kill typographical errors called TYPO, a graph plotter called GRAPH and another called PLOT to output the graph, and the list goes on, even including typesetting.

Games

No kidding, UNIX really has games! It plays chess, moo (a number guessing game that I engineered into a game called Comp5 for Milton Bradley), blackjack, tic-tac-toe (with a three-dimensional version as well), and others. There are also some extracurricular activities, such as a calendar generator for the years 0 to 9999, and a conversion program for just about any imaginable form of measurement.

Miscellaneous and Not-So-Miscellaneous Utilities

UNIX's prehistory, (the undocumented period before the announcement of UNIX by Bell Labs) goes back to the creation of programming tools in the fashion of Kernighan and Plauger's *Software Tools*. The tools and utilities perform wide and varied tasks, such as searching, sorting, and formatting; file splitting and appending, both horizontally and vertically; comparing, copying, and deleting files; directory routines; archiving; and the list goes on.

The Primary System (OS)

The monumental job of handling multiuser, multi-task operations, and in the process, communications such as pipes and signals, is the heart of the operating system or OS. The heart of the OS in UNIX is the kernel. It must handle scheduling and swapping, the "mountable" file systems, the file directories, the tree structures involved in handling the directories through the system manager and users, and the tree structure process invocation.

The documentation of the UNIX system is a library in its own right, comprising nearly 50 distinct manuals, tutorials, an overview, papers, and so on. Creating UNIX was a monumental task, and the paper it has generated is monumental as well.

C Under UNIX

Until this chapter, we have been looking at C as it runs under CP/M and CP/M-like operating systems. C is not the same when it runs under UNIX. The programs no longer look the same. It's not that something is missing; something is added. That something is I/O.

One key to UNIX is I/O redirection, the ability to take the "normal" input and output of the program and redirect it to someplace else. Operating under UNIX, C can take its input one character at a time from stdin (standard input), assumed to be the console, and sends it to stdout (standard output), also assumed to be the console. Most I/O is done by way of getchar ( ) and putchar ( ), either directly or through an I/O function that uses them.

Let's look at C (under UNIX) doing its most basic thing:

```
/ * ito copy input to output * /

main ( )
{
    int c;

    while ((c = getchar ( )) ! = EOF)
        putchar (c);
}
```

If you haven't been exposed to UNIX, it is hard to believe that that is a program. It copies its input to its output. You CP/M users must be saying "What kind of a program is that?" But under UNIX, this two-liner will do wonders. The UNIX command line

```
ito < file1 > file2
```

will copy file1 to file2 by way of the minuscule program ito.

THE UNIX SHELL

The miracles of UNIX, at least those that are readily apparent to the user, are in the Shell. In CP/M terms, the Shell is most closely related to the CCP, the console command processor. Its purpose is to intercept, interpret, and act upon the command lines, and make the desired actions happen.

The UNIX Shell

The Shell is a command language and a programming language which provides an interface to the operating system. It is the language of the Shell that takes up where the C program left off in the previous example.

Input/Output Redirection

UNIX makes continuous analogy to plumbing hardware, pipes, tees, and valves (to turn on or off). This is because of its ability to redirect much in the same manner as hydraulic devices redirect. This is unique in the field of computing and so is its terminology. The analogy starts with simple redirection. The program flow intended for the console is redirected to an alternate file. The flow can be redirected only in one incoming and one outgoing direction.

```
process1 <infile >outfile
```

Not that this is any small feat, but what if we now want to direct the program flow to yet another executable file, say a "filter" to remove some character from the file passing through it? The flow cannot be redirected and then redirected a second time, so it must be *piped* to the filter.

```
process1 <infile | filter >outfile
```

The pipe is in reality a temporary "file"[1] that is created and used by the Shell and then erased as soon as it is no longer needed. Continuing the analogy, there is a device known as a *tee* that is the same as a pipe but leaves the temporary file unerased after use.

In its simplest form, the symbols < and > redirect the file into and out of the program respectively:

```
progn < progdat
```

inputs the data from the file progdat to the program progn.

```
progn > progdat
```

causes progn to execute and output its data to progdat.

```
progn < datin > datout
```

executes progn by reading datin into the program and redirecting its output to datout.

Redirection can become considerably more complex. The command line

```
progn < indat | sort | uniq > dfile
```

reads the file indat into progn, which processes the data. Then it is piped to sort, which sorts it and passes the sorted data to uniq, which filters out reoccurrences of data before outputting the results to dfile.

The UNIX Shell uses the following characters for redirection:

    <   Direct a file to a command or an executable file

    >   Direct output from a command file to a file

  >>   Concatenate (add) to an existing file

    | Pipe the output to the input of another command or executable file

    ;   Command separator

UNIX has commands like CP/M's. For example, dir (for directory) becomes ls (for list directory). Following are a few UNIX commands without the switches:

ls	List directory
date	Give the time and date
tty	Give the terminal name
pwd	Give the full path name to the current working directory
ps	Give process status
du	Summarize disk usage
df	Show disk free space
file	Return the file type
cal	Print a calendar

Now let's look at some of the more commonly known UNIX commands implemented in many UNIX emulators such as Unica and MicroTools, and discussed in *Software Tools* by Kernighan and Plauger:

sort	Sort a file
split	Split a file into 1000-line pieces
uniq	Search identical lines and delete (from a sorted file)
wc	Word count (also lines and characters)
grep	This is find in disguise. It finds patterns in a data stream.
diff	Compare text files
dd	Convert and copy.
echo	Echo shell file commands to the console
tee	Save the intermediate data as a pipe disk file

This is only a quick glance at UNIX, but it is enough to see the similarities between UNIX and its emulators. Putting the UNIX Shell to use to get a sorted listing of the files (a directory) in the third, or owner's, field only:

    ls −l | sort +3−4

or to run a word filter, we will program and create a dictionary

    wftr < filedat | sort | uniq > dict

As you will see, with the exception of a few utility names, the UNIX Shell commands are quite similar to MicroShell's commands.

UNIX, UNIX-like operating systems, and the concept of the Shell are going to be with us for a long time to come. The intrinsic benefits of Shell files used in combination with the tools of the system and with short, powerful C programs make it possible to write extremely powerful systems[2] with relatively little new code.

UNIX Utilities

UNIX includes a library of utility programs to perform functions like sorting, word counting, formatting, and so on. The combination of its resident utilities, the versatility of the Shell, and the easy interaction between C and the Shell creates a programming environment where high productivity and versatility abound. Once one has been exposed to UNIX, conventional operating systems somehow never seem the same. To get a feel for UNIX, let's look at some of its commands and utilities.

Just to say "hello," UNIX wants you to log into the system. CP/M doesn't care who you are, but UNIX does. So get a log-in name from whoever is running the system, and UNIX will allow you to log on:

    −> login:
    −> jasbond
    −> $

You have been accepted when you see the $ sign.

Entering command lines in UNIX is reasonably straightforward. Type them in, and if you make an error, cancel the previous character with the addition of the number sign:

    −> jac#sbond

If you get totally frustrated, or simply make too many errors, the @ sign erases the whole thing, just as a ^X does in CP/M:

    −>javsvomd@
    −>

Once you have logged in, you are in UNIX. How do you get out? Enter a control-d (^D).

UNIX EMULATORS

To fill the need for UNIX-like operating environments, a number of UNIX emulators have been created. An ideal form of emulation would have the internals of an operating system as familiar as CP/M and still have a UNIX-like Shell and UNIX-like utilities. Fortunately, there are such systems. A very good one is MicroShell, which is remarkably compact. An older and larger system is Carousel MicroTools.

The Shell of MicroShell replaces CP/M's CCP, the console command processor. It stays in residence below BIOS and processes all Shell command lines. For the most part, the only differences between the UNIX Shell and MicroShell are syntactic. Following is a listing of MicroShell command line characters and a brief explanation of their function:

>	Output redirection (console)
>*	Output redirection (printer)
<	Input redirection
|	Pipe output to input of next command file
^	Precedes control character
:	First character in a comment of a Shell file
;	Command separator
+	Echo redirected output to the console
–	Return character ready (status) to console input status calls
"	Encloses tokens to be treated as a single argument
\	Causes any special meaning of the next character to be ignored
$	CP/M's traditional argument-substitution character, as in $1 for file name in a SUBMIT file
!	Put the Shell into edit mode
$t	Redirect input back to the console
$p	Redirect output to the printer

Let's put these MicroShell commands to work. Imagine that you are assigned the task of creating a technical dictionary for a spelling program like SpellStar or The Word. You have scores of files of text and programs that contain the words, spelled correctly, and you want to put them together into a single dictionary, in alphabetical order, with no repetitions. There are resident programs to sort the words and discard repetitions. You need a program to read the file, extract the words, and delimit them with newlines.

This sort of a program is called a filter, so I'll call the program in Figure 15.1 wftr (for word filter). The command line works like this:

wftr < src.fil | sort | uniq > dic.fil

In this case wftr reads the file src.fil and pipes its output to sort. The sort program sorts the words filtered by wftr and pipes them to uniq, which throws away every recurrence of a word, making all the words unique.

```
/*
                        WFTR.C

            filters words from text files


*/

#include "bdscio.h"

int c;

main ( )
{
        int inspace, inword;

        inspace = FALSE;
        inword  = FALSE;
        while ((c = getchar ( )) != EOF)
        {
            if (c == ' ' || c == '\n' || c == '\t')
            {
                inword = FALSE;
                if (!inspace)
                {
                    c = '\n';
                    putchar (c);
                    inspace = TRUE;
                }
                else
                continue;
            }
            else
            {
                inword = TRUE;
                inspace = FALSE;
                if (isalpha (c))
                    putchar (c);
            }
        }
}
```

Figure 15.1: A Word Filter Using MicroShell

uniq's output is now redirected from the screen, which would be its normal output, to the file dic.fil. That's all there is to it. For the trouble of writing a small filter, you can have a dictionary.

Writing a C program to run within the Shell in MicroShell is noticeably different from writing a conventional C program under CP/M. Notice the difference in I/O.

Except for a couple of flags, the program has but one variable, c, the character to be input and output. The only I/O commands are getchar and putchar. Therein lies the key to writing under a Shell. The standard input and standard output in UNIX is the console. The getchar and putchar functions are the mechanisms that cause streams of input or output to flow between the program and the console.

First the variable c and two flags are declared:

```
int c;

main ( )
{

    int inspace, inword;
```

The flags keep track of the character stream passing into the program, to see whether the character being examined is in a word or in white space. At the start of the program, both flags are initialized to FALSE:

```
inspace = FALSE;
inword = FALSE;
while ((c = getchar ( )) ! = EOF)
{
```

The while loop keeps the character stream coming into the program, assigning each incoming character to the variable c. When c is the CP/M end-of-text mark (^Z), execution quits the loop.

Then the character is tested to see if it is a white-space character:

```
if (c == ' ' || c == '\n' || c == '\t')
{
    inword = FALSE;
    if (!inspace)
    {
```

If it is, it is not in a word, so inword is set to FALSE (inword is initialized to FALSE, and it gets toggled on and off at each white-space character or group beginning). There is also a logistical problem. A newline should be inserted after each word in the output stream, in order to delimit the words, but you don't want multiple newlines. inspace will be false when a word is exited, so it is tested to see whether it is false. If it is, the output character will be a newline:

```
c = '\n';
putchar (c);
inspace = TRUE;
```

To prevent another newline from being issued, inspace is set to TRUE. Had inspace been true, the continue would cause execution to return to the while loop.

```
}
else
continue;
```

Had the test for a white-space character failed, the else would now be the program path:

```
else
{
    inword = TRUE;
    inspace = FALSE;
    if (isalpha (c))
        putchar (c);
```

The else signifies that you are within a word, in which case inword is TRUE and inspace is FALSE. One last test is made to see whether the character is an alphabetic character. If it is, it is allowed into the output stream.

UNIX and MicroShell supply a working environment for the program that rids it of the need for specific I/O attributes. Because the above program is intended to be a macro, the program is not entirely free-standing. Granted, were it used alone, it would work, more or less, by taking in "sentences" from the console and outputting words. But its real function is as a utility, and its intended environment is the Shell.

SHELL PROGRAMS

The Shell has a programming language of its own. It is a command line interpreter, interpreting command lines and acting upon them. As such, it is not very different from an interpreter language like BASIC. In BASIC, command lines can be acted upon individually, like this:

```
LPRINT "HELLO"
```

Or they can be grouped into a chain of numbered command lines and run as a program. The Shell works in the same fashion, except that there is no line numbering. A file is created just as if it were a SUBMIT file.[3] In fact, in MicroShell the file extension sub is used.

Here is a "true-to-life" type of programming problem: an author writes using the WordStar word processing program, but he needs plain, double-spaced, numbered pages. His printer is old and will not microjustify, and therefore will not respond to the WordStar dot command to double space.

One solution would be to write a C program that resets the seventh bit while it reads the file, to "neutralize" the file. (WordStar manipulates the seventh bit in order to prepare the text for formatting. The WordStar text file must be stripped of the high-order bit [seventh bit] to be used by pr, the tool that will double-space the output text.) Then the lines preceded by dot commands would be filtered out. Then all control characters would be filtered out, and finally a printer driver would be written. A program like that is more than an introductory exercise, and it is not appropriate for the scope of this book.

Luckily, there is another way, and it demonstrates the power of the Shell nicely. It uses the reformatting and printing programs resident with the Shell. Because this task will be performed frequently, it is well worth the time it takes to write a subfile.

The file looks like this:

```
: ptrfmt.sub
deform −s $1 proof
pr −do8 proof > $p
era proof
```

The first line, preceded by a colon, is a comment. The second line calls the program deform, which reformats the file specified in the command line. deform uses the s switch, which strips control characters, thereby removing all the fancy printer controls in the text, and then stores the output to a temporary file called proof. Next another resident program, pr, is called with a d flag to double-space and an o flag to offset the right margin eight spaces. Its output is sent to the printer. Lastly, the temporary file proof is erased. To get the Shell program to work, the invocation

```
ptrfmt ch24.txt
```

is typed to the console, and a numbered, double-spaced, plain hardcopy is produced from the WordStar file ch24.txt.

Shell files can be treated like any other program. They can be nested within another Shell file, and they can be redirected. Using the last program, ptrfmt, the output can be redirected to the console by

```
ptrfmt ch24.txt > *
```

MICROSHELL FLAGS

As you build features into the Shell, sometimes they have a tendency to come back and haunt you. For example, Verbose[4] is a feature that echoes the redirected input to the terminal. It is handy for checking Shell files to see whether argument substitution has occurred, as in the Shell file ptrfmt.

```
0001    :          ptrfmt.sub
0002    deform –s $1 proof
0003    pr –do8 proof >$p
0004    era proof
0005
```

The line

```
deform –s $1 proof
```

will appear on the screen as

```
deform –s ch24.txt proof
```

when ch24.txt is being deformatted. Without Verbose on, the substitution of ch24.txt for $1 cannot appear on the CRT. On the other hand, when running the word filter program wftr (Figure 15.1), every character is doubled with Verbose. Therefore the word *verbose* would appear as

```
vveerrbboossee
```

To keep this from happening, when pipes are used the Shell automatically turns Verbose off. But when the user simply invokes the filter, Verbose is still active:

```
wftr thefile.txt > newfile.txt
```

newfile will contain twice as much as thefile, and it will be really strange-looking text. Now no good system would allow this to happen without giving you a chance to fight back. The way to win the battle is with a flag. The default condition for Verbose is on. To turn it off, merely type

```
–v
```

A multiple command line is created like this:

```
–v ; wftr thefile.txt > newfile.txt ; +v
```

Verbose is turned off, the word filter creates newfile.txt from thefile.txt, and Verbose is turned on again.

To give you an idea of the flags and functions available, here is a brief listing. Note that each flag can be turned on with a +, off with a −. Consult the MicroShell manual for further details.

Flag	*Function*
d	Delay
f	File search
g	Gobble line feeds
l	Log-in disk
m	Mode
p	Prompt change
s	Status report (flags)
t	Transparency character flag
u	Uppercase command flag
v	Verbose
x	Exit the shell

SUMMARY

While MicroShell is not line-for-line UNIX, it allows the UNIX features to be available to the CP/M user, at the same time allowing the system to retain the CP/M features and full CP/M–MP/M compatibility. Once you have programmed with the Shell or MicroShell program, you will never be the same again.

Another UNIX-like series of tools and a Shell are found in Carousel Microtools. An extremely extensive collection of tools and utilities, the entire package was written in RATFOR (RATional FORtran). This intriguing package creates a "virtual" operating system, the theory being that running under its Shell, the program gains freedom from the physical operating system. Note that there are two Microtools packages. One was written by Phil and Debby Scherrer, which was Unicorn Systems and is now Carousel Microtools. The other, written by Don Graff, is called MicroTools, and is either free-standing or used with Rick Rump's MicroShell, which has no utility/tool package of its own. If you are looking for a UNIX-like overlay, both Carousel Microtools and MicroShell/MicroTools are well worth looking into.

16:

A Comparison of C Compilers

Since C left the sheltered confines of Bell Labs and went out into the world, several subsets have been created to meet the needs of the computing public. To the best of my knowledge, all but the smallest and most unpopular languages exist in numerous differing versions. Computer languages are rarely static or permanent. They are "living" entities that regularly produce multiple offspring, and sometimes the offspring bear only a distant resemblance to their parents.

SUBSETS AND SUPERSETS

These offspring generally take one of two forms: they are either subsets or supersets. Subsets are abbreviated versions of larger languages, and often they are created to make languages created for 16-bit or 32-bit machines accessible to the majority of people with 8-bit and 16-bit micros. Supersets enlarge, improve upon, and enhance an original language (usually a relatively small one) that may have been weak in some areas despite strengths in others. In spite of their advantages, supersets create portability problems. A program created on one superset will not run under another if its enhancements are different.

The primary benefit of subsets is that they make sophisticated programming languages available to more people. Subsets create no problems, only benefits, as long as they remain compatible with the full set; that is, if a program written in the subset will run on the larger subset compilers and in the original full version of the language.

C is neither a large language nor a small one. UNIX and C were written on and for 16- and 32-bit machines, but unless you have access to one of the versions of UNIX leased to various universities and organizations around the country, you must work on a subset of C.[1] Most of the 16-bit Cs currently available are very close to UNIX 7 C, and they are getting closer all the time. However, an implementation of the full set that is small enough to run on a typical 8-bit, 64-kilobyte machine is almost "the impossible dream." Because the majority of today's C programmers will learn C using one of its 8- or 16-bit subsets, as far as the computing public is concerned all of C's subsets are as important to the definition of the C language as the full-set implementations.

The potential C user must determine which subset is most appropriate for his needs. You can compare the subset to the definition of C as given by Kernighan and Ritchie, but it's more realistic to consider two main areas of C: the commands and operators in general and the functions. Because C is a function-oriented language, the functions can easily be separated from the rest of the languages for the sake of comparison, which is exactly what was done in Chapters 10 through 13 on functions. Examining the commands and operators will let you make a final determination of the completeness of a C compiler.

Before examining anyone's version of C, think about why you want to learn the language and what you are going to do with it. The first step is to define the application. Will the language be used for recreational or commercial programming? Are you writing utilities like text processors? Will the software be used for business or scientific applications? Once you determine what your programming emphasis will be, you can make sure that the version of C you choose has all of the functions, operators and commands that you need.

Then comes another question, code optimization. How compact is the object code, the final code generated? If you want to create an operating system, optimizing the code will be everything, and having data types float and double won't be important. On the other hand, if you are developing large business or communications systems, tight code won't mean nearly as much as speed of compilation and the completeness of the set of operators and functions. Choosing a C compiler simply involves noting your priorities and being able to make a few compromises.

RELOCATABLE CODE

It is easier to choose a C compiler if you know how compilers work. We have seen in the Introduction that compilers grind their way from source code to object code in a number of passes. An awareness of the significance of these steps makes it easier for you to pick out the right compiler for your needs. For instance, it is important to know whether a compiler includes the step of producing relocatable code. As you recall, some compilers produce relocatable code and some do not.

Macros

This matters because you may want to create *macros* rather than freestanding programs. Let me explain that further. In many cases you don't want your program to stand alone. Often you code portions of a large program in separate modules, which you ultimately link together into a larger whole. These program modules are called macros.[2] If a macro is to be linked to another program or to other macros, it needs to be in relocatable code, particularly if it will be linked with code generated by another language. Even if you don't recognize the term macro, you have probably used them. Programming utilities are a good example of macros. Access Manager, a data base tool by Digital Research, is a fine example of a series of macro routines to be linked to a number of Digital's programming languages. Naturally, it is in relocatable code.

In simple terms, relocatable code is created like this. C packages intended for CP/M and CP/M-like systems such as C/80, SuperSoft C, Q/C, and Aztec C produce 8080 or 8086 assembly. The assembly code is in turn passed through a macro loader and converted into relocatable format or a REL (or R86) file.

The benefits of relocatable code are many. The code can be debugged by a debugger such as DDT, or SID, DRI's Symbolic Instruction Debugger in CP/M, or DB or MAXIM in UNIX. Relocatable code can be linked to anything that is linkable under M80, Microsoft's macro linker, or MAC, Digital's version of the same.

That's the good news. The bad news is that it takes a number of steps on your part to do all these things, so it takes longer to compile the code. Consequently, when it's getting quite late and you are getting very tired and the same blasted bug that has been plaguing the program is still there after the umpteenth re-editing, the drudgery of parse, optimize, macro load, and link can get to be a bit much.

On the other hand, for the serious or professional programmer there are helpful options. Using the CP/M SUBMIT command saves you from typing in each step every time. There are UNIX-like Shell utilities that reduce the drudgery in the compilation process. Hard disk and high-speed memory disk emulators markedly shorten the time required for compilation and linkage. For instance, a compilation and link that would normally take a full two to three minutes on my older CompuPro 8085/8088 with only floppy disks compiles in thirty seconds on our G & G 8/16 with hard disk and M-Drive H, in spite of the fact that they both use the same processors and memory boards.

Two-Pass Compilation

What about those compilers that skip the relocatable code process? This kind of compilation is called a *two-pass* system. The parser and compiler are brought up automatically, so one command does both jobs. The resultant code is then linked in one pass. This means just two apparent operations from source code to object code. BD Systems C and DeSmet C are compilers of this type. What is the catch? No REL (relocatable) file. The intermediate code can be linked to any other BDS C program but not, for instance, to Microsoft compatible programs. SID cannot be used. BDS does have a utility, however, to produce 8080 assembly. And fortunately, the latest version (1.5) has a debugger of its own. For most people, the lack of REL files is more than made up for by the speed of operation.

Which of the two compilation systems produces the most optimized code? That is a matter of how well the optimizer has been written, not the compilation system. Many sophisticated packages that use multiple compilation passes have a program to "manage" the compiler sections and overlays. Digital Research C utilizes a "compiler supervisory module" to invoke the preprocessor, parser and code generator, listing/disassembly file merge module, and program loader utility, so that they act as a single unit. A compiler switch allows you to invoke the linker automatically as well, to shorten overall development time.

A CLOSER LOOK AT SOME C SUBSETS

Full set or subset, that is the question. If money were no object, perhaps we all would be running UNIX 7 C on a PDP 11-70 or DEC VAX, and there would be no reason for this chapter! If you are going to run a subset, then the question is, how much of a subset? There are so many things to consider about each compiler.

Few languages have enjoyed the rapid growth in popularity that C has experienced in the last few years. As a result, the market has responded with a proliferation of C packages for myriad processors and systems. Over 20 C compilers were examined and run in the course of creating this book. A table of their attributes follows this section. The table is amplified by a quick, thumbnail sketch of each. Each compiler has its advantages and disadvantages, including price.

Eight-Bit Subsets

BD Systems C

A staple among C users since the late seventies, BD Systems C is an integer-only C. It lacks typedef, static and initializers, but functions are provided for float, initialization, and just about anything else that Leor Zolman and his supporters think might be useful. It compiles and links faster than any other compiler in "C-dom," bar none. BDS's function library is one of the largest of any C implementation, and it is very close to Kernighan and Ritchie C, except for file I/O. The source code to the functions is included.

tiny-c

tiny-c is a small C-like language that has both an interpreter and a compiler. While not a "true" C, because it does not adhere strictly to Kernighan and Ritchie's definition of C, it is close enough to be a wonderful teaching tool. The fact that an interpreter version is included places tiny-c in a class by itself. There are many syntactic differences from mainline C, and the function library is atypical as well. However, it is hard to imagine a friendlier way to get started in C than through an interactive interpreter with a compiler standing by when the interpreter has outlived its usefulness. A very small Shell is also provided with the package that does < and > redirection, but it has no pipes. tiny-c has its own editor, an interpreter for both source and object code, a compiler, and a very readable 384-page manual.

Small-C and Some of Its Offspring

A totally different branch of the C tree started with Ron Cain. Ron wrote a small set of C and published the source code in *Dr. Dobb's Journal* in 1980. Ron's version of C is called Small-C. It is an integer-only version, not having type float or type long (as indeed, most 8-bit subsets did not until 1983). It also lacks the case statement, multidimensional arrays, unions, for and while loops, and structures. Because the source code was in the public domain and the price was right, numerous C compilers proliferated from it, including Kirk Bailey's Small-C Plus, CW/C, Q/C, InfoSoft C, and C/80.

C/80

Walt Bilofsky's C/80 gives Small-C altogether new power. Originally an integer-only C, C/80 was recently updated with a package incorporating type float and type long. C/80 is a true UNIX 7 C subset containing no atypical enhancements. It has all the storage classes, structures and unions, casts, and all the good C wildness that makes C what it is.

Type double is not supported, but type float goes to 10E38 with 24 bits of precision (6 to 7 decimal digits). For accuracy fanatics, float goes to 32 bits (+ / − 2,147,483,647). The float portion is offered as an enhancement separate from the integer version of C/80. This C package has its own 8080 assembler. Its function library is small, but quite adequate. Under $100, C/80 is one of today's major software bargains.

Q/C

Jim Colvin's Q/C is also an integer-only set. It does not support typedef, sizeof, casts or bitfields. (Very few Cs support bitfields. Then again, very few programmers do bitfields.) It does handle multidimensional arrays, static, and initializers. Q/C has a fine function library, and the code is very well optimized. A definite plus is the fact that the distribution package includes the source code of the compiler as well as the function libraries. It does not have a linker.

InfoSoft C

InfoSoft C is Richard Roth's revision of Small-C. InfoSoft is not new to the software field, having marketed some impressive systems packages, including the operating system CDOS. A very powerful integer-only C (with type long), InfoSoft C lacks typedef and casts. Other than that it has most of the features of C, including command line redirection. A good intermediate-size library contains very interesting and useful functions including a quick sort, a binary tree and binary search routine, and chain and overlay functions. All the C operators are supported, as are extern and static, and initializers are allowed in most applications. A debugger, always a welcome addition, comes with the distribution package.

SuperSoft C

SuperSoft C is also integer only, but will not be for long. Version 1.2 already makes room for types long, double, and float by having the compiler recognize the types. double and float functions are part of the new library. Although the compiler does not act upon data types other than integer at this time, arithmetic functions are provided which are essentially kludges (much like those in BDS). Type float probably will be a permanent part of the compiler by the time this book is in print.

SuperSoft C lacks certain features like initialization at declaration, bitfields, and typedef. However, its fine function library, which is not only large, is compatible with both Kernighan and Ritchie's definition of C and BDS C, and supports a great deal of UNIX 7 C as well. It is also available for 8080, 8086, Z8000 processors, and it runs on MS-DOS as well as CP/M and CP/M 86. SuperSoft has a good support group.

Aztec C

This is a very nearly full set of C for 8-bit computers, supporting (here come the big ones) float, long, and double. Its large function library includes many math and transcendental functions.

Whitesmiths C

One of the oldest, and certainly one of the largest, Cs for 8-bit computers, Whitesmiths C is the full set. Whitesmiths C is clearly a commercial systems and applications package. Whitesmiths' languages, including C, are designed to be transportable among the many processors and systems that Whitesmiths supports, including its own operating system, IDRIS.

A wealth of functions exist within the Whitesmiths library, but they are not strictly limited to those set forth in Kernighan and Ritchie. This should come as no surprise when you realize that in the 8080 field alone Whitesmiths has been the only commercial C for years. To interact with, and create portability to, the numerous versions of C that have emerged in the last year or two, Whitesmiths has responded with Version 2.2. This version has an additional library called V7lib, which is very close to the UNIX Version 7 C library.

Whitesmiths C creates an intermediate code called A-natural. Microsoft compatible code can be generated for the 8080 version. Compiling and linking in Whitesmiths tend to be a bit complex, but SUBMIT files are provided to ease the task. The object code can be quite compact. If tight code is a prerequisite, your choice of a C version should include the ability to omit the redirection routines. As of this writing Whitesmiths' 8080 version of C is still the most powerful offering on the 8-bit market. It interfaces as well with Whitesmiths Pascal.

Sixteen-Bit Cs

The popularity of the IBM personal computer has made the 8088 and 8086 microprocessors a permanent part of the microcomputer landscape. Initially, not only were the new 16-bit processors without software to run, but languages with which to develop software were few and far between. That is history now. 16-bit software is abundant, and good 16-bit Cs running under CP/M, MP/M, MS-DOS and PC-DOS are plentiful. The biggest difference between 8-bit and 16-bit C versions is that most of the 16-bit Cs are closer to UNIX 7 C than the 8-bit versions, with even the most inexpensive implementations supporting data types long, float, and integer.

DeSmet C

DeSmet C is very close to a full set of UNIX 7 C. It has an intermediate size library and its own assembler, ASM 88. It has all the C operators and data types. The manual is clear and easy to read. It contains a fair amount of information on dealing with the 8088/8086 architecture and could do double-duty as an 8086 manual. The best thing about the DeSmet package is the price, $100. In the 16-bit C group, this package is certainly *the* software bargain.

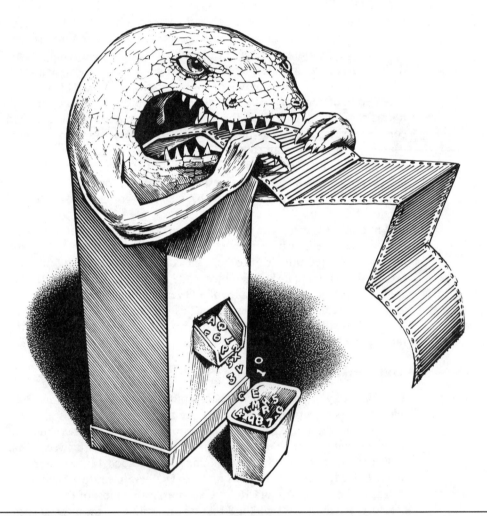

c-systems C

The c-systems C compiler package is one of the very few 16-bit versions that does not support type float and long. It has an extensive debugger called C-Window. As with most integer-only packages, there are plans to implement type float in the future.

Telecon Systems C

Telecon Systems C is available for 8080, 8086, PDP-11, and 6809 processors. The 8080 version comes both with and without float, although double is not yet implemented. It is very close to UNIX 7 C, supporting just about everything but bitfields. The intermediate size function library is similar to the library in Kernighan and Ritchie's book. Telecon C runs under many operating systems. It lacks a linker and loader.

CI-C86

Computer Innovations 8086 C is full UNIX 7 C. Written by George Eberhart, a very remarkable and talented individual, CI-C86 seems to lack nothing. It is a very complete package, including not only the usual linker, but also a (BCD) float package, an archiver, a library maintenance program, and utilities to convert from CP/M to MS-DOS and vice-versa. The function library is extremely large, almost matching BDS. George is in the process of adapting CI-C86 to the majority of processors, and presumably systems. When this comes to pass, this package will rival Whitesmiths in processor portability.

Lattice C

Another very outstanding 16-bit C is Lattice C, which is also fairly close to UNIX 7 C. There are 150 functions in all, if the special functions peculiar to the IBM PC are included.

The package, created by Francis Lynch, includes a well-written, well-organized, and complete manual, which is quite technical. A second manual, whimsically called The C-Food Smorgasbord, contains a multitude of functions and macros for all sorts of things. Decimal (BCD) arithmetic can be done with a separate package that is part of the Smorgasbord (similar to CI-C86). It does floating-point decimal work with a precision of 16 significant digits (a great help when working on the national debt). The precision of the main package is 6 to 7 figures for float and 15 to 16 for double. The functions used with the float package are peculiar to the package.

Additional functions and macros furnished with the Smorgasbord include console and list device I/O functions, IBM PC BIOS interface functions, and a very interesting package to interface the myriad terminals whose manufacturers have seemingly taken such great delight in making them incompatible with each other.

Originally written for the General Automation Company, Lattice was recoded for the 8086 in both an MS-DOS version and a CP/M-86 version. It supports the 8087 math processors, and like all 8087 language versions, will simulate the chip if it is not present. The price of this very complete package is $500 for the MS-DOS compiler and $150 for the Smorgasbord. It is available from Lifeboat Associates. You need P-LINK to use Lattice C with CP/M-86.

Digital Research C

Announced in early 1983 and billed as UNIX 7 C with no excuses, DRC sets a new standard for UNIX compatibility. Anything and everything in this definitive set is designed to produce the same results in CP/M as the C package supplied with the UNIX system on a PDP 11-70. Until now, UNIX compatibility has meant that the functions, operators, macros and so forth are essentially as defined by Kernighan and Ritchie.   Here the definition moves up a full order of magnitude.

Digital Research has formally adopted C as its in-house systems language. The implications of this major move for the corporation are broad and far-reaching. It establishes C as *the* systems language, giving it portability among the two most widely used and known families of operating systems. It also means that DRC has to be the state of the art at all times. DRI's new CP/M family of operating systems has now spread to the 68000 processor; the entire system was written in DRC.

Manufacturers have been quick to follow the lead. Most of MP/M 8/16, a multiuser operating system running on both 8- and 16-bit processors simultaneously, was written with DRI C. In my opinion this version of MP/M is not only the finest available but has begun to bridge the gap between UNIX and CP/M.

DRC is the product of Michael Lehman. The first release is for the 8086, 8087, and 8088 processors, the second is for the 68000 (68K), as a companion language to CP/M 68K. An adaptation for the Z8000 is scheduled, and no doubt there will be an 8080 (8085) version in time.

This is a full commercial package, furnished with full series of libraries for small, medium, compact, and large memory programs, a library editor, a linkage editor, and a relocatable assembler. The compiler runs under a supervisory module that virtually eliminates the need for SUBMIT files. The compiler is extremely easy to invoke and will go through all the steps of parsing, preprocessing, compiling, error output, loading, and linking with the use of a simple command line statement.

A QUANTITATIVE APPROACH TO THE COMPARISON OF C COMPILERS

Admittedly, this analysis of today's Cs has been entirely qualitative. Figures 16.1 through 16.5 offer a more quantitative approach.

Some time ago Jim Gilbreath, the head of Computer Sciences and Simulation Department at the Naval Ocean Systems Center, decided to compare various languages and compilers for operational speed. To do so, he used a program called the Sieve of Eratosthenes as a *benchmark program,* a program designed to test the capabilities of a given system. Although he may not have intended it to become *the* benchmark, his article, which appeared in *Byte* magazine, has become a classic. C was one of the fastest languages to run the Sieve, and it also had some of the most compact code. The benchmark program is an ideal test for C, and Jim Gilbreath brought out another article in *Byte,* comparing C and Pascal compilers. Some of the data following is from that article. I have added my own interpretations.

There is an intrinsic problem in reading benchmark data from Sieve tests. If the data has been compiled under different processors, or the same type of processor running at different clock speeds, or different operating systems, or different disk drive configurations (floppy vs. hard disk), DMA (direct memory addressing) vs. non-DMA, and so forth, the results will be drastically different. For example, an IBM PC will run at half the speed of a CompuPro CP/M 16 system, yet both have the same processor, an 8088. The major difference is a higher clock speed (8 MHz for the CompuPro) and DMA. MP/M systems will run slightly slower on 16-bit machines and noticeably slower on 8-bit micros, because multi-tasking chores take more CPU time. Bearing this in mind, take all Sieve data with a grain of salt unless you know it was all taken from the same system.

The Sieve program tests not only speed of operation, but the length of the object code, and compilation and load time as well. About the only thing missing is a "bug" test! Since the Sieve yields quantitative measures, it is an ideal medium to complete our comparison of C compilers. We will look at 8-bit versions first. Because compact code is one of C's greatest strengths, compilers tested by compiled length of a program, from origin to end of file, will be listed first, in kilobytes in Figure 16.2.

Length of Object Code

The offspring of Small-C do pretty well in this department, with CW/C being nothing short of miraculous. All versions of C that support command-line arguments, which is most versions of C, carry a great deal of overhead to provide for this feature. As a rule of thumb, the larger the

	C/80	Q/C	DeSmet	CC-86[I]	c-systems	SuperSoft	InfoSoft
float	✔		✔	✔			
double			✔	✔			
long			✔	✔	✔		✔
typedef			✔	✔	✔		
sizeof	✔		✔	✔	✔		✔
static	✔	✔	✔	✔	✔	✔	✔
initializers	A	B	✔	✔	✔		✔
casts	✔		✔	✔			
bitfields		✔	✔	✔		✔	
bit operators		✔	✔	✔	✔	✔	✔
structs/unions	✔	✔	✔	✔	✔	✔	✔
Number of functions	40	56	45	141	45	142	55
Length of manual	40	136	84	72	47+21	174	70
Micro-processors	8080 Z80 8085	8080 Z80 8085	8086 8087 8088	8086 8088	8086 8088	8080 8086	Z80 8080 8085
Operating systems	CP/M HDOS	CP/M	PC-DOS MS-DOS CP/M-86	CP/M-86	PC-DOS MS-DOS CP/M-86	PC-DOS MS-DOS CP/M-80 CP/M-86 CP/M+	CP/M
Has linker Other features	✔	D	✔ E,F	E	✔ G		✔ G
Price	$49.95 +29.95	$95	$100	$750	$195	$275	$59

Figure 16.1: A Comparison of C Compilers (continues)

	BDS	Aztec II	Whitesmiths	Telecon	CI-C86	Lattice	DRC
		✔	✔	✔	✔	✔	✔
		✔	✔		✔	✔	✔
		✔	✔	✔	✔	✔	✔
		✔	✔	✔	✔	✔	✔
	✔	✔	✔	✔	✔	✔	✔
		✔	✔	✔	✔	✔	✔
		✔	✔	✔	✔	✔	✔
	✔	✔	✔	J	✔	✔	✔
		✔		✔	✔	✔	✔
		✔	✔	✔	✔	✔	✔
	✔	✔	✔	✔	✔	✔	✔
	96+	77	148[C]	27	100+	102+	87
	181	81	204+200	J	142	140	168+134
	Z80	Z80	Z80	6809	8086	8086	8086
	8080	8080	8080	8080	8087	8087	8087
	8085	8085	8085	8085	8088	8088	8088
		8086	8086	8086			68000
		68000	8087	8087			
			8088	8088			
	CP/M	PC-DOS	CP/M	PC-DOS	PC-DOS	MS-DOS	CP/M-86
		MS-DOS	UNIX	MS-DOS	MS-DOS	PC-DOS	MP/M-86
		CP/M-80	RSX	CP/M-80	CP/M-86		CP/M 68K
			ISIS	CP/M			PC-DOS
			IDRIS	PDP-11			MS-DOS
			PDP-11				
			VAX				
	✔ H	✔	✔	✔	✔	✔	✔
	$150	$195	$550	$350	$395	$500	$600

[A]static only [B]extern and static only [C]plus UNIX 7 C functions [D]multi-dimensional arrays [E]assembler [F]editors [G]debugger [H]SID support [I]control-c software [J]Unknown

Figure 16.1: A Comparison of C Compilers

implementation, the larger the overhead. Many of these features can be removed at link time, usually with some difficulty for a minimal package. CW/C, on the other hand, will dump unnecessary functions and features if they are not needed, an obviously advantageous feature.

Speed of Execution

Now for speed of execution for 8-bit C compilers. To keep the results consistent, tests were run on a Z80B at 4 MHz. Time is in seconds and no attempt was made to optimize performance. The results appear in Figure 16.3.

Compiler	Program Length
CW/C	1.8K
C/80	3.1K
Q/C	3.3K
BDS	3.7K
Telecon	5.7K
Aztec	8.5K
InfoSoft	8.6K
Whitesmiths	12.0K
SuperSoft	17.7K

Figure 16.2: Compiled Program File Length

Compiler	Run Time (seconds)
C/80	25
Whitesmiths	26
Aztec	33
SuperSoft	34
Telecon	38
BDS C v1.43	40
CW/C	53
Q/C	49
InfoSoft	51
CW/C	53

Figure 16.3: Sieve Run Time for 8-bit Cs

When it comes to speed of execution, the Small-C offspring didn't fare so well, with the notable exception of C/80. Whitesmiths comes in a speedy third. New versions are being issued constantly, emphasizing code optimization for both compactness and speed of execution. Eliminating unnecessary operations from the final machine code produces both compact and fast code. Since these figures were gathered, many of the compilers tested have been issued in newer versions. Version 1.43 of BDS was tested, but the most recent version at this writing is 1.53. Therefore, you shouldn't attempt to judge performance by small differences in the test scores.

Compilation and Link Time

The last criterion is compilation and link time. When you are into some heavy development work, continually recompiling after re-editing, seconds can seem like hours. The times listed in Figure 16.4 were derived on a single-user system with floppy disks.

BD Systems C's two-pass system is hard to beat for speed of compilation. Again, C/80 is notable, particularly since it produces intermediate relocatable code. Obviously, length of generated code is closely correlated to compilation time.

16-bit C versions are noticeably different on sieve results. They run much faster and take up a great deal more memory than their 8-bit counterparts. Depending on the nature of the program, executable code running on 16-bit systems will take from one and a half times to nearly twice the storage space of its single-byte equivalent. Therefore, I have separated the

Compiler	Compile & Link Time (seconds)
BDS	21
C/80	37
Q/C	49
CW/C	71
SuperSoft	85
Aztec	86
InfoSoft	96
Telecon	201
Whitesmiths	310

Figure 16.4: Compile and Link Time for 8-bit Cs

16-bit C versions from the 8-bit versions. The results presented in Figure 16.5 were obtained on an 8088 processor running at 8 MHz under MP/M 8/16 with hard disk. Since these results are not directly comparable with the above data regarding 8-bit Cs, BDS C (v 1.53) has been added to the list for comparison. BDS was chosen for its speed, compact code, and fast compilation and execution time. Lattice C was omitted, since it has to be run on an IBM PC, thus making the results hard to compare.

This is just a partial list of the C versions available today, but it will give you an idea of what is "out there" and what to expect for your money. Before closing this chapter, and the book as well, let me leave you with a few parting thoughts about C.

- C is one of the most portable languages available today.

- There is no such thing as a "fits-all-does-all" language, but C is about as close as you are going to get for quite a while.

- C is young enough that it has not yet fragmented into multi-tudinous subsets. Major versions are reasonably compatible.

- C is going to be around for a long time.

A PARTING SHOT

Now, at the close of this book, I would like to tie up a few loose ends and make amends. For those of you to whom this book seemed too elementary in its scope, my apologies. This was meant to be but an introduction to C. For others of you for whom this book may have seemed too comprehensive in its scope, again my apologies. Some of the concepts will seem difficult at first if you haven't used a structured language before. I hope it has been a pleasant journey, not only through C and UNIX, but as an overview to programming as a whole. If you are looking for further

Compiler	Run Time (seconds)	Object Code (size)	Compile & Link Time (seconds)
BDS C	31	4 K	13
DeSmet C	10	8 K	20
Digital C	6	28 K	44
CI-86	17	16 K	26

Figure 16.5: 16-bit C Comparisons

programming examples and more understanding of advanced C, subjects such as pointers, arrays, memory allocation, and bit manipulation, I would suggest my book, *Fifty C Programs,* published by SYBEX.

I have found this book a pleasure to write. I only hope I have passed on some of that enjoyment to you.

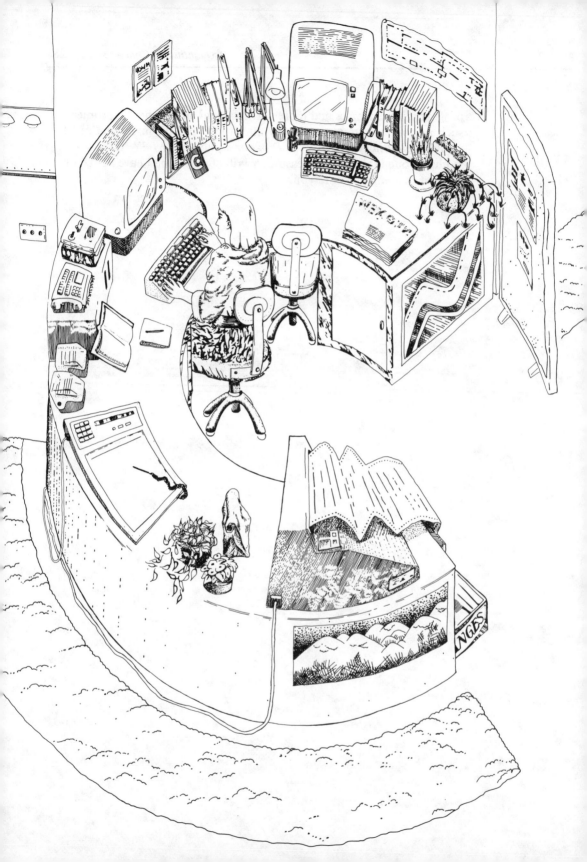

Appendix A:
Compilers

Program	Compiler	Program	Compiler
1.1	SuperSoft	6.5	BDS
1.2	SuperSoft	6.6	BDS
1.3	CI-C86*	6.7	CI-C86*
1.4	CI-C86*	7.1	BDS
1.5	CI-C86*	7.2	BDS
1.6	CI-C86*	7.3	BDS
3.1	BDS	7.4	BDS
3.2	BDS	7.5	BDS
4.2	BDS	8.1	CI-C86*
5.1	BDS	8.2	CI-C86*
6.1	BDS	14.1	Aztec II
6.2	BDS	14.2	Aztec II
6.3	BDS	14.3	Any C Compiler
6.4	BDS	15.1	BDS

---

*CI-C86 is compatible with UNIX 7 C.

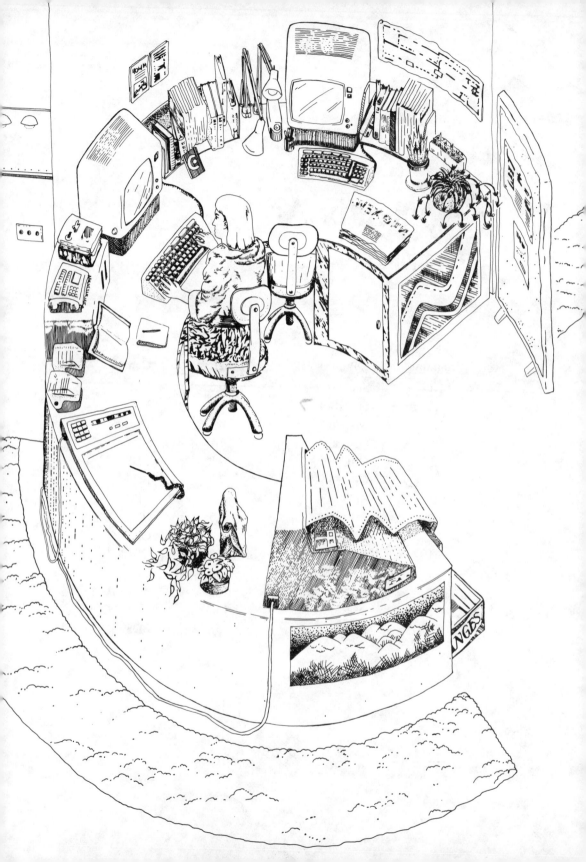

Appendix B:

C Functions—Who Has What

From the nearly two dozen C compilers reviewed for this book, I consider the compilers reviewed in the following table a representative sample of available C compilers for micros. Function names followed by an asterisk (*) are UNIX system calls, the system primitive in UNIX. All other C "functions" are UNIX subroutines. (With all C "functions" being header-defined macros, UNIX function calls or UNIX subroutines*, it is more precise to say that C under UNIX has UNIX functions rather than C functions.)

UNIX will probably be the predominant operating system within the next few years, from mainframe to micro, and this should be considered when purchasing a C compiler for micro use. If portability will be a consideration, now or in the future, strong preference should be given to those compilers closest to Version 7 (or system iii or v) C.

---

* For additional information on UNIX system calls subroutines and commands see Volume 1, *UNIX Programmer's Manual,* Bell Laboratories, Holt, Rinehart and Winston, 1979, 1983.

Function	UNIX**	Aztec II	BDS	CI-C86	CC-86	C/80	DeSmet	DRC	InfoSoft	Lattice	Q/C	SuperSoft
CPM		✔										
abort				✔	✔							
abs	✔		✔		✔			✔				✔
absval												✔
access *		✔							✔			✔
acct *		✔										
acos		✔	✔		✔							
agetc		✔										
alarm *	✔											
allmem										✔		
alloc	✔ᴬ	✔	✔	✔		✔						✔
aputc			✔									
asctime	✔											
asin	✔	✔			✔							
assert	✔				✔							✔
atan	✔	✔						✔				
atan2	✔	✔										
atof	✔	✔		✔	✔			✔				
atoi	✔	✔	✔	✔	✔		✔			✔	✔	✔
atol	✔	✔										
bdasb					✔							
bdos		✔	✔	✔	✔			✔		✔	✔	✔
bdosmw					✔							
bdosp					✔							
bdosw					✔							
bios		✔	✔		✔							✔
biosb					✔							
biosh			✔									
bioshl		✔										
blkfill										✔		
blkmw					✔					✔		
break *	✔											

** UNIX, except where noted, is UNIX Version 7, or system iii or v.

Function	UNIX**	Aztec II	BDS	CI-C86	CC-86	C/80	DeSmet	DRC	InfoSoft	Lattice	Q/C	SuperSoft
brk *	✔							✔				✔
call			✔		✔				✔			
calloc	✔			✔	✔		✔	✔		✔		✔
ccala												✔
cccall												✔
ccdos									✔			
ccera									✔			
ccexit												✔
cclose									✔			
ccren									✔			
ceil	✔				✔							
ceof									✔			
cfsize		✔										
cgetc									✔			
cgetl									✔			
cgets										✔		
chdir *	✔											
chlower											✔	
chmod *	✔							✔				✔
chown *	✔							✔				
chroot *	✔											
chupper										✔		
clear		✔										
clearerr				✔	✔							✔
close *	✔	✔	✔	✔			✔			✔	✔	✔
codend												✔
comlen												✔
comline												✔
copen								✔				
coreleft				✔								
cos	✔	✔						✔				
cosh	✔	✔			✔							
cpmver												✔
cprint										✔		

Function	UNIX**	Aztec II	BDS	CI-C86	CC-86	C/80	DeSmet	DRC	InfoSoft	Lattice	Q/C	SuperSoft
cprintf										✔		
cputc									✔			
cputs										✔		
cread									✔			
creat *	✔	✔	✔	✔			✔	✔			✔	✔
crypt	✔											
cscanf										✔		
csw			✔									
ctime	✔											
ctype								✔				
cwrite										✔		
dbminit	✔											
delete	✔											
dup *	✔											
dup2 *	✔											
ecvt	✔											
edata	✔											
encrypt	✔											
end	✔											
endext												✔
endgrent	✔											
endpwent	✔											
endtext			✔									
environ *	✔											
errno			✔									✔
etext	✔											
etpwnam	✔											
evnbrk												✔
exec *	✔		✔			✔						✔
exece *	✔											
execl												✔
execle *	✔											
execlp *	✔											
execv *	✔											

Function	UNIX**	Aztec II	BDS	CI-C86	CC-86	C/80	DeSmet	DRC	InfoSoft	Lattice	Q/C	SuperSoft
execve *	✔											
execvp *	✔											
exel			✔									
exev			✔									
exit *	✔	✔	✔	✔	✔	✔		✔		✔	✔	✔
exp	✔	✔						✔				✔
externs			✔									✔
fabort			✔									✔
fabs	✔				✔			✔				
farcall				✔								
fcbaddr			✔									
fcbinit		✔										
fclose	✔		✔		✔	✔		✔		✔	✔	✔
fcvt	✔											
fdopen	✔							✔				✔
feof	✔				✔					✔		
ferror	✔			✔						✔		✔
fetch	✔											
fflush	✔		✔	✔	✔			✔		✔	✔	✔
fgetc	✔			✔	✔	✔		✔		✔		✔
fgets	✔		✔	✔	✔			✔		✔		✔
fileno												✔
firstkey	✔											
flilno	✔											
floor	✔				✔							
fmode										✔		
fopen	✔	✔	✔	✔			✔	✔		✔	✔	✔
fork *	✔											
format		✔										
fprintf	✔	✔	✔	✔	✔			✔		✔	✔	✔
fputc	✔				✔	✔		✔		✔		✔
fputs	✔		✔	✔				✔		✔	✔	✔
fread	✔	✔		✔	✔			✔				✔
free	✔		✔		✔		✔	✔		✔		✔

Function	UNIX**	Aztec II	BDS	CI-C86	CC-86	C/80	DeSmet	DRC	InfoSoft	Lattice	Q/C	SuperSoft
freopen	✔				✔			✔		✔		✔
frexp	✔											
frext					✔							
fscanf	✔	✔	✔	✔	✔			✔		✔		✔
fseek	✔			✔	✔			✔		✔		
fstat *	✔											
ftell	✔	✔		✔	✔	✔		✔		✔		
ftellr				✔								
ftime *	✔											
ftoa		✔		✔								
fwrite	✔	✔		✔	✔			✔				✔
gcd	✔											
gcvt	✔											
get2b												✔
getc		✔	✔	✔	✔		✔			✔	✔	✔
getchar	✔		✔	✔	✔	✔	✔	✔	✔	✔	✔	
getds					✔							
getenv	✔											
getes					✔							
getgid *	✔											
getgrent	✔											
getgrigid	✔											
getgrnam	✔											
getl								✔				
getline			✔									
getlogin	✔											
getmem										✔		
getpass	✔											
getpid *	✔							✔				
getpw	✔											
getpwent	✔											
getpwnam	✔											
getpwuid	✔											
gets	✔	✔	✔				✔			✔	✔	✔

Function	UNIX**	Aztec II	BDS	CI-C86	CC-86	C/80	DeSmet	DRC	InfoSoft	Lattice	Q/C	SuperSoft
getuid *	✔											
getval			✔									✔
getw	✔	✔		✔	✔			✔				✔
gmtime	✔											
gtty *	✔											
i3tol	✔											
idexp					✔							
imax											✔	
imin											✔	
in					✔							
inb					✔							
index	✔	✔		✔	✔			✔				✔
indir *	✔											
initb			✔									✔
initw			✔									✔
inp			✔					✔				✔
inp16												✔
inportb				✔								
inportw				✔								
intrint				✔								
ioctl *	✔											
isalnum	✔			✔	✔					✔	✔	✔
isalpha	✔		✔	✔	✔		✔			✔	✔	✔
isascii	✔			✔	✔		✔			✔	✔	✔
isatty	✔							✔		✔		✔
iscntrl	✔			✔	✔			✔		✔	✔	✔
iscsym										✔		
isdigit	✔	✔	✔	✔	✔			✔		✔	✔	✔
isfd												✔
isheap												✔
islower	✔	✔	✔	✔	✔		✔	✔		✔	✔	✔
isnumeric												✔
isprint	✔			✔	✔			✔		✔	✔	✔
ispunct	✔			✔	✔			✔		✔		✔

Function	UNIX**	Aztec II	BDS	CI-C86	CC-86	C/80	DeSmet	DRC	InfoSoft	Lattice	Q/C	SuperSoft
isspace	✔		✔	✔			✔	✔		✔	✔	✔
isupper	✔	✔		✔	✔		✔	✔		✔	✔	✔
iswhite												✔
isxdigit							✔			✔		
itoa				✔								
itob											✔	
itoh				✔								
itol3	✔											
itom	✔											
itot									✔			
j^0				✔								
j^1				✔								
j^n				✔								
kbhit			✔		✔					✔		✔
kill *	✔											
ldexp	✔											
link *	✔											✔
localtime	✔											
lock *	✔											✔
log	✔	✔			✔			✔				
log10	✔	✔			✔			✔				
long											✔	
longjump	✔		✔									✔
lseek *		✔		✔				✔		✔		
ltoa				✔								
ltoh				✔								
madd	✔											
makefcb				✔							✔	
malloc	✔			✔					✔	✔	✔	
max			✔									✔
maxbrk										✔		
mdiv	✔											
min	✔											✔
mknod *	✔											

Function	UNIX**	Aztec II	BDS	CI-C86	CC-86	C/80	DeSmet	DRC	InfoSoft	Lattice	Q/C	SuperSoft
mktemp	✔											✔
moat											✔	
modf	✔				✔							
monitor	✔											
mount *	✔											
mout	✔											
moveblock				✔								
movemem			✔		✔					✔		✔
mpx *	✔											
mpxcall *	✔											
msub	✔											
nextkey	✔											
nice *	✔											✔ B
nlist	✔											
nrand			✔									
oflow			✔									
open *	✔	✔	✔		✔					✔		✔
openpl	✔											
openpoc	✔											
openport	✔											
otell												✔
out					✔							
outb					✔							
outp			✔						✔	✔		✔
outp16												✔
pause *	✔		✔									✔
pclose	✔											
peek			✔	✔	✔							✔
perror	✔											✔
pgetc												✔
phys	✔											
pipe *	✔											
pkclose	✔											
pkfial	✔											

Function	UNIX**	Aztec II	BDS	CI-C86	CC-86	C/80	DeSmet	DRC	InfoSoft	Lattice	Q/C	SuperSoft
pkoff *	✔											
pkon *	✔											
pkopen	✔											
pkread	✔											
pkwrite	✔											
poke			✔		✔						✔	✔
pokeb				✔								
pokew				✔								
popen	✔											
posit		✔										
pow	✔	✔			✔							
pputc												✔
printf	✔	✔	✔	✔		✔		✔	✔	✔	✔	✔
profil *	✔											
ptrace *	✔											
put2b												✔
putc	✔	✔		✔				✔	✔		✔	✔
putch			✔							✔		
putchar	✔	✔					✔	✔	✔		✔	✔
putdec												✔
putl								✔				
puts	✔	✔	✔	✔	✔	✔	✔	✔	✔	✔	✔	✔
putw	✔	✔		✔			✔					✔
qsort	✔		✔C	✔	✔			✔				✔
rand	✔		✔	✔				✔		✔	✔	✔
rbreak										✔		
read *	✔		✔	✔						✔	✔	✔
realloc	✔			✔	✔	✔						✔
rename		✔	✔	✔	✔		✔					✔
reset												✔
rewind	✔				✔			✔		✔		
rindex	✔			✔				✔				✔
rlmem										✔		
rpow	✔											

Function	UNIX**	Aztec II	BDS	CI-C86	CC-86	C/80	DeSmet	DRC	InfoSoft	Lattice	Q/C	SuperSoft
rsmem										✓		
rtell												✓
sbreak			✓					✓		✓		
sbrk												✓
scanf	✓	✓	✓	✓	✓			✓				✓
scarg										✓		
seek *	✓		✓			✓						✓
segread				✓								
setbuf	✓											
setes					✓							
setexit												✓
setgid *	✓											
setgtent	✓											
setint					✓							
setjmp					✓							✓
setjump	✓		✓									
setkey	✓											
setmem				✓	✓					✓		✓
settop		✓										
setuid *	✓											
shellsort					✓							
signal *	✓											
sin	✓	✓			✓			✓				
sinh	✓	✓			✓							
sleep	✓		✓									✓
softint					✓							
sprintf	✓		✓	✓	✓	✓		✓				✓
sqrt	✓	✓						✓				
srand	✓		✓				✓					✓
sscanf		✓	✓	✓				✓		✓		✓
st.....										✓D		
stat *	✓											
stccpy										✓		
stdio	✓											

Function	UNIX**	Aztec II	BDS	CI-C86	CC-86	C/80	DeSmet	DRC	InfoSoft	Lattice	Q/C	SuperSoft
stepwent	✔											
stime *	✔											
store	✔											
strcat	✔		✔	✔	✔		✔	✔		✔	✔	✔
strcmp	✔	✔		✔	✔		✔	✔		✔	✔	✔
strcpy	✔	✔		✔	✔		✔	✔		✔		✔
streq					✔				✔			✔
strlen	✔	✔	✔	✔	✔		✔	✔	✔	✔	✔	✔
strmov											✔	
strmv									✔			
strncmp	✔	✔	✔	✔	✔			✔	✔	✔		✔
strndx										✔		
strnew										✔		
strpos										✔		
strsub									✔			
strtncat	✔			✔	✔			✔		✔		✔
stty *	✔											
substr												✔
swab	✔				✔			✔				✔
switch										✔		
sync *	✔											
sys_nerr	✔											
sysinit				✔								
system	✔				✔							
tan	✔	✔			✔							
tanh	✔	✔			✔							
tell *	✔		✔									✔
time *	✔											
times *	✔											
timezone	✔											
topofmem		✔										✔
tolower		✔	✔	✔	✔		✔			✔	✔	✔
toupper		✔	✔	✔	✔		✔			✔	✔	✔
ttyname	✔							✔				

Function	UNIX**	Aztec II	BDS	CI-C86	CC-86	C/80	DeSmet	DRC	InfoSoft	Lattice	Q/C	SuperSoft
ttyslot	✔											
ubrk												✔
ugetchar												✔
umask *	✔											
umount *	✔											
unget	✔							✔				
ungetc		✔	✔	✔	✔					✔	✔	✔
unlink *		✔	✔		✔		✔	✔		✔	✔	✔
utime *	✔											
utoa				✔								
wait *	✔											✔
wpeek										✔		
wpoke										✔		
wqsort				✔								
wrdbrk												✔
write *		✔	✔	✔		✔	✔	✔		✔		✔
xmain												✔

^A alloc is a standard function in UNIX Version 6. It is present in Version 7, but under Version 7 it is standard practice to use malloc, calloc, and realloc in place of alloc.

^B nice is a *no-op* in SuperSoft C. That is, it is included to ensure compatibility, but performs no operation.

^C The operation performed by this function is not a true quicksort, but a version of Shell sort.

^D Lattice C has about 18 non-standard st... functions.

Notes

Chapter 3:
DATA TYPES, STORAGE CLASSES, AND STORAGE MANAGEMENT

1. UNIX 7 Cs use calloc and malloc.

Chapter 4:
FUNCTIONS, POINTERS, AND RELATED CONCEPTS

1. It is important to understand the concept of the assignment. The assignment operator = assigns the value of the expression on its right to the variable (lvalue) on its left. Therefore the expression

    IQ = 125

assigns a value of 125 to the variable IQ, or more precisely, puts the value 125 into the address of the variable IQ. It is the same as the BASIC expression

    LET IQ = 125

or the dBASE expression

    store 125 to IQ

Because of this, it is a convention in C to refer to variables like IQ as lvalues, and expressions like 125 as rvalues.

Chapter 5:
THE STANDARD I/O HEADER FILE

1. A *macro* is a self-contained but not free-standing block of code. Macros range from any of the small header-file-defined macros used to define functions, like

    #define abs(x) (X < 0 ? − (x) : (x))

to major tools like DRI's Access Manager, a data base management tool. Macros are discussed more fully in Chapter 16.

2. Notice the separator preceded by a space in the following header file. This syntax is used to indicate system-related functions.

3. Many versions of C drop the more general alloc( ) function for the more specific calloc( ), malloc( ), and realloc( ) functions. These are discussed in detail in Chapter 13.

Chapter 6:
BUFFERED FILES

1. The use of an I/O buffer with buffered files is peculiar to BDS C and those versions of C that emulate it. It is not part of UNIX 7 C. In UNIX 7 versions, a file descriptor, usually an integer variable, is used to keep track of the "file stream." The file descriptor is assigned at opening and used in all other functions to address the file stream.

2. fcreat ( ) is not a standard function in Kernighan and Ritchie or UNIX 7, but it is present in many 8-bit and 16-bit versions of C. Where it is not present the file is opened with

        fopen (name, "code")

The codes that may be used are "r" for read-only, "w" for write-only, and "a" for append.

3. An argument vector is a single-dimensional character array (vector or list) that holds an argument present on the command line. The invocation

        a>copy oldprog.txt. newprog.txt

has three vectors:

        argv [0] =>copy
        argv [1] =>oldprog.txt
        argv [2] =>newprog.txt

4. Note the use of uppercase letters to indicate the constant BUFSIZ.

5. C consistently uses the value -1 to indicate an error returned from a function, as well as to terminate interactive functions such as getc ( ) and getchar ( ), where it returns -1 on finding the end of the file. It is this kind of consistency that allows ERROR to be defined as -1 in the header file.

6. Some CP/M versions of C, such as DRC and CI-C86, allow the printer to be accessed as a file, by LST: or PRN:, respectively. Under UNIX, the printer is accessed through the UNIX Shell.

Chapter 7:
RAW FILES: RANDOM I/O

1. System primitives include such functions as:

Function Number	Name	Function Number	Name
13	Reset disk sys	21	Write Sequential
14	Select disk	22	Make file
15	Open file	33	Read random
16	Close file	34	Write random
19	Delete file	37	Reset drive
20	Read sequential		

These do the actual file manipulation. The commands of the language use these primitives to accomplish these tasks.

2. The UNIX 7 C versions of read and write use the number of bytes rather than the number of blocks.

    write (fd,buffer,bytes)

3. In this program, for the sake of simplicity, conventional storage has been allocated in the program data area. A more sophisticated and advanced approach would be to allocate storage dynamically on the heap, which is beyond the scope of this book.

Chapter 8:
STRUCTURES AND UNIONS

1. The number of bytes given to any particular data type depends primarily on the microprocessor in use as well as the implementation of C. Here the byte allocation is as follows:

char name[32];	32
int act_nbr;	2
char address [64];	64
char phone [12];	12
float act_bal;	4
	114 Total

2. When the pointer p is set to the address of tag

    p = &tag

p now is the address of tag. Therefore the indirect

    *p

yields the contents of the address, which is the tag. For example,

    (*p).member

is the tag.member.

Chapter 9:
AN OVERVIEW AND DEFINITION
OF THE LANGUAGE

1. In the strictest definition, UNIX 7 C's functions are UNIX's functions as outlined in Volume 1 of *The UNIX Programmer's Manual,* Sections 2 and 3. For the non-UNIX C programmer, however, the compiler's language manual will be the final definition of the version's library.

2. Octal bit patterns can be output by way of the printf ( ) functions, or puts ( ), or putchar, etc. with the use of the backslash. For example, to output the bell character, ASCII 7,

> printf ("\7")

The seven is read as octal, not decimal. This is better seen in the next example which is a clear sequence for the Televideo 920 or 950 terminal, an escape (ASCII 27) followed by a colon:

> puts ("\33:")

Octal 33 is 27 base 10. A great deal of use can be made of string constants with embedded octal numbers. The above clear sequence can be defined in the program header as

> #define CLEAR "\33:"

and used freely in the program:

> printf (CLEAR);

In this way, if the program is used on another computer, or if terminals change, the CLEAR string is all that needs changing.

3. This is true in some versions, but not in UNIX 7 C.

Chapter 10:
AN INTRODUCTION TO THE C FUNCTIONS AND FUNCTION LIBRARIES

1. UNIX 7 C regards the UNIX system calls and functions as those of C as well (*UNIX Programmer's Manual,* Vol. 1).

Chapter 11:
SYSTEM-SPECIFIC FUNCTIONS

1. Such as the BDOS and BIOS functions described on pages 196-7.

2. The uses of the Shell will be described in Chapter 15.

3. In UNIX, chmod and chown are system commands, not functions.

Chapter 14:
NUMBER CRUNCHING

1. Underflow is truncation of the value due to lack of both scale and precision. For example, the value .0000000000001 would become .0 if the limit of precision is nine decimal places.

Chapter 15:
C IN A SHELL—
THE UNIX ENVIRONMENT

1. In UNIX, as a pipe is created the data stream is buffered to memory as if it were a RAM "file". In emulators it is written to disk as an *actual* file.

2. The name *system* implies something that is larger than a program. For example, an integrated accounting package including General Ledger, Accounts Payable, Accounts Receivable, Payroll, Chart of Accounts, and related accounting utilities cannot be accurately defined as a program. They constitute an Accounting System. Similarly, a monitor that handles keyboard input is a program or process, a series of such programs including a disk operating system, I/O "program," and utilities are an operating system.

3. A SUBMIT file is a CP/M and MP/M utility that reads a text file of CP/M commands and acts upon them as if they had been typed in at the console. The utility allows primitive and simple system programs to be written. It is rather limited in what it can do, and it does not qualify as a command line language as does the Shell language.

4. Verbose in MicroShell is not dissimilar to running a shell file in UNIX with the v (Verbose) and x flags on, as in sh −vx ptrfmt ch24.txt.

Chapter 16:
A COMPARISON OF C COMPILERS

1. As of this writing, full versions of UNIX V 7, system iii, system v, and the Berkeley modifications to UNIX are available in both source licenses and binary licenses for micro, mini, and mainframe computers alike. One company alone has created over 50 adaptations just for the 68000.

2. The term *macro* as it is used here is not to be confused with a *function macro* defined in a header file.

Glossary

ADDRESS: the identification of a location in storage.

AGGREGATE: a grouping or collection of two or more data items that can be referenced individually or together, like arrays, structures and unions; the opposite of a scalar.

ALLOCATE: to grant (assign) storage.

ALPHABETIC: pertaining to a character of the alphabet.

ALPHANUMERIC: pertaining to an alphabetic or numeric character.

ANSI: American National Standards Institute.

ARGUMENT: a parameter; a data item that is passed to a function.

ARRAY: a named and ordered grouping or collection of data elements, all of which have identical attributes.

ASCII: (pronounced *ask-key*) American Standard Code for Information Interchange. All characters in microcomputers and most in minicomputers are understood by the computer in ASCII, a series of consecutive integers assigned one to each character or control code.

ASSEMBLER: a utility to translate symbolic instructions (assembly language) into binary code.

ASSOCIATIVITY: the direction in which operators are associated, i.e., right to left or left to right.

BDOS: Basic Disk Operating System; the heart of CP/M.

BINARY: 1) a number system of two numbers.
2) a condition with two possible actions.
3) an operation involving two data values.

BIOS: Basic Input Output System; CP/M's device interface.

BIT: a binary digit (may have the value 0 or 1).

BITWISE: referring to the manipulation of bits.

BLOCK: a group of commands to be executed as a single entity, e.g., a "function block," an "if block," etc.

BOOLEAN: (named after George Boole) a construct that returns a logical relationship (i.e., true or false).

BUFFER: an area of intermediate storage associated with input/output.

BUG: 1) an insect.

      2) an error made by a programmer and blamed on the computer and/or the software.

BYTE: eight contiguous bits; a half-word.

CARRIAGE RETURN: \r; a "return"; an "enter"; an ASCII 0D HEX; that character which returns the cursor to the zero position, not to be confused with a line feed.

CASE: a programming structure or form that allows multiple branching as the result of a test.

CDOS: A CP/M offspring created for Cromemco, no longer compatible with CP/M.

CHARACTER: 1) a specific element of a character set.

      2) the class of data called character as opposed to numeric.

      3) a single character as opposed to a character array.

      4) an individual, as opposed to a "team player."

CHARACTER ARRAY: an array of characters, usually a string.

COMMAND: a portion of the executable code that causes an operation to be performed.

COMMAND LINE: a line of code entered at the console to cause the one or more operations to be performed by the system.

COMMAND LINE INTERPRETER: an interpreter that is part of the system which executes command lines, like the UNIX Shell.

COMPILER: A utility to generate an assembled program from a programmer's source code.

CONCATENATION: the joining of two or more strings into one bigger string.

CONSOLE: the terminal, or keyboard and CRT.

CONSTANT: a data scalar that has a fixed value for the entirety of a program, as opposed to a variable.

DEBUG: to locate and remove programming errors.

DECIMAL INTEGER: A fractionless or whole number in base 10, usually in the range of -32768 to $+32767$ on microcomputers.

DECLARATION: the establishment of an identifier as a name; the construction of a set of attributes for a specific variable or constant.

DELIMITER: any form of punctuation or white space used to separate tokens ("words").

DOCUMENTATION: the paperwork generated by a writer of software so he won't forget what he put into a program.

DYNAMIC STORAGE: high-speed or "core" memory available for the storage of variables and capable of being freed or released back to the control of the program.

EOF: end-of-file mark.

END-OF-FILE MARK: a code returned by the system indicating that the end of the file has been reached.

END-OF-TEXT MARK: a code indicating that the physical end of a text file has been read. A control Z (^Z) in CP/M. A control Z followed by a carriage return.

EXECUTE: to carry out the program's instructions.

EXPLICIT: stated as opposed to implicit or implied.

EXPRESSION: a notation (within a program) that represents a value; a constant appearing alone; a combination of constants and/or variables and/or operators, e.g., 3.14159 or a $*$ b $*$ c or $\pi/2$, etc.

EXTERNAL: "outside of"; an external function is outside of the main body of a program.

FIELD: a section of a record separated either by format or delimiters; a logically distinct part of a record.

FILE: a (named) data set consisting of records.

FLAG: a variable, normally integer, set by the program to indicate a condition, e.g., end-page = TRUE.

FUNCTION: a statement or group of statements called by the program to perform a specific task.

GLOBAL VARIABLE: a variable known to the entire program or block.

HEADER FILE: a file written to be included in a C program during precompilation that defines program and system constants and contains macro definitions of functions.

HEAP: the "core" or high-speed storage area immediately above the program data area. The heap is the region of dynamic memory allocation.

HEX: hexadecimal.

HEXADECIMAL: a base 16 number, e.g., 1,2,3,4,5,6,7,8,9,A,B, C,D,E,F, where A = 10 (base 10), B = 11 (base 10), etc. Hex is used frequently in computer work since it is an ideal representation of a 2-byte "word."

HIERARCHY: a series of levels; order of precedence.

HIGH-LEVEL LANGUAGE: a computer language that approximates English.

IDENTIFIER: a name; a group of characters, the first being alphabetic, used to identify a variable, constant, aggregate, etc.

IMPLICIT: implied, as opposed to explicit.

INITIALIZE: to set variables, flags, switches, aggregates, etc., to predetermined value(s).

INTEGER: a nonfractional number no greater that the machine word, for example, -32768 to $+32767$ for a signed 16-bit word.

INSTRUCTION: a statement that calls for a specific action or operation.

INTERPRETER: a language that operates directly on a program that is stored in memory, generating object code from the source code on a line-by-line basis, as opposed to a compiler.

ITERATE: to repeat automatically, under program control.

INVOKE: to activate.

KEY: data that identifies a file record, an index.

KEYWORD: an identifier that, when used syntactically, has a meaning to the program.

LABEL: an identifier for a statement.

LIBRARY FUNCTION/LIBRARY ROUTINE: a special-purpose function or program that is kept in memory for a specific purpose.

LINE FEED: see NEWLINE.

LINKER: a program or process to create machine-executable (object) code from the intermediate code generated by compilers.

LITERAL: a character group, a string.

LOCAL VARIABLE: a variable that is known only within a program block.

LONG INTEGER: an integer of longer length than a short integer, usually four bytes in length, 4.295E9, a very long and accurate nonfractional number.

LOOP: the repeated execution of statements within the defined scope of the iterating block.

LVALUE: a value stored in memory with a semi-permanent address, called an lvalue because it is found on the left of an assignment statement. An expression referring to an object, a manipulatable region of storage.

MACRO: a dedicated, non-free-standing code segment whose purpose can range from a definition of a function located within the header file to an entire data base management module such as DRI's Access Manager.

NEWLINE: \n; a line feed, not a carriage return or a carriage-return/line-feed pair.

NESTING: 1) a block within a block.
        2) any group within a group.
        3) an if statement within an if or else, or a while within a while, etc.

NULL STATEMENT: a semicolon placed within the program that causes no action, sometimes used to balance if-then-if nests.

NULL STRING: ""; a string of zero length.

NULL TERMINATOR: a null byte (ASCII 0) at the end of a C string.

OBJECT CODE: the output of the linker, the executable machine code.

OCTAL: a number expressed in base eight, consisting of the digits 0 through 7.

OPERATING SYSTEM: a collection of processes, utilities, procedures, functions, routines, etc., that are organized into a program that directs the computer's operations.

OPERATOR: a symbol that specifies an operation to be performed, e.g., the arithmetic operators $+$, $-$, $*$, and $/$.

OPTIMIST: 1) a programmer who codes in ink (Joan Hughes).
        2) an operator who doesn't back up data.
        3) a purchaser who believes the software advertisements.

OVERFLOW: the result of a calculation or output that exceeds the language's capability to hold the result.

PARAMETER: an argument, a name used within a function to pass data.

PIPE: a connection between commands and/or files, originally called a pipeline. "Pipe" has come into common usage as a verb in the computer industry.

POINTER: a locator variable with the pointer attribute that identifies an exact or absolute location within memory; can also mean an address.

PRECISION: the range of an arithmetic variable; the total number of digits for float or integer, usually expressed as an exponent of 2, for example, an 8-bit integer has a precision of 16, or 2 raised to the 16th, or 65535.

PREPROCESSOR: a program, usually part of the compiler, that examines the program for preprocessor commands, and alters the source code accordingly.

PREPROCESSOR COMMAND: a command that causes the preprocessor to do specific tasks, such as substitute constants and include header files.

PROCESSOR: a hardware data processing device. The term frequently refers to the Central Processing Unit or CPU, which controls all the computer's functions.

PSEUDOCODE: a non-executable, non-compilable language that emulates a computer language, used for algorithm and program development. It can be transported from language to language.

RANDOM ACCESS: retrieving and storing data by non-sequential methods, also called direct access.

RECORD: a portion of a file consisting of one or more fields; a group of related fields that is treated as a unit within a file.

REGISTER: a storage area within the processor (the ultimate in high-speed storage).

RETURNED VALUE: the value returned by a function to the point of invocation.

RVALUE: a value that does not have a permanent address but is stored on the stack, called an rvalue because it is the result of the expression on the right of an assignment.

SCALAR: a single data item, an element, as opposed to an aggregate.

SCALE FACTOR: the number of fractional digits in floating point notation.

SCOPE: the portion or area within a program where a condition is relevant or pertinent; for example, the "scope" of a local variable is the block within which it is declared.

SEPARATOR: a delimiter, white space or punctuation separating tokens.

SHELL: a program, usually part of the operating system, that interprets user commands.

SHORT INTEGER: a nonfractional number of short length, usually the length of a machine word. A 16-bit unsigned integer has the range of 0 through 65535.

SOURCE CODE: the primary portion of a program created by a programmer, which will eventually produce object code when compiled or interpreted.

STACK: a highly dynamic area of "core" memory used by the CPU to temporarily store values. The "heap" is referred to as the "second stack."

STATEMENT: a basic element of a program that describes, names, declares, and specifies actions to be taken; always terminated with a semicolon in C.

STATIC STORAGE: storage that is permanent to the program, but unknown to external programs.

STRING: a connected sequence of characters treated as a single data item.

STRUCTURE: a set of names that refers to a data aggregate that may have the same or different data attributes.

SYNTAX: the rules governing the structure statements within a programming language.

SYSTEM CALL: a direct call to the operating system requesting an input/output or system specific function.

TOKEN: character groups in the source code; separated by C into the categories of identifiers, keywords, constants, strings, operators, and separators.

TRUNCATION: the process of cutting off, used to indicate the failure of the system to buffer the entire value (see OVERFLOW and UNDERFLOW).

UNDERFLOW: to generate a number smaller than the system's arithmetic capacity to handle it, a number like .00000000001.

VARIABLE: a named entity to which differing values can be assigned.

Bibliography

Augenstein, Moshe J., and Tenenbaum, Aaron M. *Data Structures and PL/I Programming*. Englewood Cliffs, N.J.: Prentice-Hall, 1979.

Cain, Ron. "A Small C Compiler for the 8080." *Dr. Dobb's Journal of Computer Calisthenics and Orthodontia* (#45), 5:5 (1980):5-19.

Cortesi, David E. *Inside CP/M: A Guide for Users and Programmers*. New York: Holt, Rinehart Winston, 1982.

Dolotta, T.A., and Haight, R.C. *PWB/UNIX—Overview and Synopsis of Facilities*. Piscataway, N.J.: Bell Telephone Laboratories, Inc., June 1977.

Gauthier, Richard. *Using the UNIX System*. Reston, VA: Reston Publishing Co., 1981.

Gilbreath, Jim. "A High-Level Language Benchmark." *Byte* 6:6 (1981):180-198.

Gilbreath, Jim, and Gilbreath, Gary. "Eratosthenes Revisited: Once More through the Sieve." *Byte* 8:1 (1983):283-326.

Greenburg, Robert. "The UNIX Operating System and the XENIX Standard Operating Environment." *Byte* 6:6 (1981):248-264.

Hughes, Joan K. *PL/I Structured Programming*. 2nd ed. New York: John Wiley & Sons, 1979.

Horowitz, Ellis, and Sartaj, Sahni. *Fundamentals of Data Structures*. Rockville, MD: Computer Science Press, 1982.

Hunter, Bruce H. "A Comparison of C Compilers." *Lifelines/The Software Magazine* 3:3 (1983): 15-21.

Hunter, Bruce H. "A Review of MicroShell—A UNIX-Like Utility." *Lifelines/The Software Magazine* 3:2 (1983): 17-21.

Kernighan, Brian W., and Plauger, P.J. *Software Tools*. Reading, Mass.: Addison-Wesley, 1976.

Kernighan, Brian W., and Plauger, P.J. *Software Tools in Pascal*. Reading, Mass: Addison-Wesley, 1981.

Kernighan, Brian W., and Ritchie, Dennis M. *The C Programming Language*. Englewood Cliffs, N.J.: Prentice-Hall, 1978.

Kildall, Gary. "CP/M: A Family of 8- and 16-Bit Operating Systems." *Byte* 6:6 (1981):216–232.

Knuth, Donald E. *Sorting and Searching*. Vol. 3, *The Art of Computer Programming*. Reading, Mass.: Addison-Wesley, 1973.

McCracken, Daniel D. *A Guide to PL/M Programming for Microcomputer Applications*. Reading, Mass.: Addison-Wesley, 1978.

Pournelle, Jerry. "User's Column: A Slew of Languages, a Slap at Documentation, and a Curse at Keyboards." *Byte* 7:12 (1982):235.

MANUALS

Aztec C II User Manual Release 1.05. Manx Software Systems, P.O. Box 55, Shrewsbury, NJ 07701. 1981.

Bilofsky, Walt. *C/80 2.0 Compiler and Runtime Library*. The Software Toolworks, 14478 Glorietta Drive, Sherman Oaks, CA 91423. 1982.

CC86 Reference Manual. Control-C Software, Inc., 6441 SW Canyon Court, Portland, OR 97221. 1982.

CI-C86 User's Manual v 1.32. Computer Innovations, Inc., 75 Pine Street, Lincroft, NJ 07738. 1982.

Colvin, Jim. *Q/C User's Manual*. Quality Computer Systems, 3394 E. Stiles Avenue, Camarillo, CA 93010. 1983.

c-systems Users Manual. c-Systems, P.O.Box 3253, Fullerton, CA 92634. 1983.

DeSmet C Development Package Manual. C Ware Corporation, 1607 New Brunswick Avenue, Sunnyvale, CA 94087. 1983.

Frimmel, Jim. *LC*. Misosys, P.O.Box 4848, Alexandria, VA 22303-0848. 1982.

InfoSoft "C" Compiler. InfoSoft Systems, Inc., 25 Sylvan Road South, Westport, CT 06880. 1982.

Lattice 8086/8088 C Compiler Manual. Lifeboat Associates, 1651 Third Avenue, New York, NY 10028. 1982.

MicroShell User's Manual v 2.0. New Generation Systems, Inc., 2153 Golf Course Drive, Reston, VA 22091. 1982.

Scherrer, Deborah K., and Akin, Allen. *Unicorn Systems Programmer's Manual*. Unicorn Systems, 30261 Palomares Road, Castro Valley, CA 94546. 1981.

SuperSoft C Compiler v 1.2 User's Manual. SuperSoft Inc., P.O. Box 1628, Champaign, IL 61820. 1983.

tiny-c Owner's Manual. tiny-c Associates, P.O. Box 269, Holmdell, NJ 07733. 1978.

UNIX Programmer's Manual, Vols. 1 & 2. Holt Reinhart and Winston. 1979, 1983.

Whitesmiths, Ltd. C Programmers' Manual Release 2.1. Whitesmiths, Ltd., 97 Lowell Road, Concord, MA 01742. 1981.

Zolman, Leor. *BD Software C Compiler v 1.5 User's Guide*. BD Software, P.O. Box 9, Brighton, MA 02135. 1982.

Index

Selections from The SYBEX Library

Buyer's Guides

THE BEST OF TI 99/4A™ CARTRIDGES
by Thomas Blackadar
150 pp., illustr., Ref. 0-137
Save yourself time and frustration when buying TI 99/4A software. This buyer's guide gives an overview of the best available programs, with information on how to set up the computer to run them.

FAMILY COMPUTERS UNDER $200
by Doug Mosher
160 pp., illustr., Ref. 0-149
Find out what these inexpensive machines can do for you and your family. "If you're just getting started . . . this is the book to read before you buy."—Richard O'Reilly, Los Angeles newspaper columnist

PORTABLE COMPUTERS
by Sheldon Crop and Doug Mosher
128 pp., illustr., Ref. 0-144
"This book provides a clear and concise introduction to the expanding new world of personal computers."—Mark Powelson, Editor, *San Francisco Focus Magazine*

THE BEST OF VIC-20™ SOFTWARE
by Thomas Blackadar
150 pp., illustr., Ref. 0-139
Save yourself time and frustration with this buyer's guide to VIC-20 software. Find the best game, music, education, and home management programs on the market today.

SELECTING THE RIGHT DATA BASE SOFTWARE

SELECTING THE RIGHT WORD PROCESSING SOFTWARE

SELECTING THE RIGHT SPREADSHEET SOFTWARE
by Kathy McHugh and Veronica Corchado
80 pp., illustr., Ref. 0-174, 0-177, 0-178
This series on selecting the right business software offers the busy professional concise, informative reviews of the best available software packages.

Introduction to Computers

OVERCOMING COMPUTER FEAR
by Jeff Berner
112 pp., illustr., Ref. 0-145
This easy-going introduction to computers helps you separate the facts from the myths.

COMPUTER ABC'S
by Daniel Le Noury and Rodnay Zaks
64 pp., illustr., Ref. 0-167
This beautifully illustrated, colorful book for parents and children takes you alphabetically through the world of computers, explaining each concept in simple language.

PARENTS, KIDS, AND COMPUTERS

by Lynne Alper and Meg Holmberg

208 pp., illustr., Ref. 0-151

This book answers your questions about the educational possibilities of home computers.

THE COLLEGE STUDENT'S COMPUTER HANDBOOK

by Bryan Pfaffenberger

350 pp., illustr., Ref. 0-170

This friendly guide will aid students in selecting a computer system for college study, managing information in a college course, and writing research papers.

COMPUTER CRAZY

by Daniel Le Noury

100 pp., illustr., Ref. 0-173

No matter how you feel about computers, these cartoons will have you laughing about them.

DON'T!
(or How to Care for Your Computer)

by Rodnay Zaks

214pp., 100 illustr., Ref. 0-065

The correct way to handle and care for all elements of a computer system, including what to do when something doesn't work.

YOUR FIRST COMPUTER

by Rodnay Zaks

258 pp., 150 illustr., Ref. 0-045

The most popular introduction to small computers and their peripherals: what they do and how to buy one.

INTERNATIONAL MICROCOMPUTER DICTIONARY

120 pp., Ref. 0-067

All the definitions and acronyms of micro-computer jargon defined in a handy pocket-sized edition. Includes translations of the most popular terms into ten languages.

FROM CHIPS TO SYSTEMS: AN INTRODUCTION TO MICROPROCESSORS

by Rodnay Zaks

552 pp., 400 illustr., Ref. 0-063

A simple and comprehensive introduction to microprocessors from both a hardware and software standpoint: what they are, how they operate, how to assemble them into a complete system.

Personal Computers

ATARI

YOUR FIRST ATARI® PROGRAM

by Rodnay Zaks

150 pp., illustr., Ref. 0-130

A fully illustrated, easy-to-use introduction to ATARI BASIC programming. Will have the reader programming in a matter of hours.

BASIC EXERCISES FOR THE ATARI®

by J.P. Lamoitier

251 pp., illustr., Ref. 0-101

Teaches ATARI BASIC through actual practice using graduated exercises drawn from everyday applications.

THE EASY GUIDE TO YOUR ATARI® 600XL/800XL

by Thomas Blackadar

175 pp., illustr., Ref. 0-125

This jargon-free companion will help you get started on the right foot with your new 600XL or 800XL ATARI computer.

ATARI® BASIC PROGRAMS IN MINUTES

by Stanley R. Trost

170 pp., illustr., Ref. 0-143

You can use this practical set of programs without any prior knowledge of BASIC! Application examples are taken from a wide variety of fields, including business, home management, and real estate.

Commodore 64/VIC-20

THE COMMODORE 64™/VIC-20™ BASIC HANDBOOK
by Douglas Hergert
144 pp., illustr., Ref. 0-116
A complete listing with descriptions and instructive examples of each of the Commodore 64 BASIC keywords and functions. A handy reference guide, organized like a dictionary.

THE EASY GUIDE TO YOUR COMMODORE 64™
by Joseph Kascmer
160 pp., illustr., Ref. 0-129
A friendly introduction to using the Commodore 64.

YOUR FIRST VIC-20™ PROGRAM
by Rodnay Zaks
150 pp., illustr., Ref. 0-129
A fully illustrated, easy-to-use introduction to VIC-20 BASIC programming. Will have the reader programming in a matter of hours.

THE VIC-20™ CONNECTION
by James W. Coffron
260 pp., 120 illustr., Ref. 0-128
Teaches elementary interfacing and BASIC programming of the VIC-20 for connection to external devices and household appliances.

YOUR FIRST COMMODORE 64™ PROGRAM
by Rodnay Zaks
182 pp., illustr., Ref. 0-172
You can learn to write simple programs without any prior knowledge of mathematics or computers! Guided by colorful illustrations and step-by-step instructions, you'll be constructing programs within an hour or two.

COMMODORE 64™ BASIC PROGRAMS IN MINUTES
by Stanley R. Trost
170 pp., illustr., Ref. 0-154
Here is a practical set of programs for business, finance, real estate, data analysis, record keeping and educational applications.

GRAPHICS GUIDE TO THE COMMODORE 64™
by Charles Platt
192 pp., illustr., Ref. 0-138
This easy-to-understand book will appeal to anyone who wants to master the Commodore 64's powerful graphics features.

IBM

THE ABC'S OF THE IBM® PC
by Joan Lasselle and Carol Ramsay
100 pp., illustr., Ref. 0-102
This is the book that will take you through the first crucial steps in learning to use the IBM PC.

THE BEST OF IBM® PC SOFTWARE
by Stanley R. Trost
144 pp., illustr., Ref. 0-104
Separates the wheat from the chaff in the world of IBM PC software. Tells you what to expect from the best available IBM PC programs.

THE IBM® PC-DOS HANDBOOK
by Richard Allen King
144 pp., illustr., Ref. 0-103
Explains the PC disk operating system, giving the user better control over the system. Get the most out of your PC by adapting its capabilities to your specific needs.

BUSINESS GRAPHICS FOR THE IBM® PC
by Nelson Ford
200 pp., illustr., Ref. 0-124
Ready-to-run programs for creating line graphs, complex illustrative multiple bar graphs, picture graphs, and more. An ideal way to use your PC's business capabilities!

THE IBM® PC CONNECTION
by James W. Coffron
200 pp., illustr., Ref. 0-127
Teaches elementary interfacing and BASIC programming of the IBM PC for connection to external devices and household appliances.

BASIC EXERCISES FOR THE IBM® PERSONAL COMPUTER
by J.P. Lamoitier
252 pp., 90 illustr., Ref. 0-088
Teaches IBM BASIC through actual practice, using graduated exercises drawn from everyday applications.

USEFUL BASIC PROGRAMS FOR THE IBM® PC
by Stanley R. Trost
144 pp., Ref. 0-111
This collection of programs takes full advantage of the interactive capabilities of your IBM Personal Computer. Financial calculations, investment analysis, record keeping, and math practice—made easier on your IBM PC.

YOUR FIRST IBM® PC PROGRAM
by Rodnay Zaks
182 pp., illustr., Ref. 0-171
This well-illustrated book makes programming easy for children and adults.

YOUR IBM® PC JUNIOR
by Douglas Hergert
250 pp., illustr., Ref. 0-179
This comprehensive reference guide to IBM's most economical microcomputer offers many practical applications and all the helpful information you'll need to get started with your IBM PC Junior.

DATA FILE PROGRAMMING ON YOUR IBM® PC
by Alan Simpson
275 pp., illustr., Ref. 0-146
This book provides instructions and examples of managing data files in BASIC. Programming designs and developments are extensively discussed.

Apple

THE EASY GUIDE TO YOUR APPLE II®
by Joseph Kascmer
160 pp., illustr., Ref. 0-122
A friendly introduction to using the Apple II, II plus and the new IIe.

BASIC EXERCISES FOR THE APPLE®
by J.P. Lamoitier
250 pp., 90 illustr., Ref. 0-084
Teaches Apple BASIC through actual practice, using graduated exercises drawn from everyday applications.

APPLE II® BASIC HANDBOOK
by Douglas Hergert
144 pp., illustr., Ref. 0-155
A complete listing with descriptions and instructive examples of each of the Apple II BASIC keywords and functions. A handy reference guide, organized like a dictionary.

APPLE II® BASIC PROGRAMS IN MINUTES
by Stanley R. Trost
150 pp., illustr., Ref. 0-121
A collection of ready-to-run programs for financial calculations, investment analysis, record keeping, and many more home and office applications. These programs can be entered on your Apple II plus or IIe in minutes!

YOUR FIRST APPLE II® PROGRAM
by Rodnay Zaks
150 pp., illustr., Ref. 0-136
A fully illustrated, easy-to-use introduction to APPLE BASIC programming. Will have the reader programming in a matter of hours.

THE APPLE® CONNECTION
by James W. Coffron
264 pp., 120 illustr., Ref. 0-085
Teaches elementary interfacing and BASIC programming of the Apple for connection to external devices and household appliances.

TRS-80

YOUR COLOR COMPUTER
by Doug Mosher
350 pp., illustr., Ref. 0-097
Patience and humor guide the reader through purchasing, setting up, programming, and using the Radio Shack TRS-80/ TDP Series 100 Color Computer. A complete introduction.

THE FOOLPROOF GUIDE TO SCRIPSIT™ WORD PROCESSING
by Jeff Berner
225 pp., illustr., Ref. 0-098
Everything you need to know about SCRIPSIT—from starting out, to mastering document editing. This user-friendly guide is written in plain English, with a touch of wit.

Timex/Sinclair 1000/ZX81

YOUR TIMEX/SINCLAIR 1000 AND ZX81™
by Douglas Hergert
159 pp., illustr., Ref. 0-099
This book explains the set-up, operation, and capabilities of the Timex/Sinclair 1000 and ZX81. Includes how to interface peripheral devices, and introduces BASIC programming.

THE TIMEX/SINCLAIR 1000™ BASIC HANDBOOK
by Douglas Hergert
170 pp., illustr., Ref. 0-113
A complete alphabetical listing with explanations and examples of each word in the T/S 1000 BASIC vocabulary; will allow you quick, error-free programming of your T/S 1000.

TIMEX/SINCLAIR 1000™ BASIC PROGRAMS IN MINUTES
by Stanley R. Trost
150 pp., illustr., Ref. 0-119
A collection of ready-to-run programs for financial calculations, investment analysis, record keeping, and many more home and office applications. These programs can be entered on your T/S 1000 in minutes!

MORE USES FOR YOUR TIMEX/SINCLAIR 1000™ Astronomy on Your Computer
by Eric Burgess
176 pp., illustr., Ref. 0-112
Ready-to-run programs that turn your TV into a planetarium.

Other Popular Computers

YOUR FIRST TI 99/4A™ PROGRAM
by Rodnay Zaks
182 pp., illustr., Ref. 0-157
Colorfully illustrated, this book concentrates on the essentials of programming in a clear, entertaining fashion.

THE RADIO SHACK® NOTEBOOK COMPUTER
by Orson Kellogg
128 pp., illustr., Ref. 0-150
Whether you already have the Radio Shack Model 100 notebook computer, or are interested in buying one, this book will clearly explain what it can do for you.

THE EASY GUIDE TO YOUR COLECO ADAM™
by Thomas Blackadar
175 pp., illustr., Ref. 0-181
This quick reference guide shows you how to get started on your Coleco Adam with a minimum of technical jargon.

YOUR KAYPRO II/4/10™
by Andrea Reid and Gary Deidrichs
250 pp., illustr., Ref. 0-166
This book is a non-technical introduction to the KAYPRO family of computers. You will find all you need to know about operating your KAYPRO within this one complete guide.

Software and Applications

Operating Systems

THE CP/M® HANDBOOK
by Rodnay Zaks
320 pp., 100 illustr., Ref 0-048
An indispensable reference and guide to CP/M—the most widely-used operating system for small computers.

MASTERING CP/M®
by Alan R. Miller
398 pp., illustr., Ref. 0-068
For advanced CP/M users or systems programmers who want maximum use of the CP/M operating system . . . takes up where our *CP/M Handbook* leaves off.

THE BEST OF CP/M® SOFTWARE
by John D. Halamka
250 pp., illustr., Ref. 0-100
This book reviews tried-and-tested, commercially available software for your CP/M system.

REAL WORLD UNIX™
by John D. Halamka
250 pp., illustr., Ref. 0-093
This book is written for the beginning and intermediate UNIX user in a practical, straightforward manner, with specific instructions given for many special applications.

THE CP/M PLUS™ HANDBOOK
by Alan R. Miller
250 pp., illustr., Ref. 0-158
This guide is easy for the beginner to understand, yet contains valuable information for advanced users of CP/M Plus (Version 3).

Business Software

INTRODUCTION TO WORDSTAR™
by Arthur Naiman
202 pp., 30 illustr., Ref. 0-077
Makes it easy to learn how to use Word-Star, a powerful word processing program for personal computers.

PRACTICAL WORDSTAR™ USES
by Julie Anne Arca
200 pp., illustr., Ref. 0-107
Pick your most time-consuming office tasks and this book will show you how to streamline them with WordStar.

MASTERING VISICALC®
by Douglas Hergert
217 pp., 140 illustr., Ref. 0-090
Explains how to use the VisiCalc "electronic spreadsheet" functions and provides examples of each. Makes using this powerful program simple.

DOING BUSINESS WITH VISICALC®
by Stanley R. Trost
260 pp., Ref. 0-086
Presents accounting and management planning applications—from financial statements to master budgets; from pricing models to investment strategies.

DOING BUSINESS WITH SUPERCALC™
by Stanley R. Trost
248 pp., illustr., Ref. 0-095
Presents accounting and management planning applications—from financial statements to master budgets; from pricing models to investment strategies.

VISICALC® FOR SCIENCE AND ENGINEERING
by Stanley R. Trost and Charles Pomernacki
225 pp., illustr., Ref. 0-096
More than 50 programs for solving technical problems in the science and engineering fields. Applications range from math

and statistics to electrical and electronic engineering.

DOING BUSINESS WITH 1-2-3™
by Stanley R. Trost
250 pp., illustr., Ref. 0-159

If you are a business professional using the 1-2-3 software package, you will find the spreadsheet and graphics models provided in this book easy to use "as is" in everyday business situations.

THE ABC'S OF 1-2-3™
by Chris Gilbert
225 pp., illustr., Ref. 0-168

For those new to the LOTUS 1-2-3 program, this book offers step-by-step instructions in mastering its spreadsheet, data base, and graphing capabilities.

UNDERSTANDING dBASE II™
by Alan Simpson
220 pp., illustr., Ref. 0-147

Learn programming techniques for mailing label systems, bookkeeping and data base management, as well as ways to interface dBASE II with other software systems.

DOING BUSINESS WITH dBASE II™
by Stanley R. Trost
250 pp., illustr., Ref. 0-160

Learn to use dBASE II for accounts receivable, recording business income and expenses, keeping personal records and mailing lists, and much more.

DOING BUSINESS WITH MULTIPLAN™
by Richard Allen King and Stanley R. Trost
250 pp., illustr., Ref. 0-148

This book will show you how using Multiplan can be nearly as easy as learning to use a pocket calculator. It presents a collection of templates that can be applied "as is" to business situations.

DOING BUSINESS WITH PFS®
by Stanley R. Trost
250 pp., illustr., Ref. 0-161

This practical guide describes specific business and personal applications in detail. Learn to use PFS for accounting, data analysis, mailing lists and more.

INFOPOWER: PRACTICAL INFOSTAR™ USES
by Jule Anne Arca and Charles F. Pirro
275 pp., illustr., Ref. 0-108

This book gives you an overview of Info-Star, including DataStar and ReportStar, WordStar, MailMerge, and SuperSort. Hands on exercises take you step-by-step through real life business applications.

WRITING WITH EASYWRITER II™
by Douglas W. Topham
250 pp., illustr., Ref. 0-141

Friendly style, handy illustrations, and numerous sample exercises make it easy to learn the EasyWriter II word processing system.

Business Applications

INTRODUCTION TO WORD PROCESSING
by Hal Glatzer
205 pp., 140 illustr., Ref. 0-076

Explains in plain language what a word processor can do, how it improves productivity, how to use a word processor and how to buy one wisely.

COMPUTER POWER FOR YOUR LAW OFFICE
by Daniel Remer
225 pp., Ref. 0-109

How to use computers to reach peak productivity in your law office, simply and inexpensively.

OFFICE EFFICIENCY WITH PERSONAL COMPUTERS
by Sheldon Crop
175 pp., illustr., Ref. 0-165

Planning for computerization of your office? This book provides a simplified discussion of the challenges involved for everyone from business owner to clerical worker.

COMPUTER POWER FOR YOUR ACCOUNTING OFFICE
by James Morgan
250 pp., illustr., Ref. 0-164
This book is a convenient source of information about computerizing you accounting office, with an emphasis on hardware and software options.

Languages

C

FIFTY C PROGRAMS
by Bruce Hunter
200 pp., illustr., Ref. 0-155
Beginning as well as intermediate C programmers will find this a useful guide to programming techniques and specific applications.

BUSINESS PROGRAMS IN C
by Leon Wortman and Thomas O. Sidebottom
200 pp., illustr., Ref. 0-153
This book provides source code listings of C programs for the business person or experienced programmer. Each easy-to-follow tutorial applies directly to a business situation.

BASIC

YOUR FIRST BASIC PROGRAM
by Rodnay Zaks
150pp. illustr. in color, Ref. 0-129
A "how-to-program" book for the first time computer user, aged 8 to 88.

FIFTY BASIC EXERCISES
by J. P. Lamoitier
232 pp., 90 illustr., Ref. 0-056
Teaches BASIC by actual practice, using graduated exercises drawn from everyday applications. All programs written in Microsoft BASIC.

INSIDE BASIC GAMES
by Richard Mateosian
348 pp., 120 illustr., Ref. 0-055
Teaches interactive BASIC programming through games. Games are written in Microsoft BASIC and can run on the TRS-80, Apple II and PET/CBM.

BASIC FOR BUSINESS
by Douglas Hergert
224 pp., 15 illustr., Ref. 0-080
A logically organized, no-nonsense introduction to BASIC programming for business applications. Includes many fully-explained accounting programs, and shows you how to write them.

EXECUTIVE PLANNING WITH BASIC
by X. T. Bui
196 pp., 19 illustr., Ref. 0-083
An important collection of business management decision models in BASIC, including Inventory Management (EOQ), Critical Path Analysis and PERT, Financial Ratio Analysis, Portfolio Management, and much more.

BASIC PROGRAMS FOR SCIENTISTS AND ENGINEERS
by Alan R. Miller
318 pp., 120 illustr., Ref. 0-073
This book from the "Programs for Scientists and Engineers" series provides a library of problem-solving programs while developing proficiency in BASIC.

CELESTIAL BASIC
by Eric Burgess
300 pp., 65 illustr., Ref. 0-087
A collection of BASIC programs that rapidly complete the chores of typical astronomical computations. It's like having a planetarium in your own home! Displays apparent movement of stars, planets and meteor showers.

YOUR SECOND BASIC PROGRAM
by Gary Lippman
250 pp., illustr., Ref. 0-152
A sequel to *Your First BASIC Program*, this

book follows the same patient, detailed approach and brings you to the next level of programming skill.

Pascal

INTRODUCTION TO PASCAL (Including UCSD Pascal™)
by Rodnay Zaks
420 pp., 130 illustr., Ref. 0-066
A step-by-step introduction for anyone wanting to learn the Pascal language. Describes UCSD and Standard Pascals. No technical background is assumed.

THE PASCAL HANDBOOK
by Jacques Tiberghien
486 pp., 270 illustr., Ref. 0-053
A dictionary of the Pascal language, defining every reserved word, operator, procedure and function found in all major versions of Pascal.

APPLE® PASCAL GAMES
by Douglas Hergert and Joseph T. Kalash
372 pp., 40 illustr., Ref. 0-074
A collection of the most popular computer games in Pascal, challenging the reader not only to play but to investigate how games are implemented on the computer.

INTRODUCTION TO THE UCSD p-SYSTEM™
by Charles W. Grant and Jon Butah
300 pp., 10 illustr., Ref. 0-061
A simple, clear introduction to the UCSD Pascal Operating System; for beginners through experienced programmers.

PASCAL PROGRAMS FOR SCIENTISTS AND ENGINEERS
by Alan R. Miller
374 pp., 120 illustr., Ref. 0-058
A comprehensive collection of frequently used algorithms for scientific and technical applications, programmed in Pascal. Includes such programs as curve-fitting, integrals and statistical techniques.

DOING BUSINESS WITH PASCAL
by Richard Hergert and Douglas Hergert
371 pp., illustr., Ref. 0-091
Practical tips for using Pascal in business programming. Includes design considerations, language extensions, and applications examples.

Assembly Language Programming

PROGRAMMING THE 6502
by Rodnay Zaks
386 pp., 160 illustr., Ref. 0-046
Assembly language programming for the 6502, from basic concepts to advanced data structures.

6502 APPLICATIONS
by Rodnay Zaks
278 pp., 200 illustr., Ref. 0-015
Real-life application techniques: the input/output book for the 6502.

ADVANCED 6502 PROGRAMMING
by Rodnay Zaks
292 pp., 140 illustr., Ref. 0-089
Third in the 6502 series. Teaches more advanced programming techniques, using games as a framework for learning.

PROGRAMMING THE Z80
by Rodnay Zaks
624 pp., 200 illustr., Ref. 0-069
A complete course in programming the Z80 microprocessor and a thorough introduction to assembly language.

Z80 APPLICATIONS
by James W. Coffron
288 pp., illustr., Ref. 0-094
Covers techniques and applications for using peripheral devices with a Z80 based system.

PROGRAMMING THE 6809
by Rodnay Zaks and William Labiak
362 pp., 150 illustr., Ref. 0-078
This book explains how to program the 6809 in assembly language. No prior programming knowledge required.

PROGRAMMING THE Z8000
by Richard Mateosian
298 pp., 124 illustr., Ref. 0-032
How to program the Z8000 16-bit microprocessor. Includes a description of the architecture and function of the Z8000 and its family of support chips.

PROGRAMMING THE 8086/8088
by James W. Coffron
300 pp., illustr., Ref. 0-120
This book explains how to program the 8086 and 8088 in assembly language. No prior programming knowledge required.

Other Languages

FORTRAN PROGRAMS FOR SCIENTISTS AND ENGINEERS
by Alan R. Miller
280 pp., 120 illustr., Ref. 0-082
In the "Programs for Scientists and Engineers" series, this book provides specific scientific and engineering application programs written in FORTRAN.

A MICROPROGRAMMED APL IMPLEMENTATION
by Rodnay Zaks
350 pp., Ref. 0-005
An expert-level text presenting the complete conceptual analysis and design of an APL interpreter, and actual listing of the microcode.

Hardware and Peripherals

MICROPROCESSOR INTERFACING TECHNIQUES
by Rodnay Zaks and Austin Lesea
456 pp., 400 illustr., Ref. 0-029
Complete hardware and software interconnect techniques, including D to A conversion, peripherals, standard buses and troubleshooting.

THE RS-232 SOLUTION
by Joe Campbell
225 pp., illustr., Ref. 0-140
Finally, a book that will show you how to correctly interface your computer to any RS-232-C peripheral.

USING CASSETTE RECORDERS WITH COMPUTERS
by James Richard Cook
175 pp., illustr., Ref. 0-169
Whatever your computer or application, you will find this book helpful in explaining details of cassette care and maintenance.

SYBEX COMPUTER BOOKS

are different.

Here is why . . .

At SYBEX, each book is designed with you in mind. Every manuscript is carefully selected and supervised by our editors, who are themselves computer experts. We publish the best authors, whose technical expertise is matched by an ability to write clearly and to communicate effectively. Programs are thoroughly tested for accuracy by our technical staff. Our computerized production department goes to great lengths to make sure that each book is well-designed.

In the pursuit of timeliness, SYBEX has achieved many publishing firsts. SYBEX was among the first to integrate personal computers used by authors and staff into the publishing process. SYBEX was the first to publish books on the CP/M operating system, microprocessor interfacing techniques, word processing, and many more topics.

Expertise in computers and dedication to the highest quality product have made SYBEX a world leader in computer book publishing. Translated into fourteen languages, SYBEX books have helped millions of people around the world to get the most from their computers. We hope we have helped you, too.

**For a complete catalog of our publications
please contact:**

U.S.A.
SYBEX, Inc.
2344 Sixth Street
Berkeley,
California 94710
Tel: (800) 227-2346
    (415) 848-8233
Telex: 336311

FRANCE
SYBEX S.A.R.L.
6–8 Impasse du Curé
75018 Paris
France
Tel: 01/203–9595
Telex: 211801

GERMANY
SYBEX-Verlag GmbH
Vogelsanger Weg 111
4000 Düsseldorf 30
West Germany
Tel: (0211) 626411
Telex: 8588163